Otto Preminger: Interviews

Conversations with Filmmakers Series
Gerald Peary, General Editor

OTTO
PREMINGER
I N T E R V I E W S

Edited by Gary Bettinson

University Press of Mississippi / Jackson

The University Press of Mississippi is the scholarly publishing agency of
the Mississippi Institutions of Higher Learning: Alcorn State University,
Delta State University, Jackson State University, Mississippi State University,
Mississippi University for Women, Mississippi Valley State University,
University of Mississippi, and University of Southern Mississippi.

www.upress.state.ms.us

The University Press of Mississippi is a member
of the Association of University Presses.

First printing 2021

∞

Library of Congress Cataloging-in-Publication Data

Names: Bettinson, Gary, editor.
Title: Otto Preminger: interviews / edited by Gary Bettinson.
Other titles: Conversations with filmmakers series.
Description: Jackson: University Press of Mississippi, 2021. |
    Series: Conversations with filmmakers series | Includes bibliographical
    references and index.
Identifiers: LCCN 2021016962 (print) | LCCN 2021016963 (ebook) |
    ISBN 978-1-4968-3524-6 (hardback) | ISBN 978-1-4968-3519-2 (trade paperback) |
    ISBN 978-1-4968-3523-9 (epub) | ISBN 978-1-4968-3522-2 (epub) |
    ISBN 978-1-4968-3521-5 (pdf) | ISBN 978-1-4968-3520-8 (pdf)
Subjects: LCSH: Preminger, Otto—Interviews. | Motion picture producers and
    directors—Interviews.
Classification: LCC PN1998.3.P743 A5 2021 (print) | LCC PN1998.3.P743 (ebook) |
    DDC 791.4302/32—dc23
LC record available at https://lccn.loc.gov/2021016962
LC ebook record available at https://lccn.loc.gov/2021016963

British Library Cataloging-in-Publication Data available

Contents

Introduction

In July 1970 Otto Preminger told television chat show host Dick Cavett about a recent watershed in his professional career.

> Something unheard of, for me, happened. I got a good review. I never get good reviews. People don't like me. I don't know [why]. I'm charming and nice. I do my best.

This slippery quotation typifies the Preminger mystique. Is he playful or self-pitying? Does he court praise? Are his remarks self-deprecating, disingenuous, sincere? From one angle, Preminger was nobody's idea of a critical pariah. By the time the Cavett telecast aired, his career had brought him three Academy Award nominations as Best Director. *Laura*, the sparkling film noir that enshrined his reputation in 1944, had crystallized as a "classic" of studio-era filmmaking, while a cluster of other Preminger titles—including *Where the Sidewalk Ends* (1950), *The Man with the Golden Arm* (1955), and *Anatomy of a Murder* (1959)—were destined for canonization. His esteem reached as far as France, where the critics at *Cahiers du cinéma* anointed him auteur; and England, whose *Movie* critics championed the "grace and fluidity" of his precisely controlled, democratic mise-en-scène. In the United States, Andrew Sarris's *The American Cinema* (1968) further burnished Preminger's stature, according him the imprimatur of artistic visionary. Preminger could not in good faith grouse about critical contempt, much less critical neglect.

And yet he *did* attract fervent detractors, some of whom counted among the most illustrious and influential movie critics of the period. To Pauline Kael his "films are consistently superficial and facile" (306). Judith Crist (or Judas Crist, as Preminger dubbed her) was a long-standing foe—"She has never liked anything I have done," Preminger tells Cavett—whose animus toward him peaked in a scornful review of *Hurry Sundown* (1967): "To say that 'Hurry Sundown' is the worst film of the still-young year is to belittle it. It stands with the worst films of any number of years" (quoted in Harris 288). Preminger typically operated as his own independent producer and promoter (at least since 1953's *The Moon Is Blue*), a role that his critics appeared to hold against him. Stanley Kauffmann thought him less a legitimate artist than "a commercial showman" (175), while Dwight Macdonald discerned only "a great showman who has never bothered to learn anything about making a movie" (176). Most vituperative, perhaps, was Rex Reed, a perennial adversary, to whom Preminger and his interviewers allude throughout this collection. In the 1970 interview with Cavett, Preminger all but declares Reed persona non grata, no doubt on account of the writer's possibly apocryphal backstage account of *Hurry Sundown*, published in the *New York Times*. In sum, Preminger was a wildly polarizing filmmaker, admired and derided by critics in equal measure.

Posterity threatened to slight him. Long before his death in 1986, his detractors' complaints had begun to cling to his legend, and critical support tapered off. Even his earliest advocates tempered their ardor of his work. The critics at *Cahiers du Cinéma*, as scholar Chris Fujiwara (325) observes, "got off Preminger's train at *In Harm's Way*" in 1965, the director's late period popularly characterized as one of precipitous artistic decline. Then there was Preminger's ambivalent public image. In televised interviews he exuded an easygoing if brusque charisma, but reports abounded of his tyrannical treatment of actors, particularly ingénues. Not a few critics noted that Preminger "discovered" or directed a startling number of eventual suicides: Jean Seberg, Dorothy Dandridge, Maggie McNamara, Marilyn Monroe. A martinet on the set, Preminger staged paroxysms of infamous repute. He could seem both humorless and sardonic. To his collaborators, as to his critics, he cut a paradoxical, divisive figure: some actors (Jane Fonda, Frank Sinatra) praised his methods; others (Tom Tryon, Dyan Cannon) maligned him as a bullying terror. "Preminger is the world's most charming dinner guest," said Jean Seberg, "and the world's most sadistic film director." His *Batman* costar Adam West pronounced him "one of the meanest bastards who ever walked a soundstage" (144). The insistent stories of on-set hectoring, the purported waning of his artistic powers, the lingering barbs by highbrow tastemakers—these factors propelled Preminger's cinema toward critical obscurity in the 1980s and 1990s. Not until the early 2000s did critical rehabilitation arrive, thanks to two rousing scholarly biographies (Fujiwara; Hirsch), and a string of Preminger film retrospectives launched across Europe and North America. *Otto Preminger: Interviews* is produced in this spirit of historical rediscovery and critical appreciation.

Movie criticism held an enduring fascination for Preminger. Braided throughout the interviews are incisive reflections on the film critic's function and value, a subject to which he frequently, spiritedly adverts. His views on the critical intelligentsia, and on the proficiency of particular critics, emerge most extensively in the AFI's Panel on the Critic, convened in 1969. Flanked by critics from *Variety*, the *Los Angeles Times*, and the *Saturday Review*, Preminger displays no small measure of magnanimity, not to say good humor, apropos his own films' somewhat erratic critical reception. Yet one also detects in his remarks an occasional defensiveness, a kernel of vulnerability beneath the carapace of self-possession, or at the very least an appetite for retaliation and score-settling. Note the evident relish with which he reviles the *New Republic*'s Stanley Kauffmann, whose recent, lacerating putdown of Preminger ("The Preminger Paradox") apparently looms fresh in his memory. His invective against Judith Crist on *The Dick Cavett Show* (1970) devolves into ad hominem sideswiping.

Notwithstanding these skirmishes, Preminger's cinema attracted considerable attention and appreciation from contemporary critics. His early renown hinged on *Laura*, an instant box-office and critical triumph, whose mazy gestation Preminger exhaustively recounts to Peter Bogdanovich in this collection. A string of engrossing films noirs produced at Twentieth Century-Fox—*Fallen Angel* (1945), *Whirlpool* (1949), *Where the Sidewalk Ends*—further cemented his status. In the 1950s Preminger shifted gear, galvanized by new technologies. CinemaScope and other widescreen formats helped to crystallize his visual signature, and in *River of No Return* (1954) and *Carmen Jones* (1954), he honed a distinctive set of stylistic traits: extended takes, fluid camera movement, staging in depth, and spacious framings, all of which contributed to his studied "objectivity"—a refusal to cast judgment upon his story's dramatis personae. This aesthetic drew admiration from hallowed quarters, not least the French cineastes at *Cahiers du cinéma* and the mise-en-scène analysts at *Movie*. Preminger conceded that his ostensibly theatrical style, which subordinates "disruptive" cutting to real-time duration, may have derived from his origins in the Viennese theater. (He clarifies his indebtedness to his stage mentor, Austrian impresario Max Reinhardt, in several of the interviews.) Yet, as Preminger tells *Cahiers*'s Jacques Doniol-Valcroze and Eric Rohmer, "I don't think one could accuse me of making theater in my films. On the contrary, what pleases me in the cinema are the methods that allow you to escape the theatrical perspective." Hence, his increasingly pronounced aversion to artifice, manifest in part through a penchant for location shooting and a rejection of rear-projection photography.

By chance Preminger's visual style reified André Bazin's conception of spatial realism. Long takes, mobile camerawork, multiplanar compositions, a judicious manipulation of offscreen space, the fostering of interpretive freedom—these "Bazinian" techniques are equally Premingerian principles, mobilized in movies from *Carmen Jones* to *Bunny Lake Is Missing* (1965). No wonder that Preminger's aesthetic won praise from Bazin's protégés (if not to the same degree from Bazin himself), including Jean-Luc Godard, Jean-Louis Comolli, and Jacques Rivette (whose 1953 interview with Preminger opens this volume). Nor is it surprising that the interviews reprinted from *Cahiers du cinéma* and *Movie* find Preminger expatiating on his stylistic proclivities, as do subsequent interviews assembled in this book. Encountered today his reflections on film style seem adventurous, even prescient. Of his epic war movie *In Harm's Way* (1965), Preminger tells *Movie's* interviewers: "If it were possible, I would do the whole of the film in one shot," anticipating Sam Mendes's single-take war drama *1917* (2019). His decision to postpone *In Harm's Way*'s opening titles until the film's end, seldom done in 1960s cinema, has today become de rigueur in Hollywood movies. As his adherents appreciated, Preminger's best-known work radiated bravado, restlessly pushing toward formal innovation, flaunting risqué—even impermissible—subject material, and virtuosically setting new trends in stylistic and thematic expression.

As the auteur theory coalesced, Preminger became fodder for passionate debate. For Comolli he was a bona fide auteur, a cinematic artist of the first order. For Sarris, a Preminger partisan, his achievements nevertheless failed to match those of fellow émigré directors Fritz Lang, Ernst Lubitsch, F. W. Murnau, and Josef von Sternberg. A genre pluralist, Preminger bounced from film noir and melodrama to period musical and courtroom drama, all the while permitting a singular sensibility to shine through. "Every Preminger film, even his most ill-fated, bears the signs of an overall conception and the stigmata of a personal attitude," wrote Sarris in 1968 (1996: 106). Pauline Kael, no friend of the auteur theory, demurred that stylistic consistency should not be considered a virtue in so eclectic a body of work (2016: 306). Others bristled at the nascent auteurism with which Preminger had become all but synonymous. By the end of the 1960s Warren Beatty would carp:

> To attribute [movies] wholly to their directors—not to the actors, not to the producers . . . well, that's bullshit! Those pictures were made by directors, writers, and sound men and cameramen and so forth, but suddenly it's 'Otto Preminger's *Hurry Sundown*.' . . . It's not healthy. (Quoted in Wake & Hayden 180)

Preminger, for his part, did nothing to debunk the imputed primacy of the director. In Valerie Robins's documentary *Preminger: Anatomy of a Filmmaker* (1991), he is heard to assert:

> Though it takes many people working together to make a picture, it must, I feel, be essentially the product of one man's vision, one man's initiative, one man's conviction. It is his responsibility to get the others to share his understanding and his enthusiasm.

In an interview with Gerald Pratley (not included in this volume), he observed, "The French, who have this *auteur* theory, are really right. The medium *is* a director's medium . . . It is not a medium of committees, it is one man's medium" (183).

Indeed, he tells his *Cahiers du cinéma* interlocutors that films "are the work of a single individual who has left his mark"; and before an audience at UCLA in 1969, he insists that a movie "must be the *director's* interpretation, the director's picture. The picture must be made, for better or worse, the way the director sees it."

Ultimately, John Orr suggests, Preminger ran afoul of a vehement "backlash" against auteurism led by Kael, Dwight Macdonald, and others. Nevertheless, auteurists clung to the stylistic and thematic coherence governing his oeuvre. Preminger's films thematize, as the *Movie* critics profess, the burden of taking decisions; and, as Peter Bogdanovich points out, this most "impartial," "evenhanded," and "objective" of filmmakers makes moral relativism a salient thematic motif. Preminger's celebrated detachment—the "impersonal" gaze he casts upon his characters' ambiguous morality—would sharpen into an authorial inscription; critic Donald Lyons, perhaps paradoxically, considers *In Harm's Way* "personal in its impersonality" (51). Above all, Preminger's films cohere around a consistent authorial credo: "I have a great belief in the intelligence of the audience," Preminger tells Bogdanovich. In short, his corpus displays no less "unity" and "personality" than that of Alfred Hitchcock, Orson Welles, and the other auteurs ranked highest in Sarris's taxonomy.

Preminger cultivated an authorial signature all his own, but he shared superficial affinities with Hitchcock and Welles. Like Hitchcock, he routinely engaged the skills of graphic artist Saul Bass, whose abstract, evocative poster designs and credit sequences have, since *The Moon Is Blue*, festooned Preminger movies and memorabilia. And like Welles, Preminger trained as a professional actor. Billy Wilder's *Stalag 17* (1953) supplied Preminger a memorably plum role, while pop-culture immortality beckoned as Mr. Freeze in television's *Batman* (1966). Not coincidentally, Preminger's films are honeycombed with sophisticated performances and characterization. His output showcases some of the finest dramatic work by major Hollywood stars, including Frank Sinatra (*The Man with the Golden Arm*), Marilyn Monroe (*River of No Return*), Gene Tierney (*Laura*), Dana Andrews (*Where the Sidewalk Ends*), Joan Crawford (*Daisy Kenyon*, 1947), Dorothy Dandridge (*Carmen Jones*), Deborah Kerr (*Bonjour Tristesse*, 1958), James Stewart, Lee Remick, and George C. Scott (*Anatomy of a Murder*), Sal Mineo (*Exodus*, 1960), Henry Fonda and Charles Laughton (*Advise & Consent*, 1962), John Huston (*The Cardinal*, 1963), and Laurence Olivier (*Bunny Lake Is Missing*). Preminger's transactions with actors could be fraught with conflict, but his methods, however contentious, paid off handsomely on screen. Sinatra, Mineo, Laughton, Tierney, Remick—none were better than in the films he directed. "I like actors," Preminger tells his UCLA audience, seeking to scotch rumors to the contrary.

Artistic merits aside, Preminger can be credited with impelling, seemingly by sheer pugnacity, the liberalization of American film. He agitated for, and won, industrial reform. A committed liberal, he zealously defended artistic free expression, the preservation of which is persistently espoused in this collection of interviews. Not infrequently he embraced socially progressive and proscribed subject matter, chafing at the Production Code Administration's (PCA) limits of permissibility. *Forever Amber* (1947), a studio assignment, succumbed to the censor's scalpel, but as an independent force Preminger repeatedly defied the Hays Office, releasing *The Moon Is Blue*—whose references to virginity provoked outcries from the Legion of Decency—without the Production Code's Seal of Approval, a gambit unprecedented in 1953. He mounted two black-cast musicals (*Carmen Jones*; *Porgy and Bess*, 1959) in a period of intense racial unrest. And he flouted PCA prohibitions on a clutch of forbidden topics—heroin addiction (*The Man with the Golden Arm*), rape and incest (*Anatomy of a Murder*), homosexuality (*Advise & Consent*)—thus establishing himself as a trailblazer of hard-bitten storytelling, an enemy of Hollywood puritanism, and a formidable crusader against censorship. By the 1960s critics hailed Preminger as the prime mover in the collapse of the Production Code. His interviewers eagerly solicited his attitudes toward movie censorship, none more so than William F. Buckley Jr., whose April 10, 1967, episode of *Firing Line* ("Censorship and the Production Code") most comprehensively captures Preminger's views on the subject.

"Movie Maker Hires Blacklisted Writer"—thus ran the headline of the *New York Times* on January 20, 1960. With *Exodus*, Preminger broke the Hollywood blacklist, controversially rescuing from the wilderness screenwriter Dalton Trumbo, a member of the exiled Hollywood Ten. "[Trumbo] naturally will get the credit on the screen that he amply deserves," Preminger assured the newspaper and remained true to his word. He recalls this factious period in a 1972 conversation with Kenneth Geist, published here for the first time. In remembrance of director Joseph L. Mankiewicz—president of the Directors Guild during the McCarthy era, staunch opponent of the Communist witch hunts, and a longtime Preminger intimate—Preminger recounts his presence at the infamous 1950 Directors Guild meeting, at which Mankiewicz and producer Cecil B. DeMille (along with various assembled directors) clashed over a mandatory loyalty oath forswearing Communist alliances. Opposed to blacklisting, Preminger sided with Mankiewicz. He would remain passionately outspoken in defense of America's freedoms, cautioning against the insidious erosion of US democracy, and voicing support for the antiwar student activists at San Francisco State University.

As the 1960s wore on, Preminger's film career floundered. Though historians position him as a harbinger of the New Hollywood cinema (the wave of experimental, adult-centered filmmaking that emerged after the Production Code's abolition in 1967), he failed to gain a foothold in this freewheeling landscape, and his career tipped into decline. As David Thomson argues:

By 1967, Preminger was beginning to be out of touch, yet striving to keep up with breakthroughs in censorship. . . . In just a few years Preminger had slipped from daring and modern to old-fashioned. (24)

Preminger's mastery, critics alleged, had deserted him. Formerly prized for "subtlety," he was now disparaged as "heavy handed." He acquired an unwelcome moniker: "The man with the leaden arm." Seemingly démodé, he strove for relevancy, but *Tell Me That You Love Me, Junie Moon* (1970), *Such Good Friends* (1971), and *Rosebud* (1975) fizzled at the box office. His nadir took the form of psychedelic comedy *Skidoo* (1968), castigated by critics as a humiliating and maladroit effort to entice the youth audience. In the early to mid-1960s Preminger had independently launched a string of big-budget, large-scale, star-driven extravaganzas—*Exodus, The Cardinal, In Harm's Way, Hurry Sundown*—but now he struggled to raise finance, finally pouring millions of his own dollars into *The Human Factor* (1979), his overlooked swan song. Poignantly, the late-phase interviews bring to light several tantalizing projects that withered on the vine.

As an interviewee Preminger could be feisty, acerbic, frustrating. He would claim to suffer lapses of memory so as to skirt probing questions. He could be abrasive when confronted with theoretical readings of his work: Robert Porfirio's angle of inquiry, tracing the contours of classical film noir, seems to put Preminger in ornery temper. Is it true, as some critics maintained, that Preminger begins where his sense of humor leaves off? ("He never made a great comedy," Nathaniel Rich points out [2008].) A few of the interviews compiled here seem to certify this claim. And yet still others find him in witty and impish mood, slinging gibes at fellow directors, having fun at his own expense. Like Hitchcock and Welles, Preminger was a formidable self-publicist, and—as a movie producer as well as a director—he understood the value of a candid interview. The candor of his reflections and insights makes Preminger's personal testimony ripe for rediscovery.

This book collates film-journal interviews, career profiles, private testimonies, talk-show discussions, roundtable debates, and public "Q&A" dialogue—the better to examine Preminger's discourse at a wide variety of fora. Across all platforms he demonstrates a remarkable consistency of thought—indeed, a prevailing worldview—pertaining to every aspect of films and their reception. As with other books in the Conversations with Filmmakers series, the interviews are organized in chronological sequence. For those interviews derived from televised programs (*Firing Line*; *The Dick Cavett Show*) and public appearances ("AFI's Panel on the Critic"; "Otto Preminger Speaking at UCLA"), some editing has been required in order to eliminate digressions and interruptions. All other interviews are reproduced in full. The two *Cahiers du cinéma* interviews are here published in English for the first time. I have sought to preserve the integrity of all the interviews, hence some repetition between the pieces inevitably occurs.

I gratefully acknowledge each of the authors whose interviews are included in this volume. For assistance with permissions, I am indebted to Mary Gedeon, Tim Groeling, Jill Hollis, Vishnu Jani, Sophie Mithouard, Stephen Payne, Mike Pepin, Chris Robertson, Blythe E. Roveland-Brenton, Beau Sullivan, Ouardia Teraha, Emily Wittenberg, and Patricia Zline. Appreciation is due to Joanna E. Rapf, T. Jefferson Kline, Deac Rossell, Richard Rushton, and Jonathan Munby. Special thanks to Peter Masters, and to Emily Snyder Bandy, Laura Strong, Lisa Williams, and the editorial board at the University Press of Mississippi for their steadfast guidance, enthusiasm, and support. This book is dedicated, with love, to Shirley and Robert Bettinson.

References

Fujiwara, Chris. *The World and Its Double: The Life and Work of Otto Preminger*. New York: Farrar, Straus, and Giroux, 2008.

Harris, Mark. *Scenes from a Revolution: The Birth of the New Hollywood*. Edinburgh: Canongate Books, 2008.

Hirsch, Foster. *Otto Preminger: The Man Who Would Be King*. New York: Alfred A. Knopf, 2007.

Kael, Pauline. *I Lost It at the Movies: Film Writings, 1954 to 1965*. New York; London: Marion Boyars, 2016.

Kauffmann, Stanley. *A World on Film: Criticism and Comment*. New York: Dell, 1966.

Lyons, Donald. "Preminger's Brass." *Film Comment* 26.4 (July 1990): 47–51.

Macdonald, Dwight. *On Movies*. [New York]: Berkley, 1971.

Orr, John. "Otto Preminger and the End of Classical Cinema." *Senses of Cinema* 40 (July 2006). http://senses ofcinema.com/2006/three-auteurs/otto-preminger/.

Pratley, Gerald. *The Cinema of Otto Preminger*. New York: A. S. Barnes, 1971.

Rich, Nathaniel. "The Deceptive Director." *New York Review of Books* 6 Nov. 2008. https://www.nybooks .com/articles/2008/11/06/the-deceptive-director/.

Sarris, Andrew. *The American Cinema: Directors and Directions, 1929–1968*. Oxford: Da Capo Press, 1996.

Thomson, David. "Otto Preminger: Part Two." *NFT Catalogue* (May). London: BFI, 2005. 20–25.

Wake, Sandra, and Nicola Hayden. *The Bonnie & Clyde Book*. New York: Simon and Schuster, 1972.

West, Adam, and Jeff Rovin. *Back to the Batcave: My Story*. London: Titan Books, 1994.

Chronology

1905   Is born Otto Ludwig Preminger on December 5, 1905, in Wiznitz, Romania. (Not even Preminger, it seems, knew for certain the date and place of his birth; unverified records give his birthplace as Vienna and his birthdate as December 5, 1906.)

1915   During the First World War, the Preminger family moves to Graz, Styria, before settling in Vienna in 1915.

1922   Aged seventeen, Preminger plays the role of Lysander in *A Midsummer Night's Dream* at the Burggarten.

1923   Becomes an apprentice actor to Max Reinhardt at the recently opened Theater in der Josefstadt. Enrolls in the law program at the University of Vienna.

1925   Reprises the role of Lysander for Reinhardt's production of *A Midsummer Night's Dream* at the Theater in der Josefstadt. Leaves Reinhardt to act on stage in Zurich, Prague, and elsewhere. In December, his first assignment as a theater director—Franz Grillparzer's *Weh dem, der lugt* (*Woe to Him Who Lies*)—is publicly performed in Aussig.

1927   Returns to Vienna and, in partnership with fellow actor Rolf Jahn, acquires the Modernes Theater, subsequently renamed Die Komödie. The theater's maiden production, Anton Chekhov's *The Cherry Orchard*, opens in December.

1928   Earns a doctorate of laws from the University of Vienna.

1929   Parts ways with business partner Rolf Jahn. Embarks on a new theatrical venture with actor Jakob Feldhammer, producing and directing plays at the Neues Wiener Schauspielhaus between 1929 and 1930. Splits from Feldhammer in 1930.

1930   Reinhardt hires Preminger as an assistant director at the Theater in der Josefstadt.

1931   *Die grosse Liebe*, Preminger's debut as a film director, premieres in Vienna. Preminger marries actress Marion Mill.

1933   Succeeds Reinhardt as managing director of the Theater in der Josefstadt.

1935   Courted by Hollywood mogul Joseph M. Schenck, who envisages a future for Preminger as a movie director at Twentieth Century-Fox.

At the same period, Broadway producer Gilbert Miller invites him to direct Edward Wooll's courtroom melodrama *Libel!* on the New York stage. Preminger accepts both invitations. Arrives in New York on October 21. His production of *Libel!* opens on Broadway in December.

1936   Arrives in Los Angeles in January. Under Darryl F. Zanuck's auspices at Twentieth Century-Fox, he directs the romantic comedy *Under Your Spell*, released in theaters in November.

1937–39   Directs *Danger—Love at Work* at Fox and signs a new contract with the studio. Zanuck assigns Preminger to a prestigious production—a big-budget adaptation of Robert Louis Stevenson's *Kidnapped*—but their relationship deteriorates during principal photography, and Preminger is dismissed. Effectively blacklisted by Zanuck yet still under contract to Fox, Preminger spends much of his time toggling between Los Angeles and New York. In New York, he directs a string of stage hits, including *Outward Bound*, *My Dear Children*, and *Margin for Error*, in which he also plays the role of Nazi officer Karl Baumer.

1940–42   Three subsequent New York stage productions fizzle at the box office. Preminger returns to Hollywood, accepting acting roles (and becoming typecast as a Nazi) in *The Pied Piper* (1942) and *They Got Me Covered* (1942). In Zanuck's absence he negotiates a deal to both direct and act in Fox's production of *Margin for Error*.

1943   *Margin for Error* opens in February. Preminger is granted US citizenship on August 27.

1943–44   Directs and produces romantic comedy *In the Meantime, Darling*, which opens in September 1944.

1944   *Laura* is released in October, establishing Preminger's status among the top-flight Hollywood directors. Preminger receives an Academy Award nomination for Best Director. Assigned to direct *A Royal Scandal* after the film's original director, Ernst Lubitsch, is felled by illness.

1945   Opening of *A Royal Scandal*, a commercial disappointment. Directs film noir *Fallen Angel*, released in December.

1946   Musical comedy *Centennial Summer*, featuring songs composed by Jerome Kern, opens in July. Replaces John M. Stahl as director of *Forever Amber*, a major prestige production at Fox.

1947   Release of *Forever Amber*, later described by Preminger as "the worst picture I ever made." Assumes directorial duties of *That Lady in Ermine* following the sudden death of director Ernst Lubitsch. Preminger's melodrama *Daisy Kenyon*, starring Joan Crawford, Henry Fonda, and Dana Andrews, opens in December.

1948   *That Lady in Ermine* opens in August.

1949   *The Fan*, a film adaptation of Oscar Wilde's *Lady Windermere's Fan*, is released to lukewarm critical response. Psychological thriller *Whirlpool*, reuniting Preminger with *Laura* actress Gene Tierney, opens in November. Marriage to Marion Mill ends in divorce.

1950   *Where the Sidewalk Ends*, later to be lauded as a noir classic, opens in theaters. Preminger signs a four-picture deal with Twentieth Century-Fox.

1951   Release of *The 13th Letter*, Preminger's remake of Henri-Georges Clouzot's tale of small-town intrigue, *Le Corbeau*. Directs *The Moon Is Blue* on Broadway to great acclaim. Marries model Mary Gardner.

1952   Portrays Oberst von Scherbach, a sadistic German commandant, in Billy Wilder's comedy-thriller *Stalag 17*.

1953   For producer Howard Hughes, Preminger directs *Angel Face*, starring Jean Simmons and Robert Mitchum. *The Moon Is Blue* ends its Broadway run after 924 performances. Preminger's independently produced film version of the play runs afoul of the Production Code Administration (PCA) on account of its sexually frank dialogue. Distributor United Artists releases *The Moon Is Blue* without the Production Code seal; the film becomes a box-office success.

1954   *River of No Return*, starring Marilyn Monroe and Robert Mitchum, premieres in April. It is Preminger's first film to be shot in CinemaScope. In October the all-Black musical *Carmen Jones*, another Scope feature, becomes a hit at the US box office.

1955   Directs *The Court-Martial of Billy Mitchell*, starring Gary Cooper, for Warner Brothers. *The Man with the Golden Arm*, denied a Production Code seal because of its explicit depiction of drug addiction, premieres in December.

1957   A controversial film adaptation of Shaw's *Saint Joan*, starring newcomer Jean Seberg, is derided by critics.

1958   Release of *Bonjour Tristesse*, a romance melodrama substantially filmed in Paris.

1959   Replaces Rouben Mamoulian as director of *Porgy and Bess*, produced by Samuel Goldwyn. After jockeying with the PCA, Preminger secures approval for the release of acclaimed courtroom drama *Anatomy of a Murder*, starring James Stewart. The film will earn Preminger his second Oscar nomination for Best Director.

1960   Breaks the Hollywood blacklist by giving screen credit to Dalton Trumbo, writer of *Exodus*. Directs Henry Fonda in Ira Levin's comedy *Critic's Choice* on Broadway. Preminger and Mary Gardner divorce. Marries costume designer Hope Bryce.

1962   Political drama *Advise & Consent* is granted a Production Code seal, skirting the PCA's proscriptions on homosexual subject matter.

1963   Released in December, *The Cardinal* will be nominated for six Academy Awards, including Best Director.

1965   *In Harm's Way*, starring John Wayne and Kirk Douglas, is released on April 6. Suspense thriller *Bunny Lake Is Missing* goes on general release in October.

1966   Guest stars as Mr. Freeze in twin episodes of Fox Television's *Batman*.

1967   *Hurry Sundown* is released in February.

1968   *Skidoo*, released in December, meets with critical derision.

1970   Release of *Tell Me That You Love Me, Junie Moon*.

1971   *Such Good Friends* falters at the box office.

1975   Completes *Rosebud*, another critical and commercial failure.

1977   Publishes his autobiography.

1980   *The Human Factor*, Preminger's swan song, is released with little fanfare. Later that year, Preminger is struck by a taxi cab while crossing the street in Manhattan, sustaining serious head injuries. It is rumored that he develops Alzheimer's disease in the ensuing years.

1986   Dies of lung cancer in Manhattan, April 23.

Filmography

DIE GROSSE LIEBE (1931)
Director: **Otto Preminger**
Producers: **Otto Preminger**; Emmerich Taussig
Screenplay: Siegfried Bernfeld; Artur Berger
Cinematography: Hans Theyer
Editing: Paul Falkenberg
Production Design: Artur Berger
Music: Walter Landauer
Cast: Hansi Niese (Frieda, The Mother), Attila Hörbiger (Franz), Betty Bird (Anni Huber), Hugo Thimig (Chief of Police), Ferdinand Mayerhofer (Herr Huber), Maria Waldner (Frau Amalia Huber), Hans Olden (Dr. Theolbald Steinlechner), Adrienne Gessner (Rosa)
76 minutes

UNDER YOUR SPELL (1936)
Director: **Otto Preminger**
Producer: John Stone
Screenplay: Frances Hyland; Saul Elkins. Based on stories by Bernice Mason; Sy Bartlett.
Cinematography: Sidney Wagner
Editing: Fred Allen
Production Design: Duncan Cramer
Music: Arthur Schwartz, Howard Dietz
Cast: Lawrence Tibbett (Anthony Allen), Gregory Ratoff (Petroff), Wendy Barrie (Cynthia Drexel), Arthur Treacher (Botts), Gregory Gaye (Count Raul Du Rienne), Berton Churchill (The Judge), Jed Prouty (Mr. Twerp), Charles Richman (Uncle Bob), Claudia Coleman (Mrs. Twerp).
62 minutes

DANGER—LOVE AT WORK (1937)
Director: **Otto Preminger**
Producer: Harold Wilson

Screenplay: James Edward Grant; Ben Markson. Based on a story by James Edward Grant.
Cinematography: Virgil Miller
Editing: Jack Murray
Production Design: Duncan Cramer
Music: Cyril J. Mockridge; David Buttolph; Mack Gordon; Harry Revel
Cast: Ann Sothern (Toni Pemberton), Jack Haley (Henry MacMorrow), Edward Everett Horton (Howard Rogers), Mary Bowland (Alice Pemberton), Benny Bartlett (Junior Pemberton), Walter Catlett (Uncle Alan), John Carradine (Herbert Pemberton), Etienne Girardot (Albert Pemberton), Maurice Cass (Uncle Goliath), Alan Dinehart (Allan Duncan), E. E. Clive (Wilbur), Margaret McWade (Aunt Patty), Margaret Seddon (Aunt Pitty)
84 minutes

KIDNAPPED (1938)
Director: Alfred L. Werker; **Otto Preminger**
Producer: Kenneth Macgowan
Screenplay: Sonya Levien; Eleanor Harris; Ernest Pascal; Edwin Blum. Based on the novel by Robert Louis Stevenson
Cinematography: Gregg Toland; Bert Glennon
Editing: Allen McNeil
Production Design: Bernard Herzbrun; Mark-Lee Kirk
Music: Arthur Lange; Charles Maxwell
Cast: Werner Baxter (Alan Breck), Freddie Bartholomew (David Balfour), Arleen Whelan (Jean MacDonald), C. Aubrey Smith (Duke of Argyle), Reginald Owen (Captain Hoseason), John Carradine (Gordon), Nigel Bruce (Neil MacDonald), Miles Mander (Ebenezer Balfour), Ralph Forbes (James), H. B. Warner (Angus Rankeillor), Arthur Hohl (Riach), E. E. Clive (Minister MacDougall), Halliwell Hobbes (Dominie Campbell), Montagu Love (Colonel Whitehead)
90 minutes

MARGIN FOR ERROR (1943)
Director: **Otto Preminger**
Producer: Ralph Dietrich
Screenplay: Lillie Hayward. Based on a play by Claire Boothe Luce.
Cinematography: Edward Cronjager
Editing: Louis R. Loeffler
Production Design: Richard Day; Lewis H. Creber
Music: Leigh Harline; Emil Newman

Cast: Joan Bennett (Sophia Baumer), Milton Berle (Moe Finkelstein), **Otto Preminger** (Karl Baumer), Carl Esmond (Baron Max von Alvenstor), Howard Freeman (Otto Horst), Poldy Dur (Frieda), Clyde Fillmore (Dr. Jennings), Joe Kirk (Officer Solomon), Hans Heinrich von Twardowski (Fritz), Ted North, Elmer Jack Semple, J. Norton Dunn (The Saboteurs), Hans Schumm (Karl Müller), Edward McNamara (Captain Mulrooney), Selmer Jackson (Coroner).
74 minutes

IN THE MEANTIME, DARLING (1944)
Director: **Otto Preminger**
Producer: **Otto Preminger**
Screenplay: Arthur Kober; Michael Uris
Cinematography: Joseph MacDonald
Editing: Louis R. Loeffler
Production Design: James Basevi; John Ewing
Music: Cyril J. Mockridge; David Buttolph
Cast: Jeanne Crain (Maggie Preston), Frank Latimore (Lt. Daniel Ferguson), Mary Nash (Mrs. Vera Preston), Eugene Pallette (Henry B. Preston), Stanley Prager (Lt. Philip "Red" Pianatowski), Gale Robbins (Shirley Pianatowski), Jane Randolph (Jerry Armstrong), Doris Merrick (Mrs. MacAndrews), Cara Williams (Ruby Mae Sayre), Anne Corcoran (Mrs. Bennett), Reed Hadley (Major Phillips), Heather Angel (Mrs. Nelson)
72 minutes

LAURA (1944)
Director: **Otto Preminger**
Producer: **Otto Preminger**
Screenplay: Jay Dratler; Samuel Hoffenstein; Elizabeth Reinhardt. Based on a novel by Vera Casparay
Cinematography: Joseph LaShelle; Lucien Ballard
Editing: Louis R. Loeffler
Production Design: Lyle R. Wheeler; Leland Fuller
Music: David Raskin
Cast: Gene Tierney (Laura Hunt), Dana Andrews (Mark McPherson), Clifton Webb (Waldo Lydecker), Vincent Price (Shelby Carpenter), Judith Anderson (Ann Treadwell), Dorothy Adams (Bessie Clary), James Flavin (Detective McEveety), Clyde Fillmore (Bullitt), Ralph Dunn (Fred Callahan), Grant Mitchell (Lancaster Corey), Kathleen Howard (Louise)
88 minutes

A ROYAL SCANDAL (1945)
Director: **Otto Preminger**; Ernst Lubitsch
Producer: Ernst Lubitsch
Screenplay: Edwin Justus Mayer. Adapted by Bruno Frank from the play *Czarina* by Lajos Biró and Melchior Lengyel
Cinematography: Arthur C. Miller
Editing: Dorothy Spencer
Production Design: Lyle R. Wheeler; Mark-Lee Kirk
Music: Alfred Newman; Edward Powell
Cast: Tallulah Bankhead (Catherine the Great), Charles Coburn (Chancellor Nicolai Ilyitch), Anne Baxter (Countess Anna Jaschikoff), William Eythe (Lt. Alexei Chernoff), Vincent Price (Marquis de Fleury), Sig Ruman (General Ronsky), Mischa Auer (Captain Sukov), Vladimir Sokoloff (Malakoff), Mikhail Rasumny (Drunken General), Grady Sutton (Boris), Donald Douglas (Variatinsky), Egon Brecher (Wassilikow), Eva Gabor (Countess Demidow)
94 minutes

FALLEN ANGEL (1945)
Director: **Otto Preminger**
Producer: **Otto Preminger**
Screenplay: Harry Kleiner. Based on the novel by Marty Holland.
Cinematography: Joseph LaShelle
Editing: Harry Reynolds
Production Design: Lyle R. Wheeler; Leland Fuller
Music: David Raskin
Cast: Dana Andrews (Eric Stanton), Alice Faye (June Mills), Linda Darnell (Stella), Charles Bickford (Mark Judd), Anne Revere (Clara Mills), Bruce Cabot (Dave Atkins), John Carradine (Professor Madley), Percy Kilbride (Pop), Olin Howland (Joe Ellis), Jimmy Conlin (Walton Hotel Clerk)
98 minutes

CENTENNIAL SUMMER (1946)
Director: **Otto Preminger**
Producer: **Otto Preminger**
Screenplay: Michael Kanin. Based on the novel by Albert E. Idell.
Cinematography: Ernest Palmer
Editing: Harry Reynolds
Production Design: Lyle R. Wheeler; Leland Fuller
Music: Jerome Kern; Alfred Newman

Cast: Linda Darnell (Edith Rogers), Jeanne Crain (Julia Rogers), Cornel Wilde (Philippe Lascalles), William Eythe (Ben Phelps), Walter Brennan (Jesse Rogers), Constance Bennett (Zenia Lascalles), Dorothy Gish (Harriet Rogers), Barbara Whiting (Susanna Rogers), Larry Stevens (Richard Lewis), Kathleen Howard (Deborah), Buddy Swan (Dudley Rogers), Charles Dingle (J. P. Snodgrass), Gavin Gordon (Trowbridge)
102 minutes

FOREVER AMBER (1947)
Director: **Otto Preminger**; John M. Stahl
Producer: William Perlberg
Screenplay: Philip Dunne; Ring Lardner Jr. Adapted by Jerome Cady from the novel by Kathleen Windsor
Cinematography: Leon Shamroy
Editing: Louis R. Loeffler
Production Design: Lyle R. Wheeler
Music: David Raskin
Cast: Linda Darnell (Amber St. Clair), Cornel Wilde (Bruce Carlton), Richard Greene (Lord Harry Almsbury), George Sanders (King Charles II), Glenn Langan (Captain Rex Morgan), Richard Haydn (Earl of Radcliffe), John Russell (Black Jack Mallard), Jane Ball (Corinne Carlton), Leo G. Carroll (Matt Goodgroome), Jessica Tandy (Nan Britton), Anne Revere (Mother Red Cap)
138 minutes

DAISY KENYON (1947)
Director: **Otto Preminger**
Producer: **Otto Preminger**
Screenplay: David Hertz. Based on the novel by Elizabeth Janeway.
Cinematography: Leon Shamroy
Editing: Louis R. Loeffler
Production Design: Lyle R. Wheeler; George W. Davis
Music: David Raskin
Cast: Joan Crawford (Daisy Kenyon), Dana Andrews (Dan O'Mara), Henry Fonda (Peter Lapham), Ruth Warrick (Lucille Coverly O'Mara), Peggy Ann Garner (Rosamund O'Mara), Connie Marshall (Marie O'Hara), Martha Stewart (Mary Angelus), Nicholas Joy (Coverly), Art Baker (Lucille's attorney), Robert Karnes (Jack), John Davidson (Mervyn), Charles Meredith (Judge), Roy Roberts (Quint), Griff Barnett (Will Thompson), Tito Vuolo (Dino)
99 minutes

THAT LADY IN ERMINE (1948)
Director: Ernst Lubitsch; **Otto Preminger**
Producer: Ernst Lubitsch
Screenplay: Samson Raphaelson
Cinematography: Leon Shamroy
Editing: Dorothy Spencer
Production Design: Lyle R. Wheeler; J. Russell Spencer
Music: Alfred Newman; Cyril J. Mockridge; Leo Robin; Frederick Hollander
Cast: Betty Grable (Angelina / Francesca), Douglas Fairbanks Jr. (Colonel Ladislas
Karolyi Teglas / The Duke), Virginia Campbell (Theresa), Cesar Romero (Count
Mario), Walter Abel (Major Horvath / Benvenuto), Reginald Gardiner (Alberto),
Harry Davenport (Luigi), Whit Bissell (Giulio), Edmund MacDonald (Captain
Novak), David Bond (Gabor), Lester Allen (Jester)
89 minutes

THE FAN (1949)
Director: **Otto Preminger**
Producer: **Otto Preminger**
Screenplay: Walter Reisch; Dorothy Parker; Ross Evans. Based on the play *Lady
Windermere's Fan* by Oscar Wilde.
Cinematography: Joseph LaShelle
Editing: Louis R. Loeffler
Production Design: Lyle R. Wheeler; Leland Fuller
Music: Daniele Amfitheatrof
Cast: Jeanne Crain (Lady Windermere), Madeleine Carroll (Mrs. Erlynne),
George Sanders (Lord Darlington), Richard Greene (Lord Windermere), Mar-
tita Hunt (Duchess of Berwick), John Sutton (Cecil Graham), Hugh Dempster
(Lord Augustus Lorton), Richard Ney (Mr. James Hopper), Virginia McDowall
(Lady Agatha), Hugh Murray (Dawson), Frank Elliott (The Jeweller), John Burton
(Hoskins), Trevor Ward (The Auctioneer), Patricia Edwards (An American), Eric
Noonan (Underwood)
79 minutes

WHIRLPOOL (1949)
Director: **Otto Preminger**
Producer: **Otto Preminger**
Screenplay: Ben Hecht; Andrew Solt. Based on a novel by Guy Endore.
Cinematography: Arthur C. Miller
Editing: Louis R. Loeffler
Production Design: Lyle R. Wheeler; Leland Fuller

Music: David Raskin
Cast: Gene Tierney (Ann Sutton), Richard Conte (Dr. William Sutton), José Ferrer (David Korvo), Charles Bickford (Lt. James Colton), Barbara O'Neil (Theresa Randolph), Eduard Franz (Martin Avery), Constance Collier (Tina Cosgrove), Fortunio Bonanova (Feruccio di Ravallo), Ruth Lee (Miss Hall), Ian MacDonald (Detective Hogan), Bruce Hamilton (Lt. Jeffreys), Alex Gerry (Dr. Peter Duval), Larry Keating (Mr. Simms), Mauritz Hugo (Hotel Clerk), John Trebach (Freddie), Myrtle Anderson (Agnes)
98 minutes

WHERE THE SIDEWALK ENDS (1950)
Director: **Otto Preminger**
Producer: **Otto Preminger**
Screenplay: Ben Hecht. Based on an adaptation by Victor Trivas; Frank P. Rosenberg; Robert E. Kent of a novel by William L. Stuart
Cinematography: Joseph LaShelle
Editing: Louis R. Loeffler
Production Design: Lyle R. Wheeler; J. Russell Spencer
Music: Cyril J. Mockridge
Cast: Dana Andrews (Mark Dixon), Gene Tierney (Morgan Taylor), Gary Merrill (Tommy Scalise), Bert Freed (Paul Klein), Tom Tully (Jiggs Taylor), Karl Malden (Lt. Bill Thomas), Ruth Donnelly (Martha), Craig Stevens (Ken Paine), Robert F. Simon (Inspector Nicholas Foley), Harry von Zell (Ted Morrison), Don Appell (Willie), Neville Brand (Steve), Grayce Mills (Mrs. Tribaum), Lou Krugman (Mike Williams), David McMahon (Harrington), David Wolfe (Sid Kramer), Stephen Roberts (Gilruth), Phil Tully (Ted Benson), Ian MacDonald (Casey), John Close (Hanson), John McGuire (Gertessen)
95 minutes

THE 13TH LETTER (1951)
Director: **Otto Preminger**
Producer: **Otto Preminger**
Screenplay: Howard Koch. Based on a script by Louis Chavance for *Le Corbeau*.
Cinematography: Joseph LaShelle
Editing: Louis R. Loeffler
Production Design: Lyle R. Wheeler; Maurice Ransford
Music: Alex North
Cast: Linda Darnell (Denise Turner), Charles Boyer (Dr. Paul Laurent), Michael Rennie (Dr. Pearson), Constance Smith (Cora Laurent), Françoise Rosay (Mrs. Gauthier), Judith Evelyn (Sister Marie Corbin), Guy Sorel (Robert Helier),

June Hedin (Rochelle Turner), Paul Guèvremont (Postman), George Alexander (Dr. Fletcher), J. Léo Gagnon (Dr. Helier), Ovila Légaré (The Mayor), Camille Ducharme (Fredette)
85 minutes

ANGEL FACE (1953)
Director: **Otto Preminger**
Producer: **Otto Preminger**; Howard Hughes
Screenplay: Frank S. Nugent; Oscar Millard. Based on a story by Chester Erskine.
Cinematography: Harry Stradling Sr.
Editing: Frederic Knudtson
Production Design: Albert S. D'Agostino; Carroll Clark
Music: Dimitri Tiomkin
Cast: Robert Mitchum (Frank Jessup), Jean Simmons (Diane Tremayne Jessup), Mona Freeman (Mary Wilton), Herbert Marshall (Mr. Charles Tremayne), Leon Ames (Fred Barrett), Barbara O'Neil (Catherine Tremayne), Kenneth Tobey (Bill Crompton), Raymond Greenleaf (Arthur Vance), Griff Barnett (The Judge), Robert Gist (Miller), Jim Backus (Judson), Morgan Brown (Harry)
91 minutes

THE MOON IS BLUE (1953)
Director: **Otto Preminger**
Producers: **Otto Preminger**; F. Hugh Herbert
Screenplay: F. Hugh Herbert, based on his stage play
Cinematography: Ernest Laszlo
Editing: Ronald Sinclair; Otto Ludwig
Production Design: Nicolai Remisoff
Music: Herschel Burke Gilbert
Cast: Maggie McNamara (Patty O'Neill), William Holden (Donald Gresham), David Niven (David Slater), Tom Tully (Michael O'Neill), Dawn Addams (Cynthia Slater), Gregory Ratoff (Taxi Driver), Fortunio Bonanova (Television Performer)
99 minutes

DIE JUNGFRAU AUF DEM DACH (1953)
Director: **Otto Preminger**
Producer: **Otto Preminger**
Screenplay: Carl Zuckmayer; F. Hugh Herbert
Cinematography: Ernest Laszlo
Editing: Otto Ludwig
Production Design: Nicolai Remisoff

Music: Herschel Burke Gilbert
Cast: Hardy Krüger (Donald Gresham), Johannes Heesters (David Slader), Johanna Matz (Patty O'Neill), Tom Tully (Michael O'Neill), Dawn Addams (Cynthia Slader), Gregory Ratoff (Taxi Driver), Fortunio Bonanova (Television Announcer)
90 minutes

RIVER OF NO RETURN (1954)
Director: **Otto Preminger**
Producer: Stanley Rubin
Screenplay: Frank Fenton. Based on a story by Louis Lantz.
Cinematography: Joseph LaShelle
Editing: Louis R. Loeffler
Production Design: Lyle R. Wheeler; Addison Hehr
Music: Cyril J. Mockridge
Cast: Robert Mitchum (Matt Calder), Marilyn Monroe (Kay Weston), Rory Calhoun (Harry Weston), Tommy Rettig (Mark Calder), Murvyn Vye (Dave Colby), Douglas Spencer (Sam Benson), Don Beddoe (Ben), Claire André (Surrey Driver), Jack Mather (Card Table Dealer), Edmund Cobb (Barber), Will Wright (Trader)
91 minutes

CARMEN JONES (1954)
Director: **Otto Preminger**
Producer: **Otto Preminger**
Screenplay: Harry Kleiner. Based on the musical by Oscar Hammerstein II.
Cinematography: Sam Leavitt
Editing: Louis R. Loeffler
Production Design: Edward L. Ilou
Music: Georges Bizet; Herschel Burke Gilbert
Cast: Dorothy Dandridge (Carmen Jones), Harry Belafonte (Joe), Olga James (Cindy Lou), Pearl Bailey (Frankie), Diahann Carroll (Myrt), Roy Glenn (Rum Daniels), Nick Stewart (Dink Franklin), Joe Adams (Husky Miller), Brock Peters (Sergeant Brown), Sandy Lewis (T-Bone), Maurie Lynn (Sally)
105 minutes

THE MAN WITH THE GOLDEN ARM (1955)
Director: **Otto Preminger**
Producer: **Otto Preminger**
Screenplay: Walter Newman; Lewis Meltzer. Based on the novel by Nelson Algren.
Cinematography: Sam Leavitt

Editing: Louis R. Loeffler
Production Design: Joseph C. Wright
Music: Elmer Bernstein
Cast: Frank Sinatra (Frankie Machine), Kim Novak (Molly), Eleanor Parker (Zosch), Arnold Stang (Sparrow), Darren McGavin (Louie), Robert Strauss (Schwiefka), George Matthews (Williams), John Conte (Drunky), Doro Merande (Vi), George E. Stone (Sam Markette), Emil Meyer (Detective Bednar), Frank Richards (Piggy), Ralph Neff (Chester), Ernest Raboff (Bird-Dog), Martha Wentworth (Vangie), Jered Barclay (Junkie), Will Wright (Lane), Harold "Tommy" Hart (Kvorka), Frank Marlowe (Yantek)
119 minutes

THE COURT-MARTIAL OF BILLY MITCHELL (1955)
Director: **Otto Preminger**
Producer: Milton Sperling
Screenplay: Milton Sperling; Emmet Lavery
Cinematography: Sam Leavitt
Editing: Folmar Blangsted
Production Design: Malcom C. Bert
Music: Dimitri Tiomkin
Cast: Gary Cooper (Colonel Billy Mitchell), Charles Bickford (Gen. Jimmy Guthrie), Rod Steiger (Maj. Allen Guillion), Ralph Bellamy (Congressman Frank Reid), Elizabeth Montgomery (Margaret Lansdowne), Fred Clark (Col. Moreland), James Daly (Lt. Col. Herbert A. White), Darren McGavin (Russ Peters), Jack Lord (Zachary Lansdowne), Peter Graves (Captain Elliott), Robert F. Simon (Admiral Adam Gage), Charles Dingle (Senator Fullerton), Dayton Lummis (Gen. Douglas MacArthur), Tom McKee (Capt. Eddie Rickenbacker), Stephen Roberts (Maj. Carl Spaatz), Ian Wolfe (President Calvin Coolidge)
100 minutes

SAINT JOAN (1957)
Director: **Otto Preminger**
Producer: **Otto Preminger**
Screenplay: Graham Greene. Based on the play by George Bernard Shaw.
Cinematography: Georges Périnal
Editing: Helga Cranston
Production Design: Roger K. Furse
Music: Mischa Spoliansky
Cast: Jean Seberg (Saint Joan of Arc), Richard Widmark (Charles VII, The Dauphin), Richard Todd (Dunois), Anton Walbrook (Cauchon, Bishop of Beauvais),

John Gielgud (Earl of Warwick), Felix Aylmer (The Inquisitor), Harry Andrews (John de Stogumber), Barry Jones (De Courcelles), Finlay Currie (Archbishop of Rheims), Bernard Miles (The Executioner), Patrick Barr (Captain La Hire), Kenneth Haigh (Brother Martin)
110 minutes

BONJOUR TRISTESSE (1958)
Director: **Otto Preminger**
Producer: **Otto Preminger**
Screenplay: Arthur Laurents. Based on the novel by Françoise Sagan.
Cinematography: Georges Périnal
Editing: Helga Cranston
Production Design: Roger K. Furse
Music: Georges Auric
Cast: Deborah Kerr (Anne Larson), David Niven (Raymond), Jean Seberg (Cécile), Mylène Demongeot (Elsa Mackenbourg), Geoffrey Horne (Philippe), Juliette Gréco (Night Club Singer), Walter Chiari (Pablo), Martita Hunt (Philippe's Mother), Roland Culver (Mr. Lombard), David Oxley (Jacques), Jean Kent (Helen Lombard), Elga Andersen (Denise), Jeremy Burnham (Hubert Duclos), Tutte Lemkow (Pierre Schube)
94 minutes

PORGY AND BESS (1959)
Director: **Otto Preminger**
Producer: Samuel Goldwyn
Screenplay: N. Richard Nash. Based on the stage operetta by George Gershwin, from the play by DuBose and Dorothy Heyward.
Cinematography: Leon Shamroy
Editing: Daniel Mandell
Production Design: Oliver Smith
Music: George Gershwin
Cast: Sidney Poitier (Porgy), Dorothy Dandridge (Bess), Sammy Davis Jr. (Sportin' Life), Pearl Bailey (Maria), Brock Peters (Crown), Leslie Scott (Jake), Diahann Carroll (Clara), Ruth Attaway (Serena), Claude Akins (Detective), Clarence Muse (Peter), Everdinne Wilson (Annie), Joel Fluellen (Robbins), Earl Jackson (Mingo), Moses LaMarr (Nelson), Margaret Hairston (Lily), Ivan Dixon (Jim), Antoine Durousseau (Scipio), Helen Thigpen (Strawberry Woman), Roy Glenn (Lawyer Frazier)
148 minutes

ANATOMY OF A MURDER (1959)
Director: **Otto Preminger**
Producer: **Otto Preminger**
Screenplay: Wendell Mayes. Based on the novel by Robert Traver.
Cinematography: Sam Leavitt
Editing: Louis R. Loeffler
Production Design: Boris Leven
Music: Duke Ellington
Cast: James Stewart (Paul Biegler), Lee Remick (Laura Manion), Ben Gazzara (Lt. Frederick Manion), Joseph N. Welch (Judge Weaver), Kathryn Grant (Mary Pilant), Arthur O'Connell (Parnell Emmett McCarthy), Eve Arden (Maida Rutledge), George C. Scott (Claude Dancer), Brooks West (Mitch Lodwick), Orson Bean (Dr. Smith), John Qualen (Deputy Sheriff Sulo), Murray Hamilton (Alphonse Paquette), Russ Brown (George Lemon), Don Ross (Duane Miller), Jimmy Conlin (Clarence Madigan), Ned Weaver (Dr. Raschid), Ken Lynch (Sgt. James Duro), Joseph Kearns (Mr. Lloyd Burke), Howard McNear (Dr. Dompierre), Duke Ellington (Pie Eye)
161 minutes

EXODUS (1960)
Director: **Otto Preminger**
Producer: **Otto Preminger**
Screenplay: Dalton Trumbo. Based on the novel by Leon Uris.
Cinematography: Sam Leavitt
Editing: Louis R. Loeffler
Production Design: Richard Day; Bill Hutchinson
Music: Ernest Gold
Cast: Paul Newman (Ari Ben Canaan), Eva Marie Saint (Kitty Fremont), Ralph Richardson (General Sutherland), Peter Lawford (Major Caldwell), Lee J. Cobb (Barak Ben Canaan), Sal Mineo (Dov Landau), John Derek (Taha), Hugh Griffith (Mandria), David Opatoshu (Akiva Ben Canaan), Jill Haworth (Karen), Gregory Ratoff (Lakavitch), Felix Aylmer (Dr. Lieberman), Marius Goring (Von Storch), Alexandra Stewart (Jordana), Michael Wager (David), Martin Benson (Mordekai), Paul Stevens (Reuben), Betty Walker (Sarah), Martin Miller (Dr. Odenheim), Victor Maddern (Sergeant), George Maharis (Yoav), John Crawford (Hank), Dahn Ben Amotz (Uzi), Peter Madden (Dr. Clement), Ralph Truman (Colonel)
208 minutes

ADVISE & CONSENT (1962)
Director: **Otto Preminger**
Producer: **Otto Preminger**

Screenplay: Wendell Mayes. Based on the novel by Allen Drury.
Cinematography: Sam Leavitt
Editing: Louis R. Loeffler
Production Design: Lyle R. Wheeler
Music: Jerry Fielding
Cast: Henry Fonda (Robert Leffingwell), Charles Laughton (Senator Seabright Cooley), Don Murray (Senator Brigham Anderson), Walter Pidgeon (Senator Bob Munson), Peter Lawford (Senator Lafe Smith), Gene Tierney (Dolly Harrison), Franchot Tone (The President), Lew Ayres (The Vice President), Burgess Meredith (Herbert Gelman), Eddie Hodges (Johnny Leffingwell), Paul Ford (Senator Stanley Danta), George Grizzard (Senator Fred Van Ackerman), Inga Swenson (Ellen Anderson), Paul McGrath (Hardiman Fletcher), Will Geer (Senate Minority Leader), Edward Andrews (Senator Orrin Knox), Betty White (Senator Bessie Adams), Malcolm Atterbury (Senator Tom August), J. Edward McKinley (Senator Powell Hanson), Bill Quinn (Senator Paul Hendershot), Tiki Santos (Senator Kanaho), Raoul De Leon (Senator Velez), Tom Helmore (British Ambassador), Hilary Eaves (Lady Maudulayne)
139 minutes

THE CARDINAL (1963)
Director: **Otto Preminger**
Producer: **Otto Preminger**
Screenplay: Robert Dozier. Based on the novel by Henry Morton Robinson.
Cinematography: Leon Shamroy
Editing: Louis R. Loeffler
Production Design: Lyle R. Wheeler
Music: Jerome Moross
Cast: Tom Tryon (Stephen Fermoyle), Carol Lynley (Mona Fermoyle), Dorothy Gish (Celia), Maggie McNamara (Florrie), John Huston (Cardinal Glennon), John Saxon (Benny Rampbell), Burgess Meredith (Father Ned Halley), Jill Haworth (Lalage Menton), Raf Vallone (Cardinal Quarenghi), Tullio Carminati (Cardinal Giacobbi), Ossie Davis (Father Gillis), Murray Hamilton (Lafe), Romy Schneider (Annemarie), Pat Henning (Hercule Menton), Bill Hayes (Frank), Cecil Kellaway (Monsignor Monaghan), Loring Smith (Cornelius J. Deegan), Jose Duvall (Ramon Gongaro), Peter MacLean (Father Callahan), James Hickman (Father Lyons), Russ Brown (Dr. Heller), Cameron Prud'Homme (Din), Berenice Gahm (Mrs. Rampell)
175 minutes

IN HARM'S WAY (1965)
Director: **Otto Preminger**
Producer: **Otto Preminger**
Screenplay: Wendell Mayes. Based on the novel by James Bassett.
Cinematography: Loyal Griggs
Editing: George Tomasini; Hugh S. Fowler
Production Design: Lyle R. Wheeler
Music: Jerry Goldsmith
Cast: John Wayne (Capt. Rockwell Torrey), Kirk Douglas (Commander Paul Eddington), Patricia Neal (Lt. Maggie Haynes), Tom Tryon (William McConnel), Paula Prentiss (Bev McConnel), Brandon De Wilde (Jeremiah Torrey), Jill Haworth (Annalee Dorne), Dana Andrews (Admiral Broderick), Stanley Holloway (Clayton Canfil), Burgess Meredith (Commander Powell), Franchot Tone (CINCPAC I), Patrick O'Neal (Commander Neal Owynn), Carroll O'Connor (Lt. Commander Burke), Slim Pickens (CPO Culpepper), James Mitchum (Ensign Griggs), George Kennedy (Colonel Gregory), Bruce Cabot (Quartermaster Quoddy), Barbara Bouchet (Liz Eddington), Tod Andrews (Captain Tuthill), Larry Hagman (Lt. Cline), Stewart Moss (Ensign Balch), Richard LePore (Lt. Tom Agar), Henry Fonda (CINCPAC II)
165 minutes

BUNNY LAKE IS MISSING (1965)
Director: **Otto Preminger**
Producer: **Otto Preminger**
Screenplay: John Mortimer; Penelope Mortimer. Based on the novel by Evelyn Piper.
Cinematography: Denys N. Coop
Editing: Peter Thornton
Production Design: Donald M. Ashton
Music: Paul Glass
Cast: Keir Dullea (Steven Lake), Carol Lynley (Ann Lake), Laurence Olivier (Superintendent Newhouse), Martita Hunt (Ada Ford), Noël Coward (Horacio Wilson), Lucie Mannheim (Cook), Adrienne Corri (Dorothy), Anna Massey (Elvira), Finlay Currie (Doll Maker), Clive Revill (Andrews), John Forbes-Robertson (Hospital Attendant), The Zombies (The Zombies)
107 minutes

HURRY SUNDOWN (1967)
Director: **Otto Preminger**
Producer: **Otto Preminger**

Screenplay: Thomas C. Ryan; Horton Foote. Based on the novel by Katya and Bert Gilden.
Cinematography: Milton R. Krasner; Loyal Griggs
Editing: Tony de Zarraga; Louis R. Loeffler; James D. Wells
Production Design: Gene Callahan
Music: Hugo Montenegro
Cast: Michael Caine (Henry Warren), Jane Fonda (Julie Ann Warren), John Phillip Law (Rad McDowell), Diahann Carroll (Vivian Thurlow), Robert Hooks (Reeve Scott), Faye Dunaway (Lou McDowell), Burgess Meredith (Judge Purcell), Jim Backus (Carter Sillens), Robert Reed (Lars Finchley), Beah Richards (Rose Scott), Rex Ingram (Professor Thurlow), Madeleine Sherwood (Eula Purcell), Doro Merande (Ada Hemmings), George Kennedy (Sheriff Coombs), Frank Converse (Rev. Clem De Lavery), Loring Smith (Thomas Elwell), Donna Danton (Sukie Purcell), John Mark (Colie Warren)
146 minutes

SKIDOO (1968)
Director: **Otto Preminger**
Producer: **Otto Preminger**
Screenplay: Doran William Cannon
Cinematography: Leon Shamroy
Editing: George R. Rohrs
Production Design: Robert Emmett Smith
Music: Harry Nilsson
Cast: Jackie Gleason (Tony Banks), Carol Channing (Flo Banks), Groucho Marx (God), Frankie Avalon (Angie), Michael Constantine (Leech), Frank Gorshin (The Man), John Philip Law (Stash), Peter Lawford (The Senator), Burgess Meredith (The Warden), George Raft (The Skipper), Cesar Romero (Hechy), Mickey Rooney (Blue Chips Packard), Austin Pendleton (Fred The Professor), Alexandra Hay (Darlene Banks), Arnold Stang (Harry), Doro Merande (The Mayor), Slim Pickens and Robert Donner (Switchboard Operators), Richard Kiel (Beany), Jaik Rosenstein ("Eggs" Benedict), Harry Nilsson (Tower Guard)
98 minutes

TELL ME THAT YOU LOVE ME, JUNIE MOON (1970)
Director: **Otto Preminger**
Producer: **Otto Preminger**
Screenplay: Marjorie Kellogg, based on her novel
Cinematography: Boris Kaufman
Editing: Henry Berman; Dean Ball

Production Design: Lyle R. Wheeler
Music: Philip Springer
Cast: Liza Minnelli (Junie Moon), Ken Howard (Arthur), Robert Moore (Warren), James Coco (Mario), Kay Thompson (Gregory), Fred Williamson (Beach Boy), Ben Piazza (Jesse), Emily Yancy (Solana), Leonard Frey (Guiles), Clarice Taylor (Minnie), James Beard (Sidney Wyner), Julie Bovasso (Ramona), Gina Collens (Lila), Barbara Logan (Mother Moon), Nancy Marchand (Nurse Oxford), Lynn Milgrim (Nurse Holt), Richard O'Barry (Joebee)
113 minutes

SUCH GOOD FRIENDS (1971)
Director: **Otto Preminger**
Producer: **Otto Preminger**
Screenplay: Esther Dale (Elaine May). Based on the novel by Lois Gould (adapted by David Shaber).
Cinematography: Gayne Rescher
Editing: Moe Howard
Production Design: Rouben Ter-Arutunian
Music: Thomas Z. Shepard
Cast: Dyan Cannon (Julie), James Coco (Timmy), Jennifer O'Neill (Miranda), Ken Howard (Cal), Nina Foch (Julie's Mother), Laurence Luckinbill (Richard), Louise Lasser (Marcy), Burgess Meredith (Kalman), Sam Levene (Uncle Eddie), William Redfield (Barney), James Beard (Dr. Mahler), Rita Gam (Doria), Michael Giordano III (Matthew), Oscar Grossman (The Doorman), Nancy Guild (Molly)
101 minutes

ROSEBUD (1975)
Director: **Otto Preminger**
Producer: **Otto Preminger**
Screenplay: Erik Lee Preminger. Based on the novel by Joan Hemingway and Paul Bonnecarrère.
Cinematography: Denys N. Coop
Editing: Thom Noble; Peter Thornton
Production Design: Michael Seymour; Willy Holt
Music: Laurent Petitgirard
Cast: Peter O'Toole (Larry Martin), Richard Attenborough (Edward Sloat), Cliff Gorman (Yafet Hamlekh), Claude Dauphin (Charles-Andre Fargeau), John V. Lindsay (Senator Donnovan), Peter Lawford (Lord Carter), Raf Vallone (George Nikolaos), Adrienne Corri (Lady Carter), Amidou (Kirkbane), Joseph Shiloach (Hacam), Brigitte Ariel (Sabine Fargeau), Isabelle Huppert (Helene Nikolaos),

Lalla Ward (Margaret Carter), Kim Cattrall (Joyce Donnovan), Debra Berger (Gertrude Freyer), Hans Verner (Freyer), Georges Beller (Patrice), Françoise Brion (Melina Nikolaos)
126 minutes

THE HUMAN FACTOR (1979)
Director: **Otto Preminger**
Producer: **Otto Preminger**
Screenplay: Tom Stoppard. Based on the novel by Graham Greene.
Cinematography: Mike Malloy
Editing: Richard Trevor
Production Design: Kenneth Ryan
Music: Gary Logan; Richard Logan
Cast: Nicol Williamson (Maurice Castle), Iman (Sarah), Richard Attenborough (Colonel John Daintry), Joop Doderer (Cornelius Muller), John Gielgud (Brigadier Tomlinson), Derek Jacobi (Arthur Davis), Robert Morley (Doctor Percival), Ann Todd (Castle's Mother), Richard Vernon (Sir John Hargreaves), Anthony Woodruff (Doctor Barker), Angela Thorne (Lady Mary Hargreaves), Tony Haygarth (Buffy), Paul Curran (Halliday), Cyd Hayman (Cynthia), Fiona Fullerton (Elizabeth), Tony Vogel (Matthew Connolly), Adrienne Corri (Sylvia)
115 minutes

Films in which Otto Preminger appeared as actor

The Pied Piper (1942), directed by Irving Pichel
Margin for Error (1943), directed by Otto Preminger
They Got Me Covered (1943), directed by David Butler
Where Do We Go from Here? (1945), directed by Gregory Ratoff
Stalag 17 (1953), directed by Billy Wilder

Otto Preminger: Interviews

Meeting with Otto Preminger

Jacques Rivette / 1953

Translated by Peter Masters

From *Cahiers du cinéma*, no. 29, December 1953, 7–13. Reproduced from *Cahiers du cinéma*.

Published by Cahiers du cinéma © 1953.

Kindliness is the mark of the great filmmakers. Otto Preminger offers, from the outset, living confirmation of this initial truth. But the reader doubtless cares little for politeness at the door and the formalities of greetings and introductions. So let's get straight to the subjects themselves, the reason for the visitor's imposition.

Preminger is sitting in front of me, awaiting my first questions. From his face, with marked features weathered by expressive lines, there emanates a great gentleness. This is doubtless linked to the serene clarity of his gaze. He speaks French hesitatingly, but most correctly, and explains thus: raised by a French governess, necessity required him to learn another language twenty years ago, and to then clear from his mind his preoccupations with Europe and its languages; though he intends to apply himself anew and soon recover a degree of perfection.

Then he hastily recalls, at my request, the stages of his apprenticeship: his meeting, while still young, with Max Reinhardt; the sudden and tenacious taste for the theatre. How he quickly decided to not be more than an occasional actor, to devote all his activity and all his thoughts to directing. He ends with the memory of the beautiful theater he had in Vienna. I ask him about his first time in the Austrian film studios. He is surprised, remembers nothing. As my questions become more precise, he agrees to recognize some part of the truth: one or two films, simple exercises without importance. Can't he give a name, though, a title? No, nothing interesting, he's forgotten it all. His oeuvre begins with *Laura*.

He continues his account but now abruptly breaks the thread of his biography. His arrival in New York. The direction of *Libel* on Broadway. Then he opens up about his passion for the theater. How, in spite of Hollywood, he has always applied himself to reserving six months each year to putting on plays to his taste; hence, *The Moon Is Blue*. What are the differences between the stage and the screen? Very minimal. It's the same problem in both cases. Keeping all the spontaneity of the characters, their real value; exploring movement; the invention of gestures was so accentuated in the theatre, so precise.

In 1935 comes his first stay in Hollywood, his meeting with Lubitsch. Preminger, usually so careful to affirm his full responsibility as creator, takes pains to minimize his role not only in *That Lady in Ermine*, a film stalled by the death of Lubitsch, which Preminger finished (though the essential part, he confirms, was already filmed), but also in *A Royal Scandal*, produced by Lubitsch and which illness prevented Lubitsch from directing himself. In this, too, Preminger sees himself only as the hand which realized, to the best of his ability, the concept of the films' true auteur.

Yet his biographical account is interesting him less and less. He escapes the disappointments of this first experience in Hollywood; the return to New York; the successes on Broadway. Called back to California as an actor, he then proposes the subject of *Laura*, in vain, to all the producers at Fox. The story frightens them away, and he decides to produce the film himself. He finds that if he proceeds in this manner, the majority of them will follow. This permits him to treat in his own fashion the themes of his choice.

Of *Laura* he says little, but with great tenderness. "My first," he murmurs, and, leafing through a recent edition of *Cahiers* which I gave him, he stops for a moment at the photograph in which Gene Tierney and Dana Andrews stare at each other.

I ask him about the films that we have not been able to see in Paris. *In the Meantime, Darling* was set in the area around a training camp for soldiers during the last war, in the camp for their wives. "A comedy, but with something else"— he points to his heart with a sober gesture. As for *Centennial Summer*, it was a musical film, the last one for Jerome Kern (and the only one for Preminger), shot in Technicolor as it should be. A light story interlinks several characters against the backdrop of the Centennial Exposition and the festivities celebrating the centenary of Philadelphia.

I ask for more details, but he apologizes. He has forgotten everything about these already ancient films. When I next ask him if there is one of these works which he prefers to the others, he evades the question. No, he has no opinion on the films; in truth, he casts them from his spirit. What interests him is the work itself, the filming, the difficulties. "I like to make a film, but once that is finished, the interest goes. I think of the next one. I very rarely see my finished films, only to present them to a few friends."

And *Forever Amber*? He hesitates a little, then evokes the sense of crisis which pervaded the production in the studio. How a first version directed by John Stahl with Peggy Cummins had been interrupted. How the big bosses no longer knew what action to take. How they pressured him (certainly not by imposing constraints, but by means of opinionated persuasion) to take an interest in the venture. To save the situation? "Or to ruin it," he adds, smiling. He jokes lightly about the absurdity of the undertaking, since it was about taking part in a successful scandal while leaving out everything which could scandalize. Yet he doesn't disown the picture. He took care to modify the distribution, to change the décor, to rework the script. He clarifies simply: "director."

Moving from one scandal to another, he returns to *The Moon Is Blue*. He is amused by the tale of his little war against the local censors. The film finally succeeded in being screened in all the American states, save three. Even today there is a court case in Maryland to pronounce on his fate there. The film's plot is not in question, only a few lines of dialogue, less even, just a few words: "pregnant," "professional virgin"—unheard of up to then.

But I pressure him once again to go backwards, and I confide in him my regret at never having been able to see his version of *Lady Windermere's Fan*. "You've nothing to regret," he says at once. "It was an experiment which was sadly lacking." Should I, though, still see in that a scruple of not wanting to take anything away from Lubitsch, even a subject which he formerly illustrated remarkably? However, Preminger in no way tries to dismiss this film. He adds: "It is one of my children, and the ones who are sick are not the ones whom one loves the least."

We come finally to *The 13th Letter*, a remake of *Le Corbeau*. "I admire the film by Clouzot very much, and precisely for this reason, I modified the script considerably, keeping only the general theme and the essence of the principal characters, in order to make a work totally independent of the original." A major portion of the film was shot in the real outdoors in Canada (Quebec and Montreal). What's more, it was there that Preminger made the acquaintance of the owner of this hotel, l'Avenue Montaigne, where he is hosting me. He gets up at once, opens the window, and wants me to admire Paris from his seventh floor. He exclaims less about the Eiffel Tower than about the uneven perspective of the roofs, like the image of Europe, evoking the celebrated film by René Clair [*Under the Roofs of Paris / Sous les toits de Paris*, 1930]. He refocuses at once when I ask him rather stupidly to list his favorite films: citing at random, from memory, *Sous les toits de Paris*, *All About Eve*, and *Gone with the Wind*, then adding *Rebecca*. He looks for a precise term—"a masterpiece," he affirms finally. I can barely hide my contentment.

The theater arises afresh in the conversation. In New York he has just finished the production of an opera by Von Einem, based on *The Trial*. I take the opportunity to ask: What is the link between your conception of mise-en-scène in theatre and cinema? He smiles. "That's a very old question." But he attempts it with good grace. No, he doesn't see any fundamental difference, only ambience and milieu. The true problem in the two cases remains the same; he expresses it in the word "honesty." Then it pleases him to digress slightly. "The principal difference is that in the theatre, as soon as the *metteur-en-scène* has turned his back, the actors themselves start demolishing all his work bit by bit. I succeed in getting the same precision as in the film studio, but for one evening." Still, he's not unaware of the importance of the invention of detail, of the gesture that can seem insignificant, but sometimes resumes the very idea of cinema—which only permits you to push the research to the extreme. I try to tease out some further confidences: didn't he in *Laura* introduce to Hollywood the technique of long takes filmed from the crane, which has since had such good fortune, as we know, and which CinemaScope seems now to hold sacred? He is acquiescent, but not insistent.

Suddenly he comes to life. He now talks without reticence, or the least hesitation, about *River of No Return*, a CinemaScope film he has recently shot, nine-tenths of it anyway, in the real outdoors in the emptiness of the northwest of Canada. Certainly, CinemaScope introduced "a subtle change" in the film's mise-en-scène. He appreciates that with CinemaScope there is the possibility of having a greater number of actors play at the same time, and of combining more effectively, with the movements of the camera, those of the characters *in relation* to it. But above all he seems to recognize the greater chance offered to actors by auteurs of the American cinema, the promise of considerable creative freedom, perhaps more than in Europe. I don't hide my astonishment. He makes himself even more emphatic. Being often the producer of his own films, he already knew this freedom, which he evokes with a contagious faith. However, the development of diverse processes from 3-D to widescreen, and the reduction of the total number of films being made, obliges one to think of the production of each film as one of a number of independents, for which the studio will be no more than the distributor. He takes his own case as an example: when he finished *The Moon Is Blue*, Twentieth Century-Fox submitted the script of *River of No Return*, which seduced him at once. He adapts it as he sees fit, chooses its distribution, and sets off to film with his team in complete peace in his little corner of Canada. Once the film is finished and edited under his sole auspices, it is only then screened for Darryl Zanuck, who is content to suggest a few additional details. As for the rest, no impersonal and abstract order, no absolute obligation. A producer like Zanuck is "a man with whom you can discuss things," and who can very well permit the other participant in the conversation to be in the right. You just have to be right.

The future of cinema? Preminger doesn't want to play the prophet. Personally, he has little taste for 3-D. As for Cinerama, perhaps it will evolve in parallel with CinemaScope. Nothing can confirm it or contradict it. Yet black-and-white cinema is not dead. Aside from *The Robe*, the films which are actually receiving the greatest success in the USA are two black-and-white films: *The Moon Is Blue* and *From Here to Eternity*, the last production from Fred Zinnemann-Stanley Kramer. Certain subjects, exactly like those in *The Moon Is Blue*, don't require any other treatment. Perhaps Preminger's next film will be shot in CinemaScope, perhaps in simple black-and-white; he doesn't know. He is reading. He shows me the book he has begun: *Galatea*, a recent novel by James Cain. "Perhaps this one . . ."

Interview with Otto Preminger

Jacques Doniol-Valcroze and Eric Rohmer / 1961

Translated by Peter Masters.

From *Cahiers du cinéma*, no. 121, July 1961, 1–11. Reproduced from Cahiers du cinéma. Published by Cahiers du cinéma © 1961.

This interview is the fruit of the second meeting of *Cahiers* with Otto Preminger. The propositions set forth in the course of the first, let us remember, were reported by Jacques Rivette in edition 29 in December 1953. That is why we haven't asked our interviewee any questions on films he made before that date. Moreover, there are all sorts of reasons to think that he would have eluded them with the same courtesy and firmness which he generally showed to those who report his work in too precise a manner. But the general ideas will quickly give us a pleasant base of understanding.

A first filmography of Otto Preminger was published at the end of the article by Jacques Rivette. Rather than complete it with addenda, which are too numerous, we have preferred to restart the work entirely for the comfort of the reader.

Cahiers: Can you talk to us about your years in the theater? Do you consider yourself a disciple of Max Reinhardt?

Preminger: I'm fifty-four, and I really hope that for a long time I have cut loose from all influences. Notwithstanding, I have much admiration for Max Reinhardt, to whom I was a successor as head of the Theater in der Josefstadt in Vienna from 1930 to 1934, before my departure for America. I learned a lot from him. He was a great director, especially when it came to directing actors.

It is only in the US that I began to get interested in cinema. Up until then I had never made films.

So really, from the beginning, I am a man of the theater, and my formation by the theater has marked me, I can't deny it. It means that I'm much more closely interested in the work of the actors than those of my colleagues whose "approach" starts from the scenario, the photography, or the editing. What I like is helping the actors discover ever new forms of expression, and above all to bring out agreed character types, which in Hollywood is not the easiest thing.

Progress which one must accept

But I don't think one could accuse me of making theater in my films. On the contrary, what pleases me in the cinema are the methods that allow you to escape the theatrical perspective. These methods are at the present time denied to television: the films made for television are very theatrical by the sheer fact of lack of funds, which forces you to shoot in front of painted sets. In cinema, the opposite. Thanks to modern technologies, to ultrasensitive film, we can now, whether it be in black-and-white or in color, forgo the studios and film in the places where the action takes place, as I did in *Anatomy of a Murder* and *Exodus*. I could, of course, have filmed *Anatomy* in Hollywood almost exactly as I did in Michigan. The one difference, though, is that in Hollywood extras are extras, whilst in Michigan people are people.

It's a mistake to have reservations over color and the wide screen, as has happened for a long time in America, and as crops up even more often in Europe. The critics think that a good film must by definition be in black-and-white and on a normal-sized screen! Color and widescreen represent progress which must be accepted. But I don't believe that every film should be shot in this way without exception. It depends on the subject being dealt with. My next two films will be shot in black-and-white and in the classic screen ratio. However, if you want to show an unfamiliar country, if the landscape plays a big part, it's better to use the new process. For me, color should be at the service of realism. That's how I used it in *Exodus*. I avoided color filters and excessive makeup. Eva Marie Saint seems older because she looks her real age. Among these true colors, you can't allow the presence of a made-up actress. Everything fits together: filming outside of the studio has its obligations.

Color and Scope lead to a lengthening of the film's duration. From the moment you set out to compete with the TV, you have to beat it by the length of the spectacle, in order to keep people out of their homes! But there is another reason: television stories are accustomed to be content with "types," with characters simplified to the extreme. The role of cinema should be to develop, to explain, to search out these characters, and, for that, you require two or three hours of film. I cut eleven minutes from the French version of *Exodus*, on the advice of the distributors; but even if I cut an hour, there would still be some people who said it was too long. Length doesn't measure itself by meters of film. It all depends on the subject you are dealing with. There is not an absolute rule: an hour-and-a-half, or an hour-forty, can suffice for a *policier*, for example the one I'm filming now in New York, which will be my first "suspense" film since *Laura*. It will be called *Bunny Lake Is Missing*: it's the story of a kidnapping.

Lubitsch and Shaw

Cahiers: You have collaborated with Lubitsch: do you no longer regard him as a reference?

Preminger: If Lubitsch has a successor, it is not me but Billy Wilder. His method is against my nature. Everything with him is a function of traits, comic simplification, visual gags, or "witticisms." I like the humor to come from the personality of the characters, for example, in *The Moon Is Blue*. What was funny in this film was the point of view of the young girl, the point of view of the professional virgin. The humor came from the character itself, and not from the means of showing it.

In a comedy you take a situation, and you subject it to a treatment to make it amusing, even if the treatment goes against the truth of the characters. Myself, I'm incapable of that. I find it impossible to subject everything to a comic effect. I filmed *A Royal Scandal* based on a scenario by, and in the spirit of, Lubitsch, but this is an exception in my career. That is a completely different style to mine.

If I returned to a subject like that, I would rather make it in the manner of Bernard Shaw, who always starts off from the truth of his characters. It is true that in *Saint Joan* I surrendered too much to the seduction that Shaw exercised over me. I didn't realize that his humor was too intellectual—at least for the general public. They were expecting an emotion from *Saint Joan* which does not exist in Shaw's play, nor in the film. They put all the responsibility for the film's failure on the back of Jean Seberg: this was unfair. I admit that she was not, and even now is not, a very great actress, but for this film I always thought it was more important to have a "young lady" than a very great actress. Joan was young, and it was this characteristic above all else that needed to be preserved. What's more, I don't think that Jean Seberg was as bad as they made out in America. Basically, I like my film and I'm happy that you, in France, are among those who like it too.

A film is the work of one alone

Cahiers: Directing the actors—is this the thing which counts the most for you?

Preminger: No, it's the script. At least, that's my main concern. I work in close collaboration with the screenwriter. We see each other every day. We discuss every scene in the smallest detail. But once I'm in agreement, I don't change another phrase. What's more, the quality of the script is, for me, the guarantee of the quality of the film. A script can never be worked on enough. That is what I object to with the young French directors of the "Nouvelle Vague," who, I believe, make films without a script.

The script should possess an internal cohesion, it should almost be sufficient unto itself. I don't like to write a script for this or that actor. My "interpreters" are chosen once the whole script is completely finished. The personality of the actor has to adapt to the character, and not the other way around.

Cahiers: Do you choose your subjects completely freely?

Preminger: Yes. Moreover, in America now, the development of the industry— I detest the word "industry": it's good for motorcars, not for cinema—follows, curiously, what you can see in Europe. All the important films are the product of individual enterprise, whether it's the production or the direction. The dictatorship of the big studios, the big companies, the big bosses like Zanuck no longer exist or are going to disappear.

We, the independent producers, now have complete autonomy, even in matters of publicity. In matters of publicity, the final decision rests with me: in this way I could insist on posters designed by Saul Bass. That's very important, since publicity that's too flashy or poorly adapted to the content of the film risks causing cinema to fall from its rank, if not of pure art then at least of artistic craft, to which we have painstakingly succeeded in placing it. It is precisely because our rights have been slow to gain control of that they must be defended with the utmost vigilance, against all sorts of enemies: publicity, censorship, monopolies . . . If not, the cinema will become what it was before.

We make fewer films than before. But that's an advantage, because they are more important, and above all they are the work of a single individual who has left his mark. If the film is good, he takes the credit; if it is bad, he takes the blame. In any case, there is one responsible individual. No more possible alibis.

On the other hand, I maintain the right not to consider *Forever Amber* as one of my own works. Its filming, undertaken by one of my colleagues, had been disastrous, and Zanuck, to whom I was bound by contract, called upon me to save the situation. As I was hesitating, he insisted: "I know that you don't like the subject matter, but that's unimportant. We need you. You're part of our team. We will pay you so many dollars per week. We'll carry the responsibility." It was impossible for me not to accept. A seven-year contract with Fox, that's not lightly broken. Also, I was on excellent terms with Zanuck.

Nowadays, though, if I make a choice, it is *my* choice. If the film is bad, it's my fault. The feeling of responsibility puts your heart into the work. If you make a mistake, oh well, never mind! What counts is the enthusiasm you bring to your work.

I don't want to specialize

Cahiers: But you never film original subjects.

Preminger: That's true. At least up to the present. I don't follow rules, but in general when I adapt a subject, I modify it to such a degree that one can't say if it has to do with an original story. For example, I intend to film *Advise & Consent*, a best seller published in France under the title *Les Titans*. It's a political story. I'm interested in the principle of the American elections, where the respective powers of the president and of the Senate observe a very particular type of "equilibrium" which you don't find in any other constitution in the world. I pick up the story almost as it is written, but the very idea of my film will be completely different from that of the novel.

Being American himself, the author has not shown all the originality of the relationship between the powers. For him, it was a quite natural thing. He hasn't dramatized the conflict in such a way as to make it perceivable to a non-American public.

I like to have a base: this base is generally provided me by a novel or a play. Yet if someone brought me a truly great idea, I would happily buy it.

Cahiers: Are there any a priori ideas or themes which tempt you more than others?

Preminger: My work is very diverse, and that is my wish. Of course, it would be easier for me if I specialized in a fixed genre. We are developing some formulas, and we are successful. That is not what I want, though, if only for the sake of my personal amusement. I'm intent on staying young. Each time, I like to lead a new battle, always attacking different problems: that is more exciting for the spirit. One of the privileges of the director is to enjoy the idea that he can do everything. The taste of freedom even makes me return to the theater from time to time. I've just launched a play on Broadway with Henry Fonda: *Critic's Choice*.

Each time I made a film, I have the impression I've given everything I can on this theme or in this genre. I am "empty." I absolutely have to move on to something else. I love the stories I film, and I work on them for an entire year—and sometimes even two—in the most intense state of joy. But if I had to start over again, that would be nothing more to me than a school exercise.

I don't look, I find

Cahiers: It seems that you are more and more interested by the "big problems."

Preminger: Perhaps. I don't go looking for problems, but—it's my nature—I often find them on my path. It's not the result of deliberate design. It just comes from the fact that I live in the twentieth century and I'm interested in my times.

I'm interested in Israel, in American politics, in questions of race—even via *Carmen Jones* or *Porgy and Bess*, which are really only "musicals." And these problems are more complex than one would at first think. It is from there that the ambiguity of my films comes. The situation of the blacks in the USA, for example, is not a simple thing, nor that of the Jews in Israel.

Cahiers: To sum up, each film is for you an opportunity to have an experience.

Preminger: Yes, and that's the reason why I'm always searching for new themes. Making a film is not for me the pretext for a confession but a means of enriching my spirit. These themes, I have to find them not within myself but somewhere outside of me: most often in a book. That's how I bought the rights to a novel which tells seven parallel stories of seven young men and women between the years 1945 and 1950; that's to say, between the end of the Second World War and the start of the Korean War. This takes place throughout the world, and it will really touch on important current problems (the atomic bomb, communism). When the film is finished, it will not have much apparent connection with the book. It will almost be an original work. The novel will only have served as a point of departure. It is in the same spirit that I will adapt the novel by Christian Mégret, *Carrefour des solitudes*. It concerns the story of an American soldier in France after the war. The character, who in the book is Black, with me will just become simply an American. This seems to me more interesting, for what I want to do.

It's much easier, when you possess a solid base, to explain your intentions to a screenwriter. On the contrary, you see up to ten names of authors on the script of a film built upon an original idea. Adding is less fitting and less fruitful than pruning back.

Our domain is fiction

Don't think, though, that if I tell you about these projects, I am henceforth going to specialize in sociopolitical problems. *Bunny Lake Is Missing*, which I'm filming next, will be a simple crime story. However, there is a "social" theme. The mother of the little girl who has been kidnapped is unmarried, and this story, in the way I tell it, could not happen to a mother who has a husband. This woman doesn't even have the possibility of proving that she had a daughter. The father of the child, who is a married man, pretends he doesn't know her. If you don't live in our society in a conformist manner, the law does not protect you. That is, if you will, the moral of the story, although that is only a very small aspect of the film. What interests me above all is to show a woman alone in a big city. I'll put my camera in the middle of the street like in *A bout de souffle*, which I've seen and which I like very much for its way of showing Paris, and also because it proves that Jean Seberg was not such a bad actress as all that.

Cahiers: A common trait in your characters is that they clash with society.

Preminger: Not always, but often. That is what creates the drama, the conflict—conflict between generations, between races, between moral views. In a drama worthy of the name, each of the protagonists should have the same right to express himself. I'm not saying I don't take sides, but I like to let my antagonist have his say. If you read the novel which inspired *Exodus*, you will find a large portion of it is taken up by propaganda. It is obvious that I'm *for* the Jews, since, if you make a film about a revolution, you can't be against that revolution. It goes without saying. Though I didn't hide the fact that the English—the Israelis are now convinced—showed as much "fair play" as circumstances permitted. I insistently showed the divisions among the Jews. That is why certain Jews sulked over my film. *Exodus* had immense success in England, so that on the evening of the premiere, at the end of screening, the audience saw fit to stand and sing "God Save the King."

Cahiers: *Exodus* is more serene, less critical, than your preceding films, some of which are tinted with pessimism.

Preminger: Each subject has its own tone. *Anatomy of a Murder* showed that there is no absolute justice and that, going forward, it is better to acquit the guilty than to condemn the innocent. Isn't that perhaps what you call an "ending," but is it pessimistic as such? The end of *The Man with the Golden Arm* was optimistic, and even so I was accused in America of preaching in favor of drugs. On the contrary, I wanted to show that one could heal a sickness.

I'm not looking to show absolute truth. If I succeed in attaining it, it is only by way of fiction. To please the viewer and to make him think a little bit at the same time, that is my aim. There are always ideas, if you like, behind the stories I tell, but I try not to let them appear overmuch. Otherwise, my story wouldn't be a good story.

First and foremost, I'm a man who makes films. My ideal is to express myself—perhaps that word is pretentious—through films, through stories. These stories, I don't have a rule for choosing them, but I believe they all have to some degree their truth. If not, they don't interest me.

Improvization and simplicity

Cahiers: Can you talk to us about your style of working? Do you make your actors rehearse?

Preminger: Yes. I always have two or three weeks of rehearsals before I start filming. That way I can work without haste, without spotlights, without costumes, without makeup: the actors are relaxed and have all the time to think. It's not always easy to impose these rehearsals on the cast. When I filmed *The Man with* *the Golden Arm*, Sinatra didn't want to rehearse, maintaining that he wasn't a true actor, but after a few days he got a taste for it, even to the point where he himself was proposing to me that we retake a scene.

Cahiers: We admire your camera shots. We would really like to uncover the secret.

Preminger: There is no secret, or rather it's very simple. When I film, I have two things in view. The first is to make a film where you don't sense the presence of a director. The second is to film my scene in the particular manner I have chosen, and to stick to it. I like to redo takes (sometimes I go up to thirty), but not to change the camera angle. I never count on editing to rescue me. That is the reason I use tracking shots.

Cahiers: Do you write down an editing technique, or do you improvise it?

Preminger: I improvise. But as I told you, I have rehearsed with the actors beforehand. Look at the editing of *Bunny Lake Is Missing*: that is its definitive state, and, you see, I do not have the dialogue with me on the set. Since I worked very closely on the script, I knew it by heart, and on the set, you never see me with the script in my hand. In any case, I don't like weird camera angles. I like very simple angles. I don't think that one is a great director because one photographs the sky, unless that's necessary for the story.

Cahiers: Before becoming a filmmaker, did you go to the cinema?

Preminger: No. I went only to the theater. At that time I knew nothing of the cinema. Except perhaps Garbo and Dietrich.

Cahiers: And among the modern directors, where does your taste lie?

Preminger: I don't like to judge my colleagues.

Cahiers: Even the young ones?

Preminger: I have sympathies with the Nouvelle Vague—the French, at least, since I haven't seen *Shadows* and other New York films. The future belongs to them, no contest. One should not forget that making a cheap film is an advantage, inasmuch as the public and the critics are more inclined to forgive any clumsiness. Making one's first film is also an advantage. These two advantages don't present themselves again. One can't always shoot on a low budget, and the second time, one expects more from a film director, especially concerning the rigor of the story. I must say, too, that dramatic construction is not the strength of the Nouvelle Vague. Notwithstanding, I am in general quite partisan of all experimental films, since without experiment there is no progress.

Interview with Otto Preminger

Mark Shivas / 1962

From *Movie*, no. 4, November 1962, 18–20. Reprinted by permission of Cameron and Hollis.

Q: *Advise & Consent* is primarily a moral, rather than a political, film . . .

Preminger: I think the politics in the film are really a background. People told me before I made the film—and I haven't disproved it yet—that it will not be understood easily in other countries. I don't know why people shouldn't understand. After all, the Americans don't know much about the intricacies of American politics either. But we make films in foreign countries deliberately to tell people something; you make a film about Africa, about China—why not make a film about Washington, and show its peculiarities?

Q: Recently you seem to have started a new range of subjects, the "important issues," justice, democracy and so on . . .

Preminger: I can't say this is by design. I've just bought a story by Patrick Dennis. It's a plain comedy, about a motion picture director who gets stranded in Mexico. I can't take credit for designing my life and career deliberately; I don't calculate what I'm going to do, except that I try not to fall into the trap of any formula. I feel that this would be deadly for me. I would get bored, perhaps without really knowing it, because it would become too easy. When you have new things, you have to read and research, you have to try to understand new people. It's this that makes my profession so exciting: the challenge that comes up every hour if you work on new things.

Q: Why did you do *Porgy and Bess*?

Preminger: I wanted to do *Porgy and Bess* long before Goldwyn, but my negotiations broke down because I could not see my way to pay for such an expensive property. Then when he had a conflict with the original director, he called me and I happened to be available. I knew the story, and I knew the actors, so I did it.

Q: Would it have been any different if you had produced it yourself?

Preminger: Yes, very different, because I would have changed the story considerably. When I came in, the screenplay was written. I don't think it was bad—I wouldn't have done it if it was bad—but I did not know that Goldwyn would insist on keeping it exactly as written—I might not have done it if I'd known. In my opinion it would have been much better if it had not been so "faithful" to the original play. I don't believe that in order to be faithful to the *idea* of a story or of a character you have to be really faithful to the letter. And this is what Goldwyn insisted on. This was a very good, well-written, musical comedy, but it was about thirty years old. And I feel that it was a bit dated, particularly in its humor. I tried in the direction to eliminate this as much as possible, but there are several things in it which I never liked and which I still don't like. It could have been better if it had been, like *Carmen Jones*, a film with music instead of a musical film.

Q: *Porgy* is a good deal more stylized than *Carmen Jones*.

Preminger: Yes. If I had been producing it, I would not have done it on the stage. I would have gone out more. Only because I was very insistent did I do the picnic on location. The original director planned to do even that in the studio. I think this sort of film calls for the smell of reality. The set was designed by a stage designer; it was very difficult to work in. The cameraman and I got together and repainted it every night, and when Goldwyn would come in, he was appalled that the color had been changed. This designer was a very good stage designer, but he does not understand films. For example, he designed in perspective; the windows became smaller as they went up. But that doesn't work in films, because the camera has its own perspective. When the people looked out the window, I had to have them on their knees, because there was no room for them to stand. But all this is detail, it's not important. I was very happy to work on the film, I enjoyed it, and I hope it will be a success here.

Q: Was it a success in America?

Preminger: It was a critical success, but not a financial success. It has been very successful so far in Germany, and strangely enough I think it will do much better outside America. *Carmen Jones* was a tremendous critical success in America, but it was only a financial success because it was made for very little money—I couldn't get much money for it. The rights to *Porgy and Bess* were more expensive than the whole film of *Carmen Jones*. I made *Carmen Jones* very fast, on location, in twenty-four shooting days. If it had been made for the same kind of money as *Porgy and Bess*, or for half as much, it also would not have been a profitable film. I think there is a limit to the American market here. It's not necessarily that the Americans are biased, although you can't play an all-Negro film in the South, except in Negro theaters. But the interest in Negro entertainers is limited to a certain more intelligent section of the audience.

Carmen Jones was actually the first picture with a Negro cast that was a commercial success. It was only my second independent production, and the same company for whom I had just made several million dollars with *The Moon*

Is Blue refused to touch it. I remember their exact words: this is too rich for our blood. Eventually I set it up during lunch with Zanuck. But even then the Twentieth Century-Fox brass in New York tried to nullify the agreement. These people don't have opinions, they have figures. And these figures become taboos. They don't examine a project any more. They just look at their statistics and say, "Negro picture? Out! No good." And now it is worse, because Columbia in the meantime filmed a very successful play, *Raisin in the Sun*, and that lost all the money. So I think now no one could make a Negro picture.

Q: What do locations give you that you can't get in a studio?

Preminger: I believe in them very much. Without any necessity I did all of *Anatomy of a Murder* on location. I think that it even helps the actors in a realistic drama to *feel* real. They felt like lawyers and so forth. The great advantage was that the jury and the extras were real people. I always have a tremendous argument about extras. They look like extras, they don't have any real character. They try not to work. They hide their faces, because if you see them too often, the assistant directors won't employ them again. They're a horrible race of people who've selected this profession just to be protected by their unions, and not to work. When I did *Advise & Consent* in Washington, it was wonderful because I got the *people* of Washington. When I came back to Hollywood and did this one big set, because I was not permitted to shoot in the Senate chamber, I had extras. I had horrible trouble to find the right people and to have them behave. For example, I was setting up a shot and somebody came and told me that one of the extras had his tie loosened and his collar open. He was playing a senator. So I said: "What are you doing there?" And he said: "It's hot." I said: "I know it's hot, but you are a senator. You are not an extra who is hot!" It's unbelievable! But on location you get people who are enthusiastic and interested.

Q: Why do you leave the apparent issues unresolved at the end of *Anatomy*, *Exodus*, and *Advise & Consent*?

Preminger: You couldn't say that they are completely unresolved. It is just as unresolved as life is. In *Anatomy of a Murder*, it was deliberately unresolved. What fascinated me in that story was that you never knew the truth. I wanted to show the way justice works. In our system it is better to let somebody go unpunished than to take the risk where the slightest doubt exists about a man's guilt. This, I think, is one of the greatest things civilization has created. I made Gazzara a very unpleasant character in order to make the point that he's not acquitted because he's a nice man. He's acquitted because we, the prosecutors, cannot *prove* he's guilty.

Q: How much do you improvise on the set?

Preminger: In the script hardly ever. Otherwise, I never prepare any shots. I work very closely with the writers, and I know the script by heart by the time I approve it. I visualize things: I know how I'm going to do it. But when I rehearse with actors, I often change my idea, because I like the film to come out of a rehearsal, out of a live contact, rather than to design it in advance and have it set. This is a question of system.

Q: What do you have in mind in working out your camera positions?

Preminger: I really don't do this according to any principle or design. It is a thing that forms visually in my mind. It has usually to do, when I look back on it, with the essence of the scene. I never, for any usual reason, favor a star or a woman like some people do—because they think it is better for the audience. I try to use the camera to make the point of the scene; that is about the only principle I can tell you, so it always works out differently. I believe that the ideal picture is a picture where you don't notice the director, where you never are aware that the director did anything deliberately—naturally he has to do everything deliberately. That is direction. But if I could ever manage to do a picture that is directed so simply that you would never be aware of a cut or a camera movement, that, I think, would be the real success of direction.

Q: This would include not forcing any attitudes on the audience?

Preminger: I always like to project my viewpoint on the audience, but without them knowing it. I do not think a picture should make an *obvious* statement. First of all, when it becomes obvious, people resist, they start to argue with you. It is much stronger if they don't know. But this applies to the whole thing. For instance I believe firmly that an actor can do things much better when he believes that he invented them. I never want to have an actor feel that he's directed. As a matter of fact, if there are two possibilities, and the one that the actor suggests is, in my opinion, a little less effective than the one I could suggest, I let him do it his way because I feel I will get something in exchange. It comes easier; it's more right for him, even if it could be improved. It's like a suit which you have worn a long time; it's more comfortable, it fits better than a new suit.

Q: Would you agree with *Movie's* statement that the basic Preminger theme is concerned with making decisions?

Preminger: I think it's interesting. I didn't think of it before, but I will adopt it now. There is a satisfaction that people think movies so important that they sit down and think about them and write about them and advance theories like they do about painting or writing. It doesn't matter whether, for instance, I agree when you ask me. The fact that a theory can be evolved and that it makes sense is good enough. It is not necessary that I actually started like this; but if this can be detected by other people, that gives me satisfaction so long as there is a basic truth to it. And there is something to this; that's why I said I would adopt it even if I didn't think of it before.

Q: Which of your Fox contract movies do you like now?

Preminger: I don't know. This is a personal thing. I'm very much involved while I make a film, and before I make it. It absorbs my whole life. However, when a movie is finished (that is, when I've seen the completed film the first time with an audience), I become completely detached from it. I forget, even, the story or the cast very soon. That's why I'm not very sensitive to criticism—I can take bad reviews probably better than anybody in this business.

Q: How did it happen that you weren't your own producer on *River of No Return*? It looked as if you had influenced the script a great deal.

Preminger: No, I didn't. This was the time when I changed my contract with Fox. I had a contract with them for fifty-two weeks as a producer-director; then I paid them half their money back and got half my time back in exchange. So when I came back, they had the script half ready, and it was more practical for them and for me to go into production. If you ask me which was my favorite film of this time, I know that this was not.

Q: You seemed to be more concerned with shooting it your way than with the details of Monroe's performance. She got out of her depth at times, but you didn't chop it up into short takes to make it easier for her.

Preminger: Some of it *had* to be done in short takes, because she couldn't remember her lines. I didn't want to spend my entire life in Canada. But there was no artistic difficulty with her. In spite of the fact that she had this tragic death, she was not the great genius that people want to think her. She was a sweet girl with a very small horizon.

Q: But Mitchum gave a very remarkable performance.

Preminger: We got along very well, and he is a very remarkable actor. I saw him recently in a picture called *Cape Fear*, and he was really wonderful.

Q: What is it you like about Leavitt that you work with him so often?

Preminger: It's nothing to do with liking. You see, I give the cameraman the exact setup—there is no consultation between me and the cameraman. And he's ideal for this because he doesn't care, but he's a very good craftsman, and he works fast. I also like to work with Shamroy, who is in many ways a subtler cameraman: he knows more, he's experienced, but he's also willing. Some cameramen want to have their *own* way, or at least to make suggestions. But I'm an impatient man, and as I know what I eventually want even if I'm wrong, it doesn't make any sense to discuss other things.

Q: How did you get on with Périnal on *St. Joan* and *Bonjour Tristesse*?

Preminger: Very well. He's a wonderful man. There is a great difference of quality between Périnal and Leavitt. Because while Périnal also does exactly what the director wants, he understands why the director wants it. When I met him, he was rather old, and I was warned against him. A producer friend of mine rang me up the day after I signed Périnal for *St. Joan* and told me I was crazy, because Périnal was slow, temperamental, arrived late on the set . . . none of it is true. He was the most efficient and conscientious cameraman I can imagine, and I've worked with some very good ones—Arthur Miller and Joseph LaShelle. for instance. Actually, cameraworks is now a science, not an art. It's no more a question of a *touch* in lighting; it's mathematics. If you describe what you want and the man knows his job, he can do it; there's no art about it any more.

Q: So Leavitt is just the man who does his sums fastest?

Preminger: Well he *is* fast, but it's not because of that. It's largely a matter of who's available. If I had my choice, I would probably rather use Shamroy. As a matter of fact, I wanted him for *Exodus*, but he was under contract to Fox and wasn't available. I get along with him; he is more fun. Leavitt has no sense of humor, and it's very important when you live with a man from morning to evening for fifty or sixty days to have a little fun.

Q: Are you still going to make *Bunny Lake Is Missing*?

Preminger: Sure. I'm working on a new script for it. As a matter of fact, it will probably be made in London. I'm planning to make two pictures in London, after *The Cardinal: Bunny Lake* and *The Other Side of the Coin*. They will be based in London, and *The Other Side of the Coin* will be shot in Malaya. I'm not going to direct them; I'm only going to produce them.

Preminger on *Advise & Consent*

Mark Shivas / 1962

From *Movie*, no. 4, November 1962, 26–27. Reprinted by permission of Cameron and Hollis.

Q: What was it that attracted you about the novel of *Advise and Consent*?

Preminger: It is very difficult to say what particular details struck me. I read the novel before publication, and I immediately felt that it was an interesting theme. But then the theme of the film is not quite that of the novel. I did not try to take sides or to give a picture of conservative and liberal politics in the United States. Nor did I wish to make a liberal apology. I tried to dramatize the workings of our government, which are very special, to show that the power of the executive branch, of the president, is very much checked and balanced by the power of the Senate, which represents the people. That is fascinating, because that to me is the essence of democracy—that nobody in a government has so much power that there is any danger of one overruling the others or overtaking the whole government.

Q: It is the workings of the American Constitution that you find particularly interesting?

Preminger: I would also be fascinated to make a picture about the British constitution, particularly if I lived in England. I was in Russia recently, and there were many conversations about the difference between our attitude on motion pictures and theirs. They pointed out to me that they considered motion pictures as a means of education, which is in a way also a word for propaganda. While we don't do this, it doesn't mean that we don't put any meaning into our pictures. It means that we may in a subtle way also be trying to project our thoughts, but without pushing them down the throats of the audience, leaving it to the public to draw their own conclusions. With *Advise & Consent* I think that many people can draw many different conclusions. I hope if I have succeeded with my picture, that it is not just one-sided, and that I think is what we are trying to achieve—to make people think. Where their thoughts go, we should only guide them; we should not propagandize them.

Q: You took the more blatant propaganda out of *Exodus* . . .

Preminger: It was also true of *Exodus*. In any drama all sides must have the opportunity to express their points of view. The book of *Exodus* is very propagandistic, and of course as a Jew I am in favor of the revolution in Israel, but I also tried to show the British side too. I must tell you that, for instance, all Israelis feel very friendly towards Great Britain today because they feel that if any other major power had had that mandate at that time they might never have succeeded. At the time the British were fairer to them than any other power would have been. I tried to reflect this in my picture.

Q: Would you say that *Advise & Consent* is not about political issues but more about men destroyed by the mechanism of politics?

Preminger: It is not about direct political issues; it is about moral issues. The question is this: should certain people, even with all the actual qualifications for their jobs, and with a great deal of personal integrity, be confirmed by the Senate for important assignments in the government if there have been things in their past which might have been wrong for these jobs?

I also wanted to show the cruelty of politics. It is a business, or a profession, where lives don't count when it comes to principles. I wished to demonstrate that they are being destroyed where the destruction of these lives is obviously not fair in every case. Their destruction would not be necessary if just *fairness* could be applied, if it were not necessary to apply the strictest possible principles. There are many things that I have at least tried to dramatize in this picture, and if a small percentage of this projected to the public, then I'll be very gratified.

Q: It's his lying that destroys Leffingwell (Henry Fonda) . . .

Preminger: Actually, yes. I think that the picture makes it very clear that the confirmation of the Senate is not withheld because the man was a Communist in his past, because I feel that we have passed this stage in America, this kind of hysterical McCarthyism. People who had a Communist past are not necessarily disqualified from any public office, even from the office of secretary of state, if they are now willing and able to represent our side in their job. But I feel that a man, even if he is forced to lie on the stand under oath, disqualifies himself by lying. We did show that this man was really against the wall. He couldn't help it; he would have had to sacrifice a friend. It was not possible for him to tell the truth. But we will say, regrettable as it is, and as cruel as it might be to him and terrible for his future, and in spite of the fact that it deprives the United States of a possible great secretary of state, that he should not be confirmed because he cannot compromise in questions of integrity.

Q: What destroys Brigham Anderson (Don Murray)?

Preminger: Well, the same thing . . . Brigham Anderson is really a dramatic parallel. It is really more of a symbol, this blackmail against him, because of the homosexual past that he has. What destroys him is that he sets himself up as the judge of the other man, and he also has something in his past, like many people have. But I feel that what really drives him to suicide is not the blackmail alone but the sudden realization on his part when he gets into contact again with this homosexual world, that he has inside, in spite of his struggle, in spite of his marriage and child, not quite overcome the temptation and the inclination to belong to this world. In other words, he is at once repelled and attracted. He is not adjusted enough, like many people are, and in my opinion should be, to accept their homosexual feelings. After all, there are many homosexuals who were great writers and great artists, and great politicians, and there are a number of politicians who are homosexuals and who never tried to commit suicide! But he is not adjusted enough to accept it; he doesn't want it, but at the same time he is attracted by it. This is the reason for his suicide more than the blackmail.

Q: Your last three films have been taken from best-selling novels. What's the reason for this?

Preminger: Well, first of all, I bought the last two films—the rights to *Exodus* and the rights to *Advise and Consent* long before they became best sellers. I did buy *Anatomy of a Murder* after it was a best seller, but I was interested in it long before then.

Q: Perhaps I should have said, "Why from novels rather than from original subjects?"

Preminger: That is difficult. Somehow there is a lot of material around. You see, I don't feel that I really illustrate the novel; I re-create it for the screen just as I would re-create an original story with a writer. But I feel that there is so much rich material in an interesting novel that I have no inhibitions. The novel may only serve as a useful point of departure. I would also make an original picture if somebody brought me a great idea.

Q: Your next film, *Bunny Lake Is Missing*, is an original?

Preminger: No, it is also a novel, but not so successful. It is a small story about a kidnapping. The mother of the little girl who has been kidnapped is unmarried and is unable to prove the existence of the child. The child's father will not admit to it because he is already married to another woman and pretends he does not know the mother. There is a certain social theme here: if you do not conform to the rules of society, the law does not protect you. But that is a very small part of the film.

Q: Are there any special themes that interest you?

Preminger: I cannot say there are any. I cannot generalize. I find myself very often attracted to themes of the present day more than stories of the past. I live in the twentieth century, and I am interested in what goes on around me. And my interests change. But what I try quite deliberately to do is to avoid any set formula, to avoid making one picture after another of the same kind. After *Laura*, a suspense story, it was very tempting, because the picture was a success and everybody used to send me all their suspense stories. But I try to have as much diversification as possible.

Q: Could you say anything about your manner of working? How much do you rehearse your actors before you go on set?

Preminger: That depends very much upon the subject. If possible I rehearse three to four weeks before I start shooting without even having the crew there, in order to be able to discuss things without the terrible burden of a deadline. But often that's impossible. In principle I would like as much rehearsal time as possible.

Q: When on set you work fast?

Preminger: I don't work fast. But I think I have organized myself to a point where I don't do anything unnecessary. I think that most delays in pictures, unless they are caused by force majeure, come from a certain insecurity or from a feeling that maybe I can do it two ways or three ways and then decide. I try to decide in advance when I am working with the writer on the script. And I rarely change the script, except when it is too long, which unfortunately it always has a tendency to be. Then I try to cut and not to do unnecessary scenes which I shall not be able to use. But I don't work faster than anyone else; on the contrary, once on the stage I try to give everybody the feeling that they have all the time in the world, although I know they don't, because time in our setup is a very expensive commodity.

Interview with Otto Preminger

Ian Cameron, Mark Shivas, and Paul Mayersberg / 1965

From *Movie*, no. 13, Summer 1965, 14–16. Reprinted by permission of Cameron and Hollis.

Q: Why did you choose to make *In Harm's Way*?

Preminger: Why do I ever want to make a film? This book was submitted to me in manuscript. I liked the characters, and I liked the story. This is my only reason for making films. It is my profession to make films.

However, there is another reason. Probably the story appealed to me because I felt that so many movies made recently have a terribly pessimistic outlook on our future. It seems that the only way out for us is to give in to almost any kind of demand, or blackmail, or whatever you want to call it—and when I say "us," it goes for both sides, for the West as well as for the Iron Curtain, because both have the Bomb now. And all these films or books seem to feel that any attack would finish the other side, and the world. I don't believe that. I believe that any attack that is executed by weapons invented by people, by human minds, will always find a defense that people can invent. Perhaps this story of an attack—we are attacked, we are unprepared in every way, and manage by sheer guts, character and resourcefulness, to start to work out of it—should remind us and perhaps other people that there is never any reason to give up or to give in to anything that is not right or dignified. I am as much against the war as anyone, and I hope I showed it even in this picture by showing that, of all these courageous people, just two or three are left in the end. I didn't try to make war romantic or particularly attractive, but, on the other hand, I wanted to say, perhaps unlike other people, that war does not necessarily bring the worst out in people always. It often does, but also, for the mere reason that people find themselves in the same predicament, it makes them stick together, work for each other, work together.

I don't like to mention other films, but to mention one which I think is a very wonderful film—*Dr. Strangelove*—I do feel that somehow it shows the situation only from one side. Perhaps the director, whom I like very much and admire, didn't want to show it. It cannot be true (and the film seems to imply this) that every military man in the United States is a warmonger or an idiot, or both, or crazy. Nor is it true that the president of the United States is so completely without sense. I don't mind these characters in satire—I think it is very good if there were some *balance* to it. Perhaps it could be told in another film. Let's say I don't tell my story *against* a film like *Strangelove*; I tell it to complement the film. You see, I feel that all films together, or the whole output of literature together, give a mosaic of the thinking and feeling of people. So it doesn't matter whether one film goes all the way one side and another film goes all the way the other side. It might be that people who see my film will wonder why I didn't show a character like the general in *Dr. Strangelove*—although I tried to show that the navy has not only angels.

Q: When you get a large book like *In Harm's Way*, you have to leave out a fair amount of the detail of it.

Preminger: Let me say something which I have always wanted to say but never could say quite clearly. Whether I take an original idea and pay for it, or I buy the rights to a book, and an author sells it outright, I consider this raw material, and I feel completely free to use it according to my own thinking—to filter it through my own brain, through my talent or whatever I have—in other words, to re-create whatever part of this material I want to. This thing about being faithful or not faithful to a novel should only apply if the author would say: "Look, I don't want to sell you the film rights, I want to be your *partner*. I will sell you the film rights with the condition that I have the final say, because I want to preserve the ideas." I have often been attacked: the author of *Exodus*, for instance, felt that I didn't do right by his book, and the author of *Anatomy of a Murder* felt that I did better than the book—he admired the film very much. The author of *In Harm's Way* is particularly complimentary about my handling of the son's character, one which didn't really exist in the book. He was a completely innocuous boy, who just met the father and they immediately became friends; he had no feelings about the fact that his father had left his mother eighteen years ago, and we changed that in the script. Now, all I want to say is that I consider it material, and I use what I want. In the book *In Harm's Way*, there is a lot about command decision and the great responsibility. This is interesting but very difficult to dramatize, and hardly a point that interested me here, because I'm not interested in the military mind, really. I did not make a war picture—I don't know anything about the war, and I hope I will never see another war. It was more interesting to see a group of people, characters whom I like, trapped in war, in a difficult situation, and to see how they work out of it.

Q: Why did you use Wendell Mayes?

Preminger: I think he's a very good writer. We have worked together before, and I felt that he could write this very well. You must realize also that I work very closely with writers. Particularly on this picture, we sat together and worked almost every line over. On the other hand, the writer has the advantage that, once I approve a screenplay, I do not change it any more on the set like other directors or hire other writers to improve it or, as the case may be, to spoil it.

Q: How far did the original book *In Harm's Way* delve into the political aspect, which is slightly evident in the film through the Dana Andrews character?

Preminger: The Dana Andrews character is unimportant—it is just a question of one group of people wanting to fight, and the other group of people wanting to give up. We all probably forget this (and you are probably even too young to remember), but you know, after Pearl Harbor, there was in America a tremendous group of people of any political affiliation that thought the best thing would be to make peace with Japan and not to enter the war, that we were not prepared and that we would lose. And it seems very crazy today, but at that time people in San Francisco started to move out to the East, because they felt the Japanese might land at San Francisco. I don't think that the Dana Andrews character *is* to do with anything political. But it's typical. It shows the people making use of their power, and you must admit the fact that I could get cooperation from the Defense Department, in spite of this character, in spite of Dana Andrews, and in spite of the character of Kirk Douglas, proves a certain liberal attitude. I got all the ships I needed and all the help I needed; otherwise, I couldn't have made this picture. We were shooting five days on high seas between Seattle and Hawaii on a real naval cruiser with an admiral there—it was his flagship—and he was lying there on his stomach most of the time taking photographs of us, because it was his hobby.

Q: How was it that your model shots were so much better than anyone else's model shots?

Preminger: I will tell you a secret. I had originally hired a famous specialist for these models. You know, they usually make them with ships about two or three feet long, in tanks. When I saw the beginning of his work, which was also quite expensive, I threw the whole thing away, because it didn't seem to be right. And I then proceeded to build ships, I did it myself after the picture was finished. I decided to direct it myself without any specialists, and we built ships that were between thirty-five and fifty-five feet long—they were really big ships—so that when we photographed them, the detail was very much like on the big ships. And as a matter of fact, the navy asked us, and we gave them these ships after the picture was finished for their various exhibitions. And we didn't shoot any of these miniatures in a tank. We shot the night miniatures on a lake in Mexico, because we needed the straits with mountains in the background. We shot the day battles on the Gulf of Mexico. I needed the real horizon, you know, and I think that makes a lot of difference.

Q: Is it because of the models that you didn't shoot the picture in color?

Preminger: No, I could just as well have shot it in color. The reason I didn't is because I always feel that a picture like this, a war picture, in color, has a very unreal feeling. First of all, you cannot possibly avoid the actors using makeup, particularly if they are close to middle age. A soldier in makeup always seems to me somewhat ridiculous. I know that people overlook it, that it is a convention that they accept, but a picture like this has much more impact, and you can create more of the feeling, the illusion of reality than when you shoot it in color. It's the only reason I didn't use any newsreel shots. For Pearl Harbor I got permission and put dynamite all around, and we shot this with real ships and real explosions. We didn't use any of the old stuff, because that was shown in so many pictures that I felt to show the same news clips again (because they're all the same) would be ridiculous.

Q: In the first shot of *In Harm's Way*, you start with the notice, then you go past the line of caps and along the side of the swimming pool to Barbara Bouchet dancing: I suppose it's possible, in theory, to do this in a number of cut shots, although you get a much smoother idea of getting into the story by doing it in one shot. Is that why you do it in one shot?

Preminger: If it were possible, I would do the whole of the film in one shot, because I really believe that every cut, no matter how carefully it is done, is disturbing. You may want to emphasize something through the cut (the cut is also a way to point up something); otherwise, every cut is only done because you cannot tell something in one shot. You feel a cut subconsciously. There the idea was to show that this was what was going on just before Pearl Harbor: by putting in the sound of some vessels in the background, and the parking space, the announcement of the dance, the navy hats on the long table, and the dance. Then when she behaves like she does, there are cuts and the story starts. This is already a character in the story. In order not to disturb this, I put the titles at the end, because I felt I wanted to get into the story right away and not to have all the usual clutter. I also wanted to make a point, which I don't know if people get, because they usually get up before the titles are finished: the titles go up to the atom bomb and show the future horror of possible war.

Q: Does it make any difference to you making a film for Paramount as opposed to, say, Columbia or United Artists?

Preminger: No. They only distribute the film; they have no influence on the making of my films. My contracts give me complete autonomy in the making, the casting, and the writing. They can turn down a certain property if they don't want to make it, but once we've agreed on that, they have no more say.

Q: It's good for you to ring the changes among distributors?

Preminger: Sometimes . . . they are all very nice people!

Q: *Bunny Lake* is going to be a completely different kind of film?

Preminger: *Bunny Lake* is a suspense story. It's the first suspense story I've made in a long, long time, about twenty years. It's the story of the disappearance of a child.

Q: Why are you making it here?

Preminger: First of all, it seems to me that the further away from home the mother who loses the child is, the more real the story seems. Every mystery story, you see, naturally has some holes, and it seems more believable that certain facts cannot be checked within the ten hours in which the story takes place. Also the horror of what happens to her seems to be stronger if she's away from home. Even in the original book, she is away from home; it takes place in New York. But I felt that this change would be an advantage. I had several scripts on this property. I have had this book for a long time, and I never could get the right script out of it. I wanted her to be so lost. Originally, I wanted to do it in Paris, and she didn't speak French. But this problem seemed almost insurmountable, because then the police would have to ask everything through an interpreter. That would be too difficult. So I took it here to London. I can probably also get more interesting actors to surround these two young people here than in America. We have a great shortage of really good character actors.

Q: You said you went through several scripts. What were you after that you couldn't get?

Preminger: The original book has a very weak solution. The solution is OK, but the character who commits the crime is very weak and uninteresting. We did the first script very much like the book. I did this with Ira Levin, a playwright who wrote the play that I did with Henry Fonda, *Critic's Choice*. Then I did another script with Dalton Trumbo. We had analyzed it and found that we needed another heavy, but he became very theatrical and wrong. When you talk, it is often very different from what happens when you actually write and dramatize it. I gave up this script. Eventually when I wanted to do it here, I sent the book to Penelope Mortimer because she is a novelist, and I told her what the trouble was: she came to New York for conferences and came up with a wonderful character, I think, of a heavy, which gave the whole picture a new dimension. That made me pick it up again. Then she and her husband wrote the present screenplay except for some polishing on American dialogue, which I had somebody else do. As a matter of fact, I have had the rights to this story so long that somebody said that Bunny Lake is not missing, Bunny Lake is legally dead!

Q: What will you make after that?

Preminger: A book that I bought about nine months ago; it was published in America about six or seven weeks ago. It's called *Hurry Sundown*, by [K. B.] Gilden. They're really two people, married, and they worked for fourteen years on this book. And as a matter of fact, they were so poor on the way that the husband had to work in a factory in order to support the family. The book has become a very big best seller in the United States. It has a very broad canvas. It takes place in 1946 in Georgia and shows all the problems of the Negroes and the white people and their relationships. Some critics call it a modern *Gone with the Wind*. And again, while it has no message, no immediate, present political message, it will, I think, show that all the things that happen now—civil rights and riots—this whole revolution had to come. It was the only way to solve it.

Q: In *The Cardinal* there was a tremendous compression of history into one story. How far was it this aspect rather than the central character that excited you?

Preminger: These questions become too specific, because making a film is a complete complex of things. Naturally the background was very interesting. It is the background of history but also the background of an institution like the Church and what was going on in it. I have found that the Catholic Church is really a fabulously interesting institution. It gives its various members much more autonomy than I thought before. I am not a Catholic. I don't know if it comes out in the picture—but I started to understand why the Catholic Church, in spite of always reasserting its moral purpose or at least returning to its principles, is able by compromise to survive almost any other organization. You see now their willingness to get together with non-Catholics, even with nonbelievers, which shows that they somehow realize the needs of progressing times. They are not really as conservative or reactionary as most people believe. That interested me very much.

Q: Surely these are last-minute changes, though?

Preminger: No. It is clear that any organization would hang on to its principles as long as it could, just as the monarchy in England has survived all other monarchies because it is the most liberal monarchy and gives people the right to change their government, under the Crown. The Catholic Church, too, always knows the right moment to compromise.

Q: How much do you rehearse a scene on the floor?

Preminger: That depends very much on what is necessary, on what kind of actor and what kind of scene. You see, certain kinds of pictures—in *Advise & Consent*, for instance, or *Anatomy of a Murder*, there were scenes that I rehearsed several weeks before I started, but other pictures, like for instance, *In Harm's Way*, cannot be rehearsed in advance because I cannot go out on the ship, you know, and it doesn't make sense to read these lines in a room. So I rehearse just before I do the scene, and I rehearse as long as necessary. There is no limit. Time is expensive and naturally in the back of one's mind; one cannot completely eliminate it, but I've educated myself just to forget it. Otherwise, the whole thing becomes hurried and silly. I could make every picture ten days shorter if I slough it. Some actors just need more time and more rehearsal, and some don't. Some actors, who are basically picture personalities, cannot rehearse. They become what they call stale. Really it is because they don't quite know what they are doing. You've got to catch them when they are doing it best. Some actors need a lot of rehearsal, and those are very good actors.

Q: You use a lot of long takes for dialogue scenes. Do you, as it were, let the actors dictate the length of the shot?

Preminger: No. The actors don't dictate anything. Sometimes you have an actor who can't remember more than two lines. There comes the moment where you have to compromise and give in, but usually it is not the case, because scenes are not that long. No scene can be longer than nine and a half minutes, because that's how long the film runs in the camera. Six minutes or five minutes most actors are capable of doing. Once in my career I had a difficulty like that with a seasoned actor, but otherwise I don't remember ever having difficulty.

Q: Presumably with actors like Wayne and Douglas who are personalities you didn't have to rehearse much.

Preminger: No, that isn't true. Wayne turned out—I have not worked with him before—to be the most cooperative actor, willing to rehearse, willing to do anything as long as anybody. I was surprised really how disciplined a professional Wayne is, and he liked this particular part very much. I must say, I am very lucky this way, you know; the actors I work with are not difficult, or I am more difficult than they are so that I don't notice!

Otto Preminger

Peter Bogdanovich / 1966 and 1969

The Intelligence of the Audience

"I don't *get* ulcers," Otto Preminger used to say; "I cause them." This was true in certain quarters, and so there were a lot of people who didn't like Preminger; even today, a decade after his death, he and his work are still being put down, often by folks who never knew him. Or have seen any of his films. There was the old story about Otto directing himself for a close-up in *Margin for Error* and, after he had finished the lines, supposedly saying: "Cut. Print. Excellent." Again, according to anecdote and legend, Otto could be a tyrant with actors or crew, a bully and a screamer. Another story is that he came up to his discovery Jean Seberg and bellowed into her face: "RELAX!!!" What tends to be forgotten is that the man was an exceptionally able, intelligent, resourceful, and sophisticated director, and a savvy, sharply economical producer. At least one of his films, *Laura*, is an acknowledged classic, among the best suspense dramas ever made, and a memorably ambiguous love story too. *Exodus* is as good a modern epic movie as has been done; and the undiminished power and astonishing freshness of Preminger's *Anatomy of a Murder*—featuring an amazing cast of old and new, and a brilliant score by Duke Ellington—is a testament to the director's talent and scope. It is also perhaps his most personal film: about a trial lawyer, which is what young Otto was groomed and schooled for in Vienna—his father was a famous attorney and attorney general for the Austrian Empire—before Otto rebelled and entered the theater as the great director Max Reinhardt's assistant.

From the early fifties, when he went independent and almost single-handedly ended movie censorship with his landmark cases—*The Moon Is Blue* (language), *The Man with the Golden Arm* (subject matter), *Exodus* (hiring blacklisted writers)—the Austrian Preminger became one of the most familiar and famous of American directors. His (shaved) bald head came to be nearly as well known as Hitchcock's portly frame, especially after Otto played the POW camp commandant in his friend Billy Wilder's hugely popular movie version of the hit play *Stalag 17*. This, as well as some of Wilder's remarks ("I have to be nice to Preminger because I still have relatives in Germany"), helped to foster Preminger's commercial "the-man-you-love-to-hate" image, first exploited in the teens about another Viennese Jew, named Erich von Stroheim.

I first met Otto in the mid-sixties, interviewing him at Paramount in Los Angeles, at the Hotel Bel-Air, and at his all-white-furnished offices in New York; one summer in the mid-seventies, Cybill Shepherd and I spent time with him and his family at Cap d'Antibes. His Austrian background matched my mother's Austrian heritage, his European training and viewpoint reminded me of my father's *and* mother's, so there was a lot of rapport, and he was extremely generous, warm, and friendly with me. Most of the interview we did appeared in a short-lived magazine called *On Film*, which made its single splashy appearance in 1970 with a 45 rpm recording of Preminger speaking bound into each copy.

Over the years, Preminger had his share of failures, but the successes outshone these for many years, and his economical side always kept him within reasonable limits. On his first times at the Hollywood bat, he struck out twice and didn't work in films again for over six years. Returning to the stage, he directed, and acted in, a hit Broadway comedy (*Margin for Error*), which he was allowed to do as a film, with tepid success. Another strike-out, and then, by default, he got *Laura*—as Otto relates in riveting detail over the first twelve pages of our interview. Of the next eleven pictures Preminger directed before going independent, none was a smash. Several were flops, one was notoriously panned (*Forever Amber*), and five were minor successes yet really interesting and complicated movies on a number of different levels: Alice Faye, Dana Andrews in *Fallen Angel*; Joan Crawford, Henry Fonda in *Daisy Kenyon*; the divine Gene Tierney in *Whirlpool* and *Where the Sidewalk Ends*; Jean Simmons, Robert Mitchum in *Angel Face*. It is not insignificant that Ernst Lubitsch chose Preminger to direct a picture Lubitsch was producing because he was too ill to direct—a remake of the classic Lubitsch silent comedy *Forbidden Paradise*, about Catherine of Russia, retitled *A Royal Scandal*. But "the Lubitsch touch" was a very light, Mozartian one, and nobody else had that but Lubitsch. Preminger was too down-to-earth for the romantic satire to fly. He also finished Lubitsch's last film, *That Lady in Ermine*, when the master died after the eighth day of shooting.

Eventually feeling at a dead end, Preminger returned to Broadway, directed and produced another hit comedy (*The Moon Is Blue*) and again made the film; but this time he owned the movie rights himself. At heart an innocuous little picture, *The Moon Is Blue* pioneered the use on the US screen of words like "virgin" and "pregnant," and the noisy controversy over this film made the film a smash and set up Preminger as a powerful independent. Though he still did the occasional studio assignment—*River of No Return* with Marilyn Monroe; the all-black operettas *Carmen Jones* and *Porgy and Bess*—his main energies were channeled into his own pictures; the next of these, *The Man with the Golden Arm*, starring Frank Sinatra as a drug addict, was another major success. Two infamous Jean Seberg pictures followed: *Saint Joan*, based on Shaw's best play, was a valiant effort that didn't quite work and was loudly derided in the press; and *Bonjour Tristesse*—a fascinating picture, far ahead of its time in the use of wide-screen, and of color for flashbacks with black-and-white for present-day—was generally disliked. Except in France, where it became a favorite of the New Wave directors, who embraced wide-screen mainly because of their admiration for Preminger's use of it in films like *Tristesse*. Indeed, Preminger's discovery Jean Seberg became a French sensation, explaining why Jean-Luc Godard cast her in *Breathless*—an homage to Preminger—which in turn made Seberg more acceptable to US tastemakers.

Preminger's next two independent films, however, became the greatest successes of his career, and two of the best and most enduring of the American screen: *Anatomy of a Murder* and *Exodus*—the latter as surefooted a blockbuster as was ever conceived and a serious, powerful look at the emergence of Israel after World War II. These two, back-to-back, positioned Preminger for his final ten films, not one of which hit, though at the least five of them range from damned good to brilliant. All of them are challenging and courageous in their own ways, with memorable casts: *Advise & Consent*, *The Cardinal*, *In Harm's Way*, *Bunny Lake Is Missing*, *Hurry Sundown*. Otto seemed always to be open to what he called "a little coincidence," which, as he said, "can change a lot for a person or a film or a career." This attitude gives his pictures air; though he had a knack for the big canvas, Preminger's pictures are never bloated, and his all-star casts work in a kind of harmony other "big" pictures seldom achieve. The director's use of main-title designs by Saul Bass—a stark and bold graphic design for *Golden Arm* started this—became almost a cliché of the mid-fifties through the sixties because of how often it was imitated. Preminger, however, had a way of making this kind of theatricality work. He also could make "big" pictures that retained intimacy, that were neither pretentious nor portentous, which, considering the large-scale "theme" projects he dealt with—the US justice system, US politics, the Catholic Church, the navy, southern rural politics, the formation of Israel—is quite a feat of good taste and dramatic intuition.

Anatomy has to number among the finest of American talking pictures, starring James Stewart in a definitively archetypal performance, Ben Gazzara and George C. Scott virtually brand-new and ready to take over the world from Jimmy; Eve Arden and Arthur O'Connell to help him keep it; Lee Remick standing between the two forces in her most appealingly ambiguous way; and, as the judge in this true-life rape/murder trial story, the hero of all fifties liberals: Joseph N. Welch, the man who brought down the devil himself, Senator Joe McCarthy, in the infamous Army-McCarthy hearings that held the nation transfixed via TV. To shoot the entire picture in a small Michigan community was a creative decision not many producers would have made at the time. Otto believed that real locations inspire better work from the director—if a wall can't be moved to accommodate a shot, a new solution must be found. Preminger viewed this challenge as extremely positive (and it is something I have tried to remember on every picture). The theme of *Anatomy*—that "no one is all good or all bad," nor black nor white but gray—is quite often Preminger's theme, even when unspoken, and the objectivity of his presentation invites debate from his audience.

Preminger's work, though the director was often called a "dictator" or "totalitarian" by his coworkers, usually left opinions up to the audience. Those long, extended takes of his in wide-screen (or in regular-screen format) holding everyone in the frame, letting the viewer make up his own mind; not coloring this by cutting, which immediately creates a viewpoint. (Otto said that he thought every cut was an interruption.) Preminger generally presents all sides with equal passion, like a good lawyer represents his clients, guilty or innocent; like a good actor—which Preminger was too—always on the side of his character. Ultimately, Preminger believed in the intelligence of the audience—as much as he believed in the system of trial by jury no matter how many faults the system has—no matter how many mistakes audiences make. He knew that time was the only audience that really counted, which kept him going through the present-day disappointments. Only those who take no risks risk no failure.

Otto had a cool and forbidding manner to many people, but he seemed like a pushover with his family; he was warm, amusing, and utterly charming with people he liked. At the time I was starting out, he was running into hot water at Paramount: the new regime didn't like him, and, although he was one of the princes of the lot when I first visited there, they slowly got rid of him. He didn't go quietly. Indeed, the seventies, which started out great for me, spelled the end of Preminger's career. His last four films, all released in the seventies, were box-office failures—as all but one of his seven sixties movies were—though not one of them was less than fascinating, and each of them took courageous chances. All through these times, Otto was never low or depressed; he kept on going.

To me, he was always very encouraging, interested in my activities. In 1972 he was on a TV talk show with a vicious New York critic who attacked me for *The Last Picture Show* and my *next* film (*What's Up, Doc?*), which had not even been released yet. Preminger defended *Picture Show* by saying it was clearly one of the best movies of the year, and that he personally had already seen my next and it was brilliant and destined to be a huge success. This effectively shut the critic up. The truth was, Otto had *not* seen *Doc* (no one had). He phoned to tell me he had "lied" for me, and I shouldn't let on if asked.

Even in the face of certain doom, Preminger retained his basically cheerful and optimistic nature. It seemed clear early on that *Skidoo*, his comedy with Jackie Gleason, was not going to work. But I watched Otto mixing it, finishing it off, running it the first time for the studio executives—I was at Preminger's home projection room that night, and there wasn't one laugh through the entire movie—and still Preminger acted as though nothing was wrong. If it wasn't a success, so what? Next. His exclusive deals with Columbia and then Paramount provided *complete control* for Preminger as producer and director as long as he stayed below a certain budget—I believe it was then three million dollars a film; for that figure, he could do whatever he pleased. And Preminger the producer was very strict with Preminger the director: on *Exodus*, when the shadow of a boom was spotted in dailies, it meant going back and reshooting an expensive shot; Preminger's decision was not to go back. "No one will notice it," he said, and no one did. Nevertheless, though he had a six- to eight-picture deal with Paramount, the studio froze him out after only four. He never recovered his pace again. Four years passed before he made another picture, then four years more before his last. Neither seemed to work for audiences. A couple of years later, Otto was hit by a cab while crossing a Manhattan street. This terrible accident, which he survived, seems to have triggered the onset of Alzheimer's disease. He died within a few years, just six months before his eightieth birthday. One of his most cherished projects—about the infamous Rosenberg treason case—did not get made.

I never saw the so-called cruel or ulcer-producing Preminger. Both with his young twins and young wife Hope Bryce (who had been his costume designer), and with his son by stripper/author Gypsy Rose Lee, I saw Otto as loving and warm, fatherly, concerned, patient. He was a gracious host. I visited him for the last time not long before he died. He and Hope and I had an afternoon drink at their New York apartment. He was in a cardigan sweater and appeared shrunken, bent over slightly; he had always stood very straight and tall. It had been a joke with Preminger for as long as I knew him that the problem with our relationship was that I had all the questions but that he couldn't give proper answers because he didn't remember the pictures well enough; he loved to say that I knew his films much better than he did. That afternoon, as we sat around, he joked again, but it was a dark joke because of the Alzheimer's that had already made itself felt. Yes, Hope said, Otto never could remember much about his old pictures. "Now," Otto said quietly, "I *really* can't." "But you never could, darling," Hope said. Otto smiled but his eyes looked sad and somewhat confused. We talked for over an hour about current pictures, my work, his films. He listened intently, smiled often, seemed happy to have company. When it came time for me to leave, Otto walked me to the front door without any help. We shook hands. There was great warmth in his eyes, and as friendly a smile as I had ever seen, though his eyes still looked sad. I felt just then that I would probably never see him again, and that he was feeling the same thing. He waved to me. I waved back. His last smile of affection and bewildered sadness haunts me still.

Open Questions

We did our three interview sessions in Mr. Preminger's offices at Paramount Studios and in his suite at the Hotel Bel-Air during October and November 1966, and again in mid-1969. I started by asking how and when he had begun working in the US, and I didn't have to say anything else for quite a while . . .

Otto Preminger: In 1935 I left Austria, where I had directed in the theater and made one film, and came to the United States. I was invited here by Joe Schenck, chairman of the then recently combined Twentieth Century-Fox company. I really studied when I came here, started from scratch. I spent about eight months in cutting rooms and worked with many different directors.

Then one day Darryl Zanuck, the head of the studio, asked me whether I was ready to practice on a B picture. I made two of them. One was called *Under Your Spell* [1936], with Lawrence Tibbett. Zanuck was mad at him—he didn't want to settle Tibbett's very high-priced contract—so the film was kind of a punishment. I ended up directing him.

The second was called *Danger—Love at Work* [1937]. We started out with a French actress, Simone Simon, although I protested to Zanuck. This was the time of those very fast-talking comedies, and I said, "She can't even understand what the other people are saying." But Zanuck insisted she do it. After a couple of days of looking at the rushes, he realized she couldn't do it, and Ann Sheridan replaced her.

Making these pictures was a very interesting experience, because the way B pictures were done is so reminiscent of the way people do TV shows now. My conviction is that one day the TV shows of today will have to disappear just as B pictures did. They will have to make TV shows like they have tried to make pictures—on a more individual basis. You cannot *produce* dramatic entertainment, whether it's for TV or movies or the stage, wholesale and on a treadmill. Mass production is not possible.

Zanuck liked these two pictures very much, so the third picture he assigned me to was a huge epic—the biggest picture Fox had produced to that time—called *Kidnapped*, based on the Stevenson novel. We had a budget of $750,000, which seems small now but was enormous then. But I didn't want to do it. Coming from Vienna, I was completely foreign to Scotland and that whole culture. I had barely started to learn English and become part of the American scene.

I wanted to turn it down, but a very good friend of mine, Gregory Ratoff, who was also a friend of Zanuck's and acted as a kind of go-between, said, "Don't turn it down, or he'll never talk to you again. He feels he gave you the biggest chance he has to give. Just do the picture." So I started the picture while Zanuck was in New York.

I staged the scenes—that's not too difficult—but I really felt very strange. In one scene I made a slight change. Then Zanuck came back and started a fight with me. He said, "Well, why did you change it?" But I hadn't changed it the way he thought; I had just left something out. Zanuck said, "I remember there was this and this in the scene."

I said, "You really *don't* remember!" I made a tremendous fight. I could shout just as loud as he could, which, it turned out, he had never experienced before. His secretaries came running from the outer office because they thought one of us was going to kill the other.

I didn't see Zanuck again for a long time, because he replaced me. That is, I quit. I'd only worked on it for a week or so. Alfred Werker finished the picture, which turned out to be probably the biggest disaster ever at Fox. It lost all its money and was a flop.

I still had a contract with Fox. Since they didn't make any moves to settle it, I decided to stay in Los Angeles. I went to the university and studied young people, because I still didn't know America. I even enrolled in a drama course, just to see how they did it. Because I was known through publicity and newspapers, I used another name so I could watch undisturbed. One day they discovered who I was. They considered this terrible and threw me out.

Because of the situation with Zanuck, I was practically blacklisted in Hollywood; I couldn't get a job in films for several years. So I went back to New York and started to produce plays. One of them was *Margin for Error* by Clare Boothe [Luce]. It was 1939, just before the war started. During rehearsals, the leading actor, a German star named Rudolph Forster, left. I came to rehearsals one day and found a very short note from him: "Dear Otto. Sorry—leaving to rejoin Adolf. Greetings, Rudolph." Many years later Forster played a very small part for me in *The Cardinal* [1963].

We couldn't find anybody to replace him—the part was a Nazi—and there were no Nazis available at that time. Although I'm Jewish, I can look like a Nazi if I shave my head—as I now wear it all the time. So I played the part. Then Twentieth Century-Fox started a picture called *The Pied Piper* [1942], and they offered me a part in it—again, playing a Nazi.

Meanwhile, Fox had also bought the screen rights to *Margin for Error* [1943]. They offered me the part I had played on stage at a very good salary—practically a star salary. But I told my agent, "I won't take the part unless I can also direct the picture. I'm not an actor; I'm a director. I'm not going to waste my time playing Nazis." My agent said, "That's foolish. They'll never let you direct. Take the money."

I called Bill Goetz, who was running the studio while Zanuck was in Europe for the war. I said to him, "Look, I'll do this the following way: you pay me only for the part, and I will direct the picture for free. If, after a week, you feel it's a mistake, I will resign as director, but I will continue to play the part for any other director as well as I know how." Goetz said, "Let me think about it." He called me later that afternoon and said, "It's a deal." So I started to direct the picture.

My agent got very mad at me and said, "Well, if you'd told me you were going to do it for free, *I* could have gotten you the job. Besides, you should never do anything for free; it's a mistake." It didn't turn out to be a mistake, because at the end of the first week Goetz offered me a contract as producer, director, and actor. When the picture was finished, I started to work on several projects bought for me by Fox.

Then Zanuck came back from the war and had a tremendous fight with Goetz. He accused him of treachery in several areas and refused to come back to the studio until Goetz had cleared out. After Zanuck had been reinstated, he called me to his home. We had not spoken to each other since the incident on *Kidnapped*. Whenever we had seen each other at parties, he just turned the other way.

I came to his house and was ushered to the swimming pool, where Zanuck was sitting with his back to me. He didn't get up or even turn around. He just said, "Well, you keep working on these three properties, two of which we'll keep. You can produce them, but you will never direct again as long as I am here at Fox." He assigned me to Byrnie [Bryan] Foy, who was in charge of the B pictures unit.

I knew I'd be finished at Fox as soon as my option came up. However, I had nothing to do in New York at the moment, so I decided to stay and do the best I could with these two properties. One was called *Army Wives*—finally released as *In the Meantime, Darling* [1944]—and the other was *Laura* [1944].

I started to work on the script of *Laura* with a writer named Jay Dratler. Then I hired Samuel Hoffenstein, who was a great poet, and a woman named Betty Reinhardt. Although he was not really a dramatic writer, Hoffenstein gave me some scenes which were wonderful. He really created the character Clifton Webb played—Waldo Lydecker.

We only used one gimmick from the book: when they find the dead girl, who they think is Laura, her face is unrecognizable because of a shotgun blast. The real Laura doesn't know this is going on, and she walks into the investigation. She comes back from a weekend and is then, naturally, a suspect. That was the good part of the novel. Everything else, including the characters, was newly crafted for the film. When the script was finished I sent it in. I also took it to Vera Caspary, who wrote the novel. Her reaction was, "Why do you want to make a B picture out of my wonderful story?"

All the reactions to the script were rather bad. When I sent it to Mr. Foy, he said, "No, we won't do this picture." "Why, Byrnie?" "Well, I haven't read it, but my man"—he had a boy who got fifty dollars a week to read scripts for him—"says this is not suspense; it's not a thriller. There is not one scene with the police. It has got to be completely rewritten." I said, "Why don't *you* read it? After all, I get fifteen hundred dollars a week, and your reader gets only fifty." "OK, I'll read it."

The next day I met him in an elevator. "I read it last night," he said. "It's no good." So I said, "Byrnie, do me one favor." (We were very friendly; we played gin rummy.) "Send it to Zanuck. Let him be the judge. I worked very hard on this script, and I believe in it." Byrnie said, "You know what Zanuck is going to say about your script. He's going to throw you out. This way at least you can stay here. Maybe we'll even pick up your option." "I'm not interested in staying here. I want Zanuck to read this script. If you don't send it to him, I will." "All right, I'll send it to him."

Then came a surprise twist. This type of thing happened several times on the picture, and it explains the difference between the success of Zanuck and the second-rate success of a man like Byrnie Foy. Zanuck read the script. He called Byrnie and me into his huge office, and he started to walk up and down with his little cigar and his croquet mallet. He said to Byrnie, "You don't like this script?" Byrnie said, "No, I don't . . ." But he was trying to spare me. He said that it was not my fault—it was just a bad project. Zanuck pumped him: "Why?" And Byrnie hanged himself. It turned out he really hadn't read the script to the end. So Zanuck said, "Well, if you don't like it, I'll produce it. I'll take it into my unit as an A picture." It was a great victory.

Zanuck didn't talk to me much about it, but he started to send the script around to other directors. He didn't want me to direct it. And then came a terrible thing: every director turned it down. Nobody liked the script. I remember one was Lewis Milestone, who wrote a very nice note: "Well, Preminger probably knows what to do with the script. He should direct it; I won't."

The man who finally accepted the script was Rouben Mamoulian. He also didn't like it, as it turned out, but he wanted the money. When he found out that I was not particularly in Zanuck's good graces, he started to ignore me. He began to design the sets with the art department without asking me. He started to rewrite the script, which I stopped. I said, "You accepted the script; you've got to do it." I had no hopes of directing it, however. I was just resigned to the fact that I would sit out my contract and at least produce this film which I liked.

Then came the casting. Zanuck assigned Gene Tierney, and I agreed to Dana Andrews. Neither of them was a big star at the time. He assigned Laird Cregar to the part that Clifton Webb eventually played. I went to see Zanuck alone, without Mamoulian, and I said, "Look, this whole thing is wrong if you have Laird Cregar. You must have a man who either is unknown or has never played heavies before. Otherwise, the audience will know right away, and there will be no chance to suspect Gene Tierney." It kind of appealed to him, but he didn't make a decision. Then I suggested Clifton Webb, who at that time was playing downtown in *Blithe Spirit*.

Clifton Webb's career in films had been a complete flop. He had been at Metro for eighteen months with a very high salary and never made a film. But he was a big stage star, and always a social event—he had many friends. A very good friend of mine, an agent named Felix Ferry, introduced me to him. I told Clifton that I wanted him to play this part. That was against all the rules at Fox, because a producer was not supposed to talk to an actor without the casting department first giving him the script. Webb liked the part and said he'd do it.

When I went to Zanuck and suggested him, the reaction was completely negative. A casting director named Rufus LeMaire was present. He said, "I was at Metro when Webb made a test there, and he 'flies'"—implying that he was homosexual—"you can't have him in the film."

So I started this fight for Clifton Webb. I wanted him for the part, because he was new. Also, at that time, when a picture supposedly took place in New York, it would still have that Los Angeles feeling. People didn't really bother to capture that kind of big-town sophistication. Clifton was ideal for it. I said to Zanuck, "Couldn't I make a test of him?" "No. What do you need a test for? We'll ask Rufus to bring the Metro test."

This went on for a couple of weeks. The test from Metro never arrived. In the meantime, I had been admitted to the executive dining room, where conversation was public. One day Zanuck argued about Clifton Webb in front of everyone and made some rather vulgar remarks. He said that when the picture played in the Middle West, Webb would be laughed off the screen. [Ernst] Lubitsch, who had become a good friend of mine, took me aside after lunch and said, "You have a chance to produce this big picture. You have Mamoulian. Why do you fight? Why do you have to be so difficult? You will cut your throat again. They threw you out once; they'll throw you out again."

But, by that time, having directed on stage in New York and acted in these pictures, I had a certain standing. I was not just a nobody as I had been when I came from Vienna, where my past was a matter of record but nobody cared about it. So I said, "No, I want Clifton Webb."

I told Felix Ferry about the test. He came back to me and said, "You will never see this test." "Why?" "Because I talked to Clifton last night. He never made a test. He's never faced a camera."

Rufus LeMaire had been lying. So, with great care, dramatizing it, I waited for lunch the next day. Zanuck was sitting at the head of the table. Rufus Le-Maire and Lubitsch and [director] Henry King and most of the other producers were there. I asked Rufus, "When are you going to get that test?" "Tomorrow, definitely." I said, "You're lying, Rufus. You won't get it." "What do you mean?" "What I mean is that this test was never made. You just don't like Clifton Webb, and you don't want him in the part and you're sabotaging him, that's all."

Then, once again, Zanuck proved to be a very interesting man. He said, "Is that true, Rufus?" And Rufus had to admit it. So Zanuck said, "Well, you wanted to make a test with Clifton. Make the test." He gave me permission to get Gene Tierney and direct the test—Mamoulian was not in town.

Elated, I went that same evening to Clifton Webb's dressing room at the Biltmore, so we could pick a scene from the script for the test. And Clifton said, "My dear boy, if your Mr. Zanuck wants to see me, he can come here himself. I'm not going to test. And I certainly won't test with this young lady whom I don't know. Who is this Gene Tierney?" He was very difficult. I said to him, "Well, will you do a scene from the play which you've already learned?" "Yes, that I will do."

I went back to Zanuck. I didn't dare tell him about this, because Clifton would have been out. Instead I said, "Maybe it would be easier if we didn't use Gene Tierney for the test. There's a beautiful monologue in the play where Clifton is all by himself on the stage. After all, what you mainly want to see is not whether he can act, but whether his particular movements fit the part." Zanuck said, "If I wanted to see him on the stage, I would go downtown. Besides, I want to see him in this scene of yours. I want to see how the script plays." His belief in the script had been shaken because so many directors had turned it down.

Not caring too much about my position at Fox, I used the monologue from the play and shot the test without Zanuck's permission, which was a capital crime. When it was finished, I took it to Zanuck's projection room, absolutely ready to be fired, and ran it for him. It was beautifully photographed—we put Clifton in half light and half shadow—and he played it very well. He knew what Zanuck's objection might be, and he avoided all that completely. When Zanuck saw the test, he said, "All right, he can play the part."

Then Mamoulian started to direct the picture, ignoring me completely. He didn't even let me come on the stage, said I made him nervous because I was also a director. He behaved in a very silly way, because I only could have helped him. I knew the script, and I knew where he was missing. I don't think Mamoulian is a bad director, but he just didn't understand the picture. For instance, he put Judith Anderson in long, waving robes—almost like a period play. But this was all meant to be very crisp and contemporary, like New York. Also, Judith Anderson has to be held down on the screen; she is not basically a screen actress. Dana Andrews and Gene Tierney were new; they needed help. And Mamoulian and Clifton Webb didn't like each other because Webb had heard that Mamoulian was against him.

Zanuck was in New York, and the rushes were sent to him. They were so bad you couldn't believe it. I received a wire from Zanuck which I'll never forget. He blamed me for everything: "This Dana Andrews whom you sponsored is an amateur without any sex appeal, and Clifton Webb is 'flying.' Judith Anderson should stay on the stage, and you should have stayed in New York or Vienna, where you belong."

Zanuck came back and called Mamoulian and me into his office. He was ready to abandon the picture. Mamoulian had an alibi for everything. He said, "The script is bad. It cannot be directed differently." So I, being a director, played it for Zanuck. I said, "Now let's take this scene. This is the way it should be done." I knew the lines by heart. "This line was read like this by Miss Anderson. That's wrong—she has to throw it away." Zanuck was apparently impressed by it. He said to Mamoulian, "Well, I think he's right. Try again tomorrow. I'll give you another chance." Mamoulian tried again the next day, and again it was bad.

The following day at lunch, in front of eighteen people, Zanuck asked me, "Do you think we should take Mamoulian off the picture?" It was a terribly embarrassing thing to do to anybody. And I said, "Yes." Just like that. Zanuck said, "OK." Then the whole group walked back to the administration building. Zanuck always walked in front with his mallet. He called to me, "Come here." When we reached his office, he said, "You can start directing."

Then came the most horrible thing: Mamoulian had told Dana Andrews and Gene Tierney and Judith Anderson about my criticism with Zanuck, but he made it sound as though I had been criticizing them. He didn't tell them that I was really criticizing his direction. So there was the atmosphere of an iceberg when I arrived on the set. Miss Anderson said to me, "Mr. Premincher"—deliberately mispronouncing my name—"if you know how to play this so well, why don't you show me how?"

I said, "That is exactly what I am going to do, and you will do it exactly like this. Then I will take you to see the rushes tomorrow, and you will be the first one to agree that I was right. I'll show you both scenes: the way you did it before, and the way you're going to do it now." Being an actress, she did it—they all did. I took them the next day to see the rushes, and they were all convinced. I had no more difficulties, and we had a wonderful time. And, of course, Clifton had been on my side from the beginning. We threw out everything Mamoulian had directed, and I finished the picture.

It was customary at Fox for the director to make the first cut, which was then shown to Zanuck. The routine was that Zanuck and the director and the cutter sat in the front row of the projection room. The next three rows were filled with yes-men, real sycophants who had learned croquet so they could play it with Zanuck. They had also learned to read—from the way Zanuck sat or the way his neck wrinkled—whether he liked a picture or not. So, before he could say something, they were usually in agreement with him.

When the screening of *Laura* was over, nobody had laughed, nobody had said anything. It was like a funeral. Zanuck turned to me and said, "Well, Byrnie was right. We missed the bus on this one." Then he left. I walked out to the Fox parking lot with my cutter, Lou Loeffler, who liked the film very much. We both couldn't believe the reaction to it. I remember we stood out there in the rain for an hour discussing the picture: "It can't be all that bad . . . But this scene was good . . . How could they not like it?"

All those yes-men started to write memos to Zanuck with suggestions which were unbelievable. He showed them to me the next day. He said, "We've got to do something. I don't think we can save the picture, but at least we can save Gene Tierney. She's an extra in this picture; you've made an extra out of my new star."

He called in a writer who was under contract, and he started to dictate a new last third to the picture. In the original version, there was one narration by Clifton Webb, and one narration by Dana Andrews. Now Zanuck added a narration by Gene Tierney which negated everything that had happened in the picture. She was to say it was not true—it had all been in Clifton Webb's imagination. It was just unbelievable.

At one point, I made a face and Zanuck said, "Well, if you don't want to direct it, I'll get somebody else." I said, "No, no. I'll do anything you say." I was tired. This new script was written in a few days, and we did about a week or ten days of retakes, which I directed. The new script was so bad that the actors laughed. They had started to like me and believe in me, and they were happy with their performances. But I made them do the new scenes, which were cut into the film, and a showing of the new version was scheduled for Zanuck.

Then something happened which shows how, in our profession, a little coincidence can change a lot for a person or a film or a career. At that time, Walter Winchell, as a gesture of friendship, had an office at Fox. He was very close to

Zanuck. He arrived from New York and had lunch with Zanuck, who said to him, "Walter, I'm very busy all day, but I'd like to talk to you. Come over tonight. I'm running a new film, and after the picture we can sit down and talk. You can bring somebody if you like."

So Walter Winchell arrived at the projection room. None of the yes-men were there. They had given up; they had written off the picture. Zanuck, Loeffler, and I sat in the front row, and in the last row were Winchell and a young lady he had brought. The picture started and, for the first time in its history, there was a reaction. Winchell laughed at many of the lines which were very New Yorkish. He made remarks and Zanuck looked back—he couldn't understand it.

When the picture was over, Winchell went up to Zanuck, shook his hand, and praised him. He always speaks very fast, staccato. "Big time," he said. "Big time. Great." And Zanuck looked at me. He was confused. Then Winchell said, "But the ending. I didn't get it. You've got to change it." He turned to the girl and said, "I didn't get it, I didn't get it—did you get it?" "No," she said, "no."

Then, once again, Zanuck proved that his success is deserved because he's a very flexible man. He's not stubborn when it comes to admitting a mistake. He turned to me, in front of Winchell, Loeffler, and this girl and said, "Do you want to have your old ending back?" "Of course." "OK." And we put it back the way it had been originally.

Through these circumstances, we avoided Zanuck's usual cutting. At that time in his career, he cut all motivations out of pictures. When you protested, he would say, "Let the audience think." "But they won't know why the character did this." "Let them think. They'll make up their own story." Just nonsense, of course.

Then we put the music in, which was also a stroke of luck. Because the picture was not considered a possible success, Alfred Newman, who was head of the music department and scored all the bigger pictures himself, assigned a young man named David Raskin, who had never done a motion picture score before.

For the main theme I wanted to buy "Summertime" by Gershwin. I love that melody. But Gershwin was dead, and his brother Ira didn't permit it. He figured it would hurt a possible filming of *Porgy and Bess* in the future. So Raskin came into my office one day and played this tune on the piano—"Laura." I said, "I really don't know enough about music to judge, but I like it. Let's put it in." Later, Johnny Mercer wrote a lyric to it, which is not in the film, and it became a success.

About a month after the screening with Winchell, we had the first preview. It was on a Jewish high holiday, and I was scared because I felt there would be no Jews there, and we'd have an unmixed audience. In spite of this, the preview was a tremendous success. And Zanuck was very fair. He said, "This is your success. I concede."

Peter Bogdanovich: What particularly interested you about *Laura*?

Preminger: The gimmick. You see, a suspense picture depends mainly on finding a new gimmick. There are very few new plots. If you can find something different, as in this case, where a girl you thought was dead automatically becomes a murder suspect by walking into her own apartment—that helps.

Bogdanovich: Do you agree with certain critics who felt Andrews was disappointed in the real Laura for not living up to his illusion of her?

Preminger: I couldn't tell you, because I don't remember the film that closely anymore. I always have to try to disassociate myself from a film when it's finished. This helps me a lot because, unlike other people, I'm not as depressed by failure, and I'm not as elated by success.

Bogdanovich: Did you consciously draw a parallel between Clifton Webb and Dana Andrews in *Laura*?

Preminger: Well, I am always trying to know the characters in my films, and to make people interested in learning about them. Naturally, when they have a relationship with each other, you might compare them somewhat. I cannot direct a character unless I understand him to the extent that I can identify myself with him, whether he is a murderer or an angel, a woman or a man. I have to understand their motivations. That makes them part of me, and that might be a reason why you find these things in my pictures.

Bogdanovich: Have you found, in later years, that the success of *Laura*, coming so early in your film career, was more of a hindrance with critics than an asset?

Preminger: I don't ever think of anything in terms like those. Besides, *Laura* became a classic only later on, which is a great satisfaction for me. I got very mixed reviews at first—some really bad ones, in fact. I met one of the reviewers after he retired, and he told me, "I saw *Laura* on TV the other day, and it is one of the greatest pictures I've ever seen." I didn't have the heart to remind him that he wrote an absolutely devastating review of it when it opened.

Bogdanovich: When you first started making pictures, were there certain directors whose work influenced you?

Preminger: Nothing I do is that deliberate. Naturally, I am influenced by whatever I see, whether in life or on film or in the theatre. I try to see as many pictures as possible, good or bad, because I think it's necessary for anybody in any profession to keep abreast of the times.

To give you an example, when the Nouvelle Vague came, they cut out all the opticals, all the dissolves and fades, not as an experiment but because they had no money. When I saw these films, I decided that dissolves slow up a film unless they are used with great discretion and not just automatically to denote a passage of time. So in my last films I haven't used them. In *Hurry Sundown* [1966], for instance, there isn't one dissolve—and only two fades, which are used because they work out nicely with the mood of the scene, not in the sense of a conventional "fade-out." In other words, I think that things should change, and when I see a deliberate experiment I like, I am influenced by it.

But I never went in for hero worship. While I admired Ernst Lubitsch, for example, I never tried to work in his style. On the contrary—he chose me, which was a great honor, to direct a film he had prepared called *A Royal Scandal* [1945]: his doctor wouldn't let him direct it himself. I had many difficulties, friendly difficulties, with him because I directed it differently than he would have. In other words, I didn't try to make it a Lubitsch film. When I felt I was going too much into his style, I tried to avoid it. On the other hand—and this is one of my few principles—I have never deliberately tried to create a style, by using certain camera angles all the time, or something like that. Direction should not impose an arbitrary style.

Bogdanovich: But your films do have a very definite style.

Preminger: Naturally, there might be a common denominator which could be called, if you want to be nice, the style of a man. But I never worked at it deliberately, and I don't want to know about it, because that would only limit me. I want to do every single film the way I feel at that moment.

Bogdanovich: How closely did Lubitsch work with you on *A Royal Scandal*?

Preminger: The script was already done—it was completely Lubitsch's. Whatever changes I made were very small.

Bogdanovich: Did he come on the set every day?

Preminger: No, but we saw the rushes together and discussed them. He was very easy, actually; he was the only producer with whom I had no conflict.

Bogdanovich: Because he was a director?

Preminger: He was also a man who really *knew*, unlike, say, Milton Sperling or Sam Goldwyn—who in spite of his great name really doesn't know anything about production. Sam Goldwyn came on the set of *Porgy and Bess* [1959] four weeks after the start of shooting and said to me, "The rushes for the 70 mm version are very beautiful, but they are too dark. On the second version, the 35 mm version, you should have more light." I said to him, "Sam, we shoot only one version." "What do you mean? What am I going to show in the smaller theaters that don't have 70 mm?" I said, "You're going to print it down. We shoot it in 70 mm Todd-AO, and then we reduce it to 35 mm. That's done optically, just as I can blow up 35 mm." *The Cardinal* was shot in 35 mm and blown up to 70 mm. But Goldwyn didn't believe me; he thought I was teasing him. He went to the cutter and checked, and he became the laugh of the lot because he really thought there were two cameras shooting all the time. That was the reason I had confidence in Lubitsch on these matters. There could never be any arguments, because he *knew*.

Yet there's a great difference between us. Lubitsch had a wonderful gift for taking a situation and making it funny, but—and this is where our main difference lay—he did it by distorting character. In *A Royal Scandal*, he had scenes where the empress of Russia didn't act like an empress. Now, even in a comedy, an empress should stay an empress. In the pictures I directed for him, the characters were distorted for the sake of a gag—their nobility was hurt. Also, you know, these things don't pay off. I remember the preview of *A Royal Scandal*. I went there with Lubitsch and Zanuck, and when we came out they felt this was the biggest success ever, because they had never heard such laughs. I was pessimistic; and I told them, "I didn't feel that we got the audience. They laughed, but when they left they took nothing with them." As it turned out, *A Royal Scandal* wasn't a very big success.

Bogdanovich: How did you come to make *Forever Amber* [1947]?

Preminger: Well, after *Laura*, I didn't have many difficulties with Zanuck, except that I became his friend. He began inviting me to Palm Springs. One time I played croquet with him and Howard Hawks, although I didn't know how to play—they couldn't find anyone else. Hawks played so well that he and I together always beat Zanuck and whoever else was on the other side.

But the only difficulty was that being so close to Zanuck, I couldn't turn him down. One day I came to Palm Springs and he said to me, "I have a terrible problem. You have to help." He explained that he had spent two million dollars on a film based on *Forever Amber*, and that he had to stop production and start from scratch. He said, "If you want to recast or rewrite it, you can do anything you want, but you've got to do the picture." I said, "I can't direct this. This is a horrible book." He said, "Look, you're part of the team. Your contract still has six years to go. We are stuck with you, but you are also stuck with us." He had this very persuasive manner, and I finally agreed to do it.

We did recast it. I wanted Lana Turner for the part, and Zanuck had been insisting on Linda Darnell. So, very much in the Hollywood manner, I invited Lana Turner and Zanuck to a dinner party so she could persuade him—and she was practically sitting on his lap. She wanted it. But she was at Metro, and Zanuck wouldn't give it to anybody he didn't have under contract. He said, "If you think Lana Turner is right, then we'll dye Linda Darnell's hair blond, and she'll be exactly like her." So she played the part, and she wasn't so bad. It wasn't her fault.

The Legion of Decency really emasculated the picture. There was an incredible scene in Spyros Skouras's office. The head of the Legion of Decency didn't even want to see the picture. He said to Skouras, "We banned the book. Why did you buy it and make a picture?" And Skouras literally went down on his knees and said, "Father, please, we invested six million dollars in this picture. Please. Go and look at it with Mr. Preminger." The man said, "Change the title," because they felt it was very irreverent of Twentieth Century-Fox to make a film of a book that was banned. Finally, we had to put on a foreword that spoke about sin and how it is punished ("The wages of sin is death"). Then, whenever two people kissed, we had to dissolve or cut as their lips approached. Anyway, I don't think the film was a masterpiece one way or the other.

Bogdanovich: Obsession seems to be a recurring theme in your pictures. Clifton Webb is obsessed with Laura, Dana Andrews in *Where the Sidewalk Ends* [1950] is obsessed with arresting Gary Merrill, Charles Boyer in *The 13th Letter* [1951] is obsessed with sex, and so on.

Preminger: Well, obsession is a very dramatic thing and a very human thing. We are all obsessed with our work, our lives.

Bogdanovich: Dana Andrews in *Where the Sidewalk Ends* struck me as being somewhat like Don Murray in *Advise & Consent* [1962] in that he has no pity for someone who has a similar weakness. He sets himself up as a judge, and this becomes his downfall. Have you ever noticed that similarity?

Preminger: No. But you know me so well now—you can always answer for me.

Bogdanovich: How did you come to make *Angel Face* [1952]?

Preminger: I got a call one day from Zanuck, and he told me that Howard Hughes wanted to borrow me for this story. Hughes called me, and I told him, "I don't like it." He said, "Look, you come into the studio tomorrow morning. You just walk in like Hitler, and you take over." He thought that would impress me, forgetting that I am Jewish. And Zanuck asked me to do it because he was indebted to Hughes. We revamped the story, and we made it, and it was fun making it.

Bogdanovich: The idea of the car going into reverse . . .

Preminger: That was taken from my personal experience. You see, I'm not a very good driver. I remember stopping at an intersection once, and I passed the line. I reversed and pulled back a little. When the light changed, I had forgotten to shift, and I went backward. That gave me the idea to have this trick for the murder. It worked out very well.

Bogdanovich: Do you often use things from your personal experience?

Preminger: I think everything you do—whether you make pictures or write books or whatever—is somehow related to your personal experience. I mean, it's never completely foreign to me.

Bogdanovich: Were any of your studio films tampered with or recut after you had finished?

Preminger: No. After *Laura* I had a very good relationship with Zanuck. He really didn't do anything to hurt my feelings. If he wanted to do something which I didn't like, I could always talk him out of it.

Bogdanovich: Why did you choose *The Moon Is Blue* [1953] as your first independent production?

Preminger: I had produced and directed the play, so it was natural for me to do the picture. Also, people were just beginning to do independent production then, and it wasn't so simple to do one. This was a small picture, and I could get the rights reasonably. In fact, I didn't have to pay anything for it—the author became my partner.

Bogdanovich: How do you think the publicity you got from not allowing any cuts to be made affected the reception of the film?

Preminger: As you know, we released it without the seal, without the approval of the Legion of Decency. That helped the picture in some places, but there were small towns where the police stood in front of the theater and put down the names of people who went in.

Bogdanovich: I thought David Niven was the only really honest, sympathetic character in the film, unlike William Holden, or, especially, Maggie McNamara. Would you agree?

Preminger: Well, you just don't like girls who remain virgins.

Bogdanovich: Which of your functions—director or producer—do you consider more important?

Preminger: That's all one function. I consider producing to be just an extension of directing. Although today the producer is often only a packager, an agent who has discovered he can make 50 percent instead of 10.

Bogdanovich: What interested you in *River of No Return* [1954]?

Preminger: *River of No Return* was an obligation. I wasn't particularly interested in it, but I still had to make some films for Fox. It was simply an assignment, and I liked the script fairly well.

Bogdanovich: When Marilyn Monroe loses her things from the raft, it represents the loss of all her material possessions—but you don't punctuate it at all—you don't even show the stuff drifting off down the river.

Preminger: Well, that's true—I have a great belief in the intelligence of the audience. I try to do things as subtly and with as little punctuation as possible.

Bogdanovich: Did you welcome the use of CinemaScope?

Preminger: Yes. But it really didn't make that much difference. It is actually more difficult to compose in CinemaScope and Panavision. I mean, when you go to a museum, you find that very few painters choose those proportions. But somehow it embraces more—you see more. So I've been doing all my recent pictures in Panavision, which I think is a better lens than CinemaScope.

Bogdanovich: It would seem to fit your long-take technique better.

Preminger: It's true that on a very wide screen, cuts shock you more. I don't believe in cutting too much or doing too many reaction shots.

Bogdanovich: Did you have troubles with the producer of *The Court-Martial of Billy Mitchell* [1955]?

Preminger: No, I didn't have troubles with him—he had troubles with me. He's actually a very nice, intelligent man, but he had a tremendous inferiority complex. Whenever he suggested something, and we liked it and incorporated it in the script, he came back the next day and changed it again. This went on until neither Ben Hecht nor I had the patience to go through with it. He was the only man I ever saw Gary Cooper get angry at. Because he has this strange negative quality.

Bogdanovich: Would you agree that *The Man with the Golden Arm* [1955] is a much less objective film than most of your others?

Preminger: Why?

Bogdanovich: I thought it was much more of a character study and much more colored to Sinatra's viewpoint than is usual in your films. The sets seemed more artificial as well.

Preminger: Well, I would have liked to make this film on location in Chicago. Unfortunately, there were many financial reasons why I couldn't do it. At that time, it was very difficult to make pictures on location.

Bogdanovich: How did you decide to cast Sinatra for the part?

Preminger: When I had about thirty or forty pages of the script ready, I gave one copy to Sinatra's agent and one to Marlon Brando's agent—just to give them an idea of what the picture was about. I got a call the next day from Sinatra's agent, who said, "He likes it very much." I said, "All right, I'll send him the rest of the script as soon as I have it." He said, "No, no. He wants to do it without reading the script." I said, "Fine."

Three or four days later, I called Brando's agent and told him I already had somebody else. He couldn't believe me—he thought I was bluffing. That's how Sinatra came to play the part—he made the decision very quickly. And I must say, it was a wonderful experience. I've never enjoyed working with anybody more than Sinatra. All these stories I hear about him delaying a picture, doing only one take and then walking out, I just can't believe.

Bogdanovich: What interested you most about the book?

Preminger: I think there's a great tragedy in any human being who gets hooked on something, whether it's heroin or love or a woman or whatever.

Bogdanovich: Again, it's obsession, isn't it?

Preminger: Perhaps.

Bogdanovich: Was *Saint Joan* [1957] a pet project of yours?

Preminger: Well, I loved the play by Bernard Shaw. I always wanted to make a picture of it. Perhaps that was the great mistake: I loved the play so much that I didn't analyze it. I realized only later that the play is actually a very intellectual, analytical rendition of the story of Saint Joan. It's not an emotional story, and it just wasn't moving enough to get the masses to follow. Even the play, as I found out later, was never a big popular success. But I would do it all over again, and probably the same way, because I love the play.

Bogdanovich: Do you feel that Joan is guided by reason or by vision?

Preminger: You never quite felt that Shaw believed it was vision—that is what makes the play interesting for intellectuals but not quite convincing for the masses. Something is missing—something that could make people cry. Perhaps Joan is too convinced herself. You just don't believe that she is a saint—that everything is vision and instinct and passion. There is too much reason in it for pictures.

Bogdanovich: In his preface, Shaw says that he thinks Joan was a complete realist; do you feel that way?

Preminger: Probably. You see, that was the reason I tried to get a girl who was as young as Saint Joan. On the stage, it's usually played by a very mature actress, because it's a difficult part to play. I felt that on the screen you have to come close to her, and she must be young. I don't blame [Jean] Seberg for anything that happened. I don't think she had the depth, but I really don't think she was as bad as most people say.

Bogdanovich: It's been pointed out that the saint is a recurring motif in your films: Laura herself, Alice Faye in *Fallen Angel* [1945], Gene Tierney in *Whirlpool* [1949], Deborah Kerr in *Bonjour Tristesse* [1958], Kathryn Grant in *Anatomy of a Murder* [1959], Jill Haworth in *Exodus* [1960] are all saints in a certain sense—women who suffer but are not evil in any way.

Preminger: They are not evil, but that's not a saint—they have their weaknesses . . .

Bogdanovich: Well, so does Joan.

Preminger: Perhaps that's why she was not completely a saint. Anyway, I like women.

Bogdanovich: In *Bonjour Tristesse*, why did you use color for the memory scenes and black and white for the present?

Preminger: I'm not particularly fond of flashbacks, so I probably tried to make it more agreeable or interesting by doing that. *Bonjour Tristesse* is a film I like. I rarely say this, but I really don't think the American critics did it justice. You know, it was a very big success in France, and in America the critics said it wasn't French enough, which is very funny.

Bogdanovich: The film seems to imply a more incestuous relationship between David Niven and Jean Seberg than the book did.

Preminger: Really?

Bogdanovich: There's a line where Mylène Demongeot is talking to Niven and Seberg, and she says, "You two don't even need words: the perfect marriage."

Preminger: Don't you realize that if I still remembered everything I did in *Bonjour Tristesse*, I would be terribly hampered in making a film now? When I'm finished with a picture, I'm finished. The first time I see a picture with an audience is the most thrilling moment, and then I forget it. Let me tell you a true story: I was dressing, my wife was not ready, we were going out for dinner. I turned on the TV, and *Fallen Angel* was on. I got fascinated, because it was like a new story to me. Then my wife was ready, and we had to go out. I turned it off, and I realized I didn't know the end of the picture.

Bogdanovich: Would you have done *Porgy and Bess* differently if you had produced it?

Preminger: Completely. I would have made it all on location, and I would have made the story into a film—as I did in *Carmen Jones* [1954]—rather than stick so closely to the book of the musical. It would have been the same story, but I would have built it differently.

Bogdanovich: More realistically?

Preminger: Yes.

Bogdanovich: Do you think you were influenced by your law studies? Many of your films have trials in them.

Preminger: It's not so much my law study as my whole youth. My father was a district attorney and attorney general for the Austrian Empire. He was always connected with big trials and, very early in life, I was permitted to go and watch him. Trials are much more flamboyant in Europe, where the speeches are long and big. So naturally my education and background influenced me—much more so than my law studies, because I studied law very mechanically. Maybe twice in my life did I go to lectures.

Bogdanovich: But you have a particular interest in the clarity that law strives for.

Preminger: I will say that I feel very grateful to my father, because the philosophy of law gives you a certain outlook on life. I can give you an example. When I went to Russia at the invitation of their picture makers, I took two pictures with me, and one of them was *Anatomy of a Murder*. I was a guest at the Russian Academy of Film; there were eight hundred young people there, and I showed them the film. They were very sharp, and they started to criticize the film. They said that this man is horrible and his wife is a prostitute—why should he be acquitted at the end? I tried to explain to them that the basic idea of the film was to show how in our system of law a man is considered innocent until he is proven guilty. They couldn't understand it for a long time. They said, "What do you mean? He was obviously guilty." "But the state could not prove it," I said. "We believe it is better to let a hundred guilty people go free than convict one innocent person." It was very difficult to explain to people who are not brought up with this principle.

Bogdanovich: Would you agree that each of your films is a trial in which the audience is the jury?

Preminger: In a way, that's true of any drama. When you present a story on stage or film, unlike in a book or a poem, you present it objectively and let the audience judge.

Bogdanovich: If you had cast Lana Turner in *Anatomy of a Murder*, as you planned, would you still have cast Ben Gazzara as her husband?

Preminger: Yes, because in the book the woman was older than the man. And I *did* cast Lana Turner—she was signed. We had a conflict because I selected a pair of slacks, and she didn't want to wear them. She wanted to have her costumes done by Jean Louis. I felt that the wife of a second lieutenant couldn't afford Jean Louis. Her agent came to talk to me, and I said, "Look, if she doesn't like it, she can turn the picture down." He thought I was bluffing.

Bogdanovich: Everybody always thinks you're bluffing.

Preminger: But I never am. He called me back and said she wouldn't wear the trousers. So I signed Lee Remick.

Bogdanovich: Do you think it would have been more interesting if she had been older?

Preminger: No, I don't think it matters.

Bogdanovich: What made you decide to shoot everything on location? Was this the first time you'd done it?

Preminger: Yes, I think it was the first time. You see, I feel realistic films gain by being shot on location in two ways. It's not only verisimilitude—certainly you can copy almost any location. I could have gone there, photographed the courtroom, and had a replica built here in Hollywood. But if you shoot on location, you can't shoot in every way you want; you can't move walls, you have ceilings, you can't light exactly the way you want to. That makes you direct in a more realistic way. You have to be more inventive; it's a challenge.

The second thing is that I feel professional extras are usually disgruntled people who don't care much anymore. Either they wanted to be actors and didn't make it, or it's kind of a profession—they go from one picture to another and put on the same makeup and the same laughs and the same moves. But there is a reality if you have the real people—if you go to the Upper Peninsula of Michigan and get real people to sit in that courtroom—and the jurors are real people. Somehow it influences everybody; it influences the other actors. It gives them a reality and a feeling which they wouldn't get otherwise.

Bogdanovich: Do you endorse the terrorist tactics in *Exodus*?

Preminger: I believe that whether I approve of it or not—and I don't approve of any violence—the state of Israel would not have come into being without terrorists. Every revolution needs some kind of terror or violence in order to unseat the regime. That's why I also understand what's going on in the Negro movement now, but I don't approve of it. It might momentarily hurt the Negro cause, but a revolution is not something logical that you can figure out.

I had a big argument in Israel when I made the picture. The ruling group did not like the idea that I gave any credit in the picture to the terrorists. Later, the terrorists also made it difficult for me. They felt they did not get *enough* credit and even threatened to picket that big scene I did on the square with forty thousand people. I didn't let myself be swayed by either side, and I felt that it was the right balance.

When I did *Exodus*—this also happened on *The Man with the Golden Arm*—the original author denounced me. When we started, I had engaged Mr. Uris to write the screenplay. I very quickly realized he couldn't write it, at least not the way *I* wanted it. I don't think he can write dialogue. I think he has a very good imagination—he's what I'd call a "passionate storyteller." But in telling a story he becomes too much of a partisan.

You see, I would be willing to defend my film of *Exodus* against some really big enemies of Israel, like Nasser. I would be willing to sit down with him, and let him tell me why he felt this picture is unfair. Because I know it isn't. But the book by Uris has a pox against all the enemies of the Jews in it, and that is difficult to defend. This is part of my whole outlook on the world; I am basically an optimist. I don't believe that there are any real villains. If somebody is a villain, I try to find out why. I don't necessarily excuse him, but I try to understand him.

People often come to me and ask if the film is going to be "faithful to the book." Once an author sells—and "sells" is a very hard word—the film rights, he gives up any claim to have somebody do it "faithfully." By that time, my mind and my talent and my heart are in charge of this story and these people. They become my raw material, and I can only re-create them the way I see them. It would be different if the author came to me and said, "Look, you want to do this book; let's be partners. Let's do it together, and we will have equal say."

Bogdanovich: Chances are you wouldn't make it then.

Preminger: I might not do it—that's true. But then he would have a right to complain.

Bogdanovich: Do you think Eva Marie Saint's development in the picture is basically the form of the film?

Preminger: That's difficult to say. It was meant to mirror, hopefully, the change of an audience which in the beginning might not be completely caught up with the hero and what was happening but in the end would agree.

Bogdanovich: You had Paul Newman almost throw away his last speech.

Preminger: Well, it's a difficult speech. I didn't want to make it too heroic and too declamatory. I didn't want him to speak like Moses. I think he did it very well.

Bogdanovich: Wasn't there also the implication that this wasn't by any means the end of the story?

Preminger: Oh, sure—that was there—they drove on.

Bogdanovich: What would you say is the theme of *Advise & Consent*? Is it the idea of checks and balances in the government?

Preminger: Yes, this was the basic theme. For me, there's an interesting story in showing how American government *functions*. The film has some very sharp criticisms of our way of government, and it was wonderful that I had the freedom to do this. It's amazing that the American government permits a picture like this to be made. This film proved to me that, in spite of all the beefs you hear, this is really the only free country, where you have free expression. Making *Advise & Consent* was very important to me in that sense.

Bogdanovich: Why did you shoot the scene where Don Murray first hears about the blackmail threat in the bathroom? Was it to anticipate his suicide?

Preminger: Well, his wife's in bed, and the scene showed that they have a normal, intimate marital life, because the homosexual incident is in the past. It was good to show that they don't live like strangers.

Bogdanovich: But you seem to imply that they have not had a completely happy life together. She says, "I know we haven't had a very exciting marriage."

Preminger: No, I disagree with you there: I think this happens in many marriages. If you read stories, you can find that nearly 50 percent of all women are not particularly fond of continuous sexual relations. So she feels guilty and accuses herself. The Murray character was not particularly aggressive, so he was probably more attracted to a woman who wouldn't demand too much. She, on the other hand, now feels it was her fault.

Bogdanovich: When Lew Ayres announces the death of the president, you don't cut to the rest of the Senate for their reaction. You often leave out reaction shots in your films.

Preminger: The old, classic picture technique always cuts to reaction shots, particularly in comedies. I feel that underrates the audience. It's like putting in mechanical laughter on TV.

Bogdanovich: There's another example in *In Harm's Way* [1964]: when John Wayne tells Paula Prentiss that her husband is missing, one expects you to cut to her reaction, since she's facing away from camera—but you don't. After a few seconds, she turns into the camera, which was much more effective than a cut.

Preminger: That has to do with my conviction that every cut interrupts the flow of storytelling. When I want a close-up, I either have the people come closer to the camera or move the camera closer to them. But always with some motivation, not wildly. You can cut without being too obvious, but it still interrupts the illusion, unless you want to use a cut to shock the audience. But this is only a theory, and I am an enemy of theory.

By the way, that was Paula Prentiss's last scene in the picture, and she so much wanted to be good that she kept unconsciously kicking herself in the ankle. When the scene was over, she suddenly couldn't walk, and she was taken to the hospital. She had broken her ankle, but she was concentrating so hard on the scene that she didn't realize it.

Bogdanovich: What was your purpose in making *The Cardinal*?

Preminger: I read the book thirteen years before I made it. I was fascinated by it, because I'm fascinated by institutions, from the Senate of the United States to the Catholic Church. I think the Catholic Church is a political institution—forget religion, it's a political unit. The way it's organized and works is ingenious. The Church is not a completely totalitarian government, as you might think. It's true that the pope has the final say on everything, but the wisdom is that he never acts like Adolf Hitler. You see, he always gives the lower echelons a lot of autonomy. It's an interesting mixture of totalitarianism and, perhaps not democracy, but individual autonomy.

Bogdanovich: You made no attempt in *Bunny Lake Is Missing* [1965] to create a London mood; you don't show any evocative shots of London. In fact, you usually avoid that sort of thing in your films.

Preminger: I think people notice *Bunny Lake* is placed in London, but the fact that the story plays there is not particularly essential. It only made it easier because these two Americans were isolated. There were no friends, there were no people they knew from the past, and that made the suspense angle better. That's why I moved the story to London.

Bogdanovich: Why did it take so long to develop the script for *Bunny Lake*?

Preminger: It was very difficult to make it reasonable. When I worked on the original story, I found that the villain, the old woman who stole the child—the former teacher of the school—was uninteresting. It's a completely arbitrary solution; it doesn't make much sense. Then we created a rich heiress who manufactured this whole thing because she had no children and wanted a child. This also turned out to be terribly phony. I finally came to the conclusion that it would have to be somebody very close from the beginning. That was the third and final attempt.

Bogdanovich: Do you think the implication of the ending is that Carol Lynley's character is not really healthy?

Preminger: Naturally, she is influenced by this thing. She has the child, and she will live for this child, but I think she is shaken by this experience with her brother. Without knowing it, she was part of this relationship. It is a tragedy for her, without doubt.

Bogdanovich: What was the purpose of the Noël Coward character?

Preminger: It was derived from a character in the book—unreal, as in every suspense story. If anything, this character is a weakness; it's a red herring.

Bogdanovich: Do you tell your cameraman the specific kind of lighting you want?

Preminger: Yes. Not the lighting—I don't know anything about that—but the mood. For example, there is a little scene in *Hurry Sundown* [1966] where Jane Fonda says, "Maybe I would like to have more children." I told the cameraman I'd like to go into complete darkness while she walks up, because she's inhibited about saying it. She wants other children, but she doesn't want to admit that this first child is retarded. She opens up a little more than she really wants to.

Bogdanovich: What is the overall theme of *Hurry Sundown*, as you see it?

Preminger: The theme is like *Advise & Consent* and *Anatomy of a Murder*: part of American life. When I read the book, I felt that this particular time—the end of World War II—was historically very important for the development of civil rights in America. The picture is not really about civil rights, though. This young farmer who comes back is certainly not a wild, liberal civil rights fighter. But, having been around with the army in Europe, he has seen that all these prejudiced ideas he was brought up with about Negroes are wrong.

I think this is the general trend of what's happened during the last twenty years. Not so much the freedom fighter, the intellectual who comes from the East and marches, but a man who finally realizes that his future does not depend on keeping Negroes down. So I deliberately didn't bring in anything of civil rights, no propaganda from the East or the North.

Bogdanovich: You made a character, like the bigoted judge Burgess Meredith plays, not completely unsympathetic.

Preminger: No, deliberately not. I think that a character like the judge very much believes he's right. On the other hand, the sheriff is the same kind of character. You see, villains are too easy. This sheriff really likes Negroes. There is a line in the picture that I'm proud of. The sheriff tells this old Negro schoolteacher, who today would be called Uncle Tom-ish, "I'll always be like a father to you people." And this man of about seventy says to him, "I don't know. I haven't been in need of a daddy for a long time."

Bogdanovich: Do you think more of a financially successful picture like *Anatomy of a Murder* than you do of a commercially disappointing picture like *Advise & Consent*?

Preminger: I don't think in those terms. I don't sit around and say, "Was this a good picture, a bad picture?" I leave that to the people who will write my obituary—I let them worry about it. As a matter of fact, if I really sat down and analyzed it, I personally think that *Advise & Consent* is a better picture than *Anatomy of a Murder*. Besides, when we speak about success or failure, we always talk about the box office. It is not always true that a picture which doesn't attract many people is unsuccessful. If the things that I wanted to communicate came through, then for me it is successful.

Bogdanovich: *Skidoo* [1968] is a rather controversial picture; some people hate it, and some people adore it.

Preminger: No, I don't think many people adore it. Except my wife, who adores all my pictures, because that's what you get married for. I do believe that the picture has some funny things in it, and some interesting things. But, if you ask me my honest opinion, I don't think it was altogether successful in projecting what I wanted to project.

Maybe one of the faults was that while I worked very well with [Jackie] Gleason, while he's a very professional actor, there was still a kind of wall between us. While I could not argue with Gleason about what he was doing—it was all *correct*—it still did not really . . . I mean, there is such a difference between us—in the texture of our characters—and if he should read this, he would probably say he's very happy about the difference. There is a different attitude toward life, toward our profession, toward men, toward women, toward friendship, toward love, toward war, toward peace, toward politics—toward *everything*. This made it impossible to project the meaning which I felt lay *underneath* the comedy. That's why for me the picture is not really successful.

Bogdanovich: The strange thing about *Skidoo* is that even the people who like it don't think it's funny: they think it's not supposed to be funny. Others, for example, say, "Look what he did to Carol Channing!"

Preminger: What I did to Carol Channing? Look at what Carol Channing did to me! No, Carol Channing even more than Gleason—I like her very much, but there, too, I made a mistake. I think she was miscast; I think Gleason was miscast. Now, I'll never complain about the actors in [*Tell Me That You Love Me,*] *Junie Moon* [1970], whether the film is successful or not, because they were able not only to laugh and cry and move to the right when I told them to go to the right, but to execute what I *felt* about the characters.

Bogdanovich: What interested you about *Junie Moon*?

Preminger: I read the novel, and it fascinated me: the three characters, their courage, the idea of three disabled people meeting and deciding, as they say in the film, to "pool their disabilities" and make a life for themselves, not to depend on charity or pity. The humor of the story; it just fascinated me.

Bogdanovich: When I first heard about *Junie Moon*, I thought it was an odd subject for you to do.

Preminger: No subject is odd for me—except a western—that's the only thing I couldn't do.

Bogdanovich: Why?

Preminger: Because I'm not interested in horses. I mean, I hardly ever go to see a western. To me, they all seem the same. It's always the same saloon, the same guns, and who draws faster . . .

Bogdanovich: Maybe you're too European for westerns.

Preminger: Some Europeans love westerns. No—it's just my nature; I'm not an outdoor man. That's why I love to live in New York, not Los Angeles.

Bogdanovich: I understand you're planning a picture about the Ethel and Julius Rosenberg spy case [unrealized project]. Have you decided on the title?

Preminger: Yes. *Open Question.*

Bogdanovich: That's a real Preminger title; is it a project you've had in mind for a long time?

Preminger: For a very long time. It fascinates me, because it really *is* an open question. The more I read about it, the more I feel it is impossible to say, honestly, that they were innocent. It is also impossible, however, to say that they were guilty. But, remember, they were *killed*—they were executed.

I think this case is really the greatest argument against the death penalty. Because if they were alive, instead of making a picture about them, we could open the case now and find out if they were really guilty, in an atmosphere which is not as bad as it was then, with the Joe McCarthy hearings, and all that. Maybe they *were* guilty. It could be. But, certainly, if you examine the court records, it was not proven that they were guilty—beyond a reasonable doubt.

Otto Preminger: Censorship and the Production Code

William F. Buckley Jr. / 1967

From *Firing Line* with William F. Buckley Jr., Program 054 "Censorship and the Production Code," Hoover Institution Archives. Reprinted by permission.

C. Dickerman Williams: Ladies and gentlemen, our topic for discussion tonight is production codes and censorship. Our guest is Mr. Otto Preminger, the motion picture producer. Our student guests are from Queens College. Mr. Buckley, will you proceed?

William F. Buckley Jr.: Mr. Chairman, Mr. Preminger is, of course, the famous movie producer, and I know he will not want me to waste any time in advising you that his latest picture, *Hurry Sundown*, is now playing at your local theater, in spite of the movie critics.

(Laughter)

Mr. Preminger loves to tease the censors. He was reportedly delighted that the Motion Picture Production Code was denied to his *The Moon Is Blue*. He showed it anyway. Ditto, *The Man with the Golden Arm*; and now there is a fuss over *Hurry Sundown*, and hurry and find out what it's all about, is Mr. Preminger's position. Exactly what Mr. Preminger's views are on codes, censorship, and the like is not exactly clear; and the purpose of this discussion is to attempt to find out.

Now, Mr. Preminger, you have said that you aren't in favor of—quote—"immoral films." What do you mean by "immoral films"?

Preminger: I don't know when I said this thing about immoral films, and it's probably taken out of context. I don't know about it.

Buckley: It was issued by your office.

(Laughter)

Preminger: Really? Then my office is often out of context . . .

(Laughter)

I would say, however, that an immoral film is a film that does not conform to the morality that we all in our community adopt. That is an immoral film, and an immoral film may be the better expression, of course, than an obscene film. And I certainly am against obscenity in any way, just as much as I'm against censorship of any kind.

Buckley: In other words, you are against immoral films, but what steps would you take to discourage their production?

Preminger: It is not necessary to discourage the production of an immoral or obscene film; if an obscene film is shown in any theater, the police and the district attorney would immediately confiscate it and indict the producer, the theater owner, everybody connected . . .

Buckley: That's censorship, isn't it?

Preminger: No, that's not censorship. It's the law against obscenity. They would do the same thing if we did it on Fifth Avenue—the same act of obscenity—or if you did it here, or if you did it on the front page of the *New York Times* or even of the *National Review*. You cannot commit obscenity in any way.

[. . .]

Buckley: I am anxious, Mr. Preminger, to pursue this, and suppose I quote what you are alleged by your office to have said, in its entirety. You said—are quoted as saying—"Many people think that because I have had censorship trouble that I am in business to make dirty pictures. This is not true. Nobody can make a success with immoral films. The public will not accept them. No one ever got rich selling French postcards. I want to make adult films, not immoral films; and if it's necessary, I will fight for the right to make them."

Now, you seem to be saying there, as I understand it, that you're against immoral films because they are unsuccessful, but you'd be against them even if they were successful?

Preminger: Yes. I would be against them under all circumstances.

Buckley: You would, all right.

Preminger: Only in the context of this quote I have said that an immoral film also could not be successful because I think there is morality built into any dramatic medium, whether it's a play, a television show . . . You cannot tell me one successful play or film where the bad principle won. This is morality. Generally, the bad principle must always lose in the end.

Buckley: Well, I think that's extremely interesting, and I'm anxious to get back to that, but, first of all, I want to find out what it means when you say, "I, Otto Preminger, am against immoral films." Does that mean that assuming the existing laws that you cited a moment ago were to come up for review tomorrow and there was a plebiscite, would you vote yes or no that you wished those laws to continue in being?

Preminger: I would want them to continue in being.

Buckley: Well, but then you are in favor of certain kinds of censorship . . .

Preminger: No. No. Censorship is a great difference. Censorship is if the government, the state, a city, wants to see the film or the book or the newspaper or the magazine before it is shown to the people, and wants to tell you—or me—whether we can publish this magazine or whether I can show this film before it is shown. That is censorship.

If, on the other hand, somebody [produces] a film and commits in the film or through the film a violation of the law, let's say, obscenity, then he has committed something which is against the law and then . . . you know, it's like stealing or any other violation of the law; and the normal agencies start to do their job and arrest him and confiscate the film. That is not censorship. It is like any other violation of the law. Now, that is necessary in any society. Without that, society couldn't exist any more than without laws against murder.

Buckley: Well, when you say—quote—"I have had censorship trouble," what were you alluding to?

Preminger: I was alluding to illegal censors who tried to stop me from doing what I attempt to do. For instance, the Motion Picture Producers Association has a censor, a so-called self-censor. I am not a member of the Motion Picture Producers Association; only my distributors are members. Now when, for instance, *The Moon Is Blue* was finished, my distributor United Artists showed the picture to the censors. The censor said, "No, I cannot permit this picture, because there are two words which I would like you to cut." The words were "virgin" and "pregnant"; we can now freely use [these words] on television even, and everywhere. I said, "I will not cut these two words." Now, mind you, I don't believe that this film or any film is so sacred that it would be ruined if a line or even a whole scene were cut. I only feel that in my area I am supposed, or I am obligated, to defend that freedom of expression that is guaranteed to us by the law, by the same law that would put me in prison if I committed an act of obscenity. This same law says that I have the right to my freedom of expression.

I'm the only judge, what I can do, what I cannot do. I feel that this is very important because without this freedom of expression, we couldn't sit here and talk. And if the same freedom of expression were guaranteed to the people in Russia or in Nazi Germany, the government of Russia and Nazi Germany—or of China—couldn't exist. This is, in my opinion, the greatest safeguard of our way of life.

[. . .]

Buckley: All right. You are in favor of obscenity laws, but you're also in favor of always leaving to the individual the initiative of deciding for himself whether or not he's excluded by those laws.

Preminger: No, no, no. It is the responsibility of the picture maker to decide whether he offends the law or not; certainly I wouldn't do anything deliberately to offend the law. If then a judge in a court decides that I have offended the law, I must take the punishment. It's very simple; it's just like any other crime.

[. . .]

Buckley: Now Mr. Preminger says here with his usual sense of assurance that there isn't such a thing as obscenity floating around America, as witness the fact that otherwise the attorney generals would have come up and interdicted the fate of [obscene films]. Of course, that's not true. It is true [that] courts have a difficult time exactly objectifying that which is obscene and that which isn't; but, for instance, take the recent experience in England. *Lady Chatterley's Lover* made it, but *Last Exit from Brooklyn* [sic] didn't make it. Now *Last Exit from Brooklyn* [sic] is nevertheless on sale all over the United States. So is *The Story of O*, so are a number of books which if Mr. Preminger couldn't be gotten to say that he judged them as obscene would end me up with a conviction that Mr. Preminger doesn't think anything at all is obscene.

Preminger: Well, I think many things are obscene and . . .

Buckley: How about *The Story of O*?

Preminger: I'm afraid I haven't read *The Story of O*, and I will tell you something very strange. Somebody gave me *The Story of O*, and I started to . . .

Buckley: Want to make a movie?

Preminger: No, no. Just privately. I started to read it, and it bored me so that I couldn't continue reading it. Now you will say I am jaded, hum?

(Laughter)

[. . .]

Preminger: Censorship is for many reasons . . . In England, the film censor gave an A certificate, meaning everybody can see this, to the same film *Hurry Sundown* that the Catholic Legion of Decency condemned here. And in England there was a film with Marlon Brando, *The Wild One*, which played here without any objection by anybody; it still hasn't played in England because the industry censor finds that the excessive violence in that film is very bad and it shouldn't be shown. So there are different standards everywhere. It's not about obscenity . . .

Buckley: Not only that but contradictory ones often, I agree.

[. . .]

Williams: Mr. Preminger, a student has a question for you.

Student: Mr. Preminger, since before you stated that there really is no censorship in the United States, that you have this freedom and with this freedom you've been very famous for using very subtle and mundane means of professing a point in a movie, do you plan in the future to use these means to settle with present-day problems? Let's say, as in *The Cardinal* you dealt with Nazism, do you plan to deal with, let's say, communism?

Preminger: If I have a chance, yes. You know, I would like to make a film . . .

Buckley: What are you waiting for?

Preminger: Well, a story. You see, I make films; I basically need as in *The Cardinal* a personal story.

Buckley: How about *I Chose Freedom*?

Preminger: Well, I might be interested.

Williams: Mr. Preminger, we have another student question for you.

Student: Mr. Preminger, I'm sort of confused about exactly what is art and what is the dividing line between art and obscenity.

Preminger: I don't think art has anything to do with obscenity, but to say what is art in connection with motion pictures is something that I think only the future can decide. I think only pictures that will survive, you know, the present day, the actuality, will eventually be considered as art. In other words, of the three hundred or four hundred pictures that are being made every year, I don't think that you can now decide really—really decide—which ones are art and which ones are not art.

Buckley: Well, courts in fact do, don't they? Always have.

Preminger: Not about art.

Buckley: Oh, sure they do. Well, they decided they were obscenity. For instance, very recently the California court said that *Un chant d'amour* by Genet was obscene and therefore could not be shown.

Preminger: But that does not mean it is not art, you know. The courts have often decided about great, great paintings that later on became very valuable; great paintings were kept in museums. At the time they were painted, they were obscene.

Buckley: And vice versa. A lot of people pay a lot of money for paintings that end up being trash, right?

[. . .]

Student: On one other interview show you were on, you said that you thought you had raised your children so well and given them an idea of what was good . . .

Preminger: I didn't say that, you know. My children are only six and a half years old, you know; I have quite a way to go. I advocated in this show, wherever I said it, that parents should be warned; in other words, I am for telling parents, "This is a film that I recommend only for adult audiences"—that, I think, is my responsibility; so that the parents don't take or permit their children to go. But on the other hand, I think in my way to educate my children, I hope that I will give them a sense of value, you know, so valid, that they know what is good and bad, what is right or wrong, so they can see a film even if it is considered only for adults and they will know, let's say, by the age of thirteen or fifteen, that this is bad. They won't believe that excessive violence, for instance, is good; they won't imitate it, I hope.

Williams: Mr. Buckley, a student has a question for you.

Student: Mr. Buckley, as an author yourself, how much success have you had with self-censorship?

Buckley: Well, very little, to judge from what the critics say.

(Laughter)

But I do think that self-censorship, *le frein vital*, as advocated by [Paul Elmer More], is an extremely important instrument of art, even of pedagogy; and that one of the characteristic difficulties of the twentieth century is not a lack of spontaneity so much as it is too much spontaneity, too little discipline, too little craft.

Williams: Mr. Preminger has a comment.

Preminger: You have mentioned during this show, several times, critics. What do you think the function of critics is, and how important is this function? For any art form or form of entertainment or communication?

Buckley: I think there are so many listed responses to that question I'd have to ask you to be a little bit more specific. Some critics who are obviously, let's say, your peers as moviemakers can criticize, let's say, a movie by you and teach you something. That's just one role.

Preminger: Right. I agree. I agree.

Buckley: Another critic wants to, let's say, inform me, knowing my tastes whether or not I would be wasting my time going to see your latest movie. He's got to know me awfully well to be able to speak to me, or I know him. Then, of course, the other critics who simply criticize in order to make a living. This is sort of their way of getting into the act. Those I tend to be less patient with.

Preminger: And do you feel that critics, you know, who are not able to guide their readers—their readers go to see these plays or movies or read the books in spite of the critics—do you feel that they don't fulfill their function, and should be replaced? Or do critics never fail?

Buckley: Oh no, I think it's obvious that they often fail, but it's also obvious that something can be a lousy, stinking production and still be extremely popular.

Preminger: Why?

Buckley: Well, because . . .

Preminger: How? Don't you believe that the people . . . why should they go to see it if the critic warned them or if it is lousy, shouldn't the critics be able to warn them in such a way that they wouldn't?

Buckley: I think that's a very naive question.

Preminger: I'm asking you . . .

Buckley: I think, for instance, that *Forever Amber* is a lousy book . . .

Preminger: It's also a lousy picture, I made it . . .

(Laughter)

And while I made it, I knew it was a lousy picture. I was then under contract, and I had to make it.

Buckley: Yes. But it's a lousy book, and it sold a billion copies or something. If it sold ten billion copies, it'd still be a lousy book. So what?

Preminger: That is true, but don't you think that then the critics should be able to communicate to their readers not to read it?

Buckley: Well, the point is . . .

Preminger: Otherwise, the book must have something that makes people buy it.

Buckley: There is a market for a lot of goods, both intellectual and material, that simply aren't any good. And as long as we have a . . .

Preminger: Any good from what point of view?

Buckley: Any good from any point of view that is defensible.

Preminger: I agree with you about the book. *Forever Amber* was not a well-written book. I don't think it was an entertaining book. And still so many people bought it. I also don't think it was particularly sexy or obscene or anything like that; it was a naive book. Why did so many people buy it in spite of all the critics?

Buckley: Well, why do so many people buy comic books?

Preminger: Why do people buy, for instance . . . there is a film running—I don't know if you have seen it—called *The Sound of Music.* The original play got very bad reviews and ran forever, for three years; and then the movie got worse reviews and is probably the movie that will gross more than any movie ever in the history of movies. How come?

Buckley: Well, because . . .

Preminger: Who is failing?

Buckley: The critics can certainly err, but it doesn't follow also that the people's judgment is necessarily vindicated simply because they turn out for something in great numbers. We know that *Confidential* magazine had a circulation of thirteen million copies in 1954 . . .

Preminger: Besides, *Sound of Music* has none of the characteristics of *Confidential* magazine . . .

(Laughter)

Williams: Mr. Preminger, let me try to answer your question about the popularity of *Forever Amber.* It was a book of escape; it came out in the middle of the war, if I recall correctly; and I think people wanted to get away from the tenseness of the war and found a certain measure of escape in *Forever Amber.* At any rate . . .

Preminger: What about *Sound of Music*?

Williams: I don't know anything about it; I haven't got a theory on that.

Buckley: Well, *The Sound of Music* is very good, wholesome entertainment, and it's quite true that a lot of critics in order to guard their chic have to be against anything that is wholesome and entertaining.

Preminger: All of them. Unanimously.

Buckley: Yeah. Which was also true of . . .

Preminger: And you say now as a critic, and I agree with you, that it is good entertainment.

Buckley: Yeah. It's what they also said of *Margin for Error*, which you made into a very successful movie, am I correct?

Preminger: I did the play first and then the movie.

Buckley: Yeah. And they were both panned and both very successful, so again—what else is new? This, I think, happened, and you also find a lot of acknowledged masterpieces were panned . . .

Williams: Gentlemen, I don't propose to censor this most interesting discussion, but because we have a shortage of time, I've got to say that we must end it. Thank you, Mr. Preminger. Thank you, Mr. Buckley.

AFI's Panel on the Critic

Arthur Knight / 1968

From AFI's Panel on the Critic © 1968, used courtesy of American Film Institute.

Arthur Knight: I'm particularly pleased to find myself flanked this afternoon by Art Murphy, who writes film reviews and also film articles for *Variety*; by Charles Champlin, who does the same function for the *Los Angeles Times*; and by at least a representative of those who sometimes feel the brunt of this writing, the producer Mr. Otto Preminger.

Otto, can you tell us about your past . . . ?

Otto Preminger: My past is simple. I wanted to be an actor at age nine but didn't start then. At seventeen I got a job as an actor in a new theater in Vienna that was founded there by a German director, a very famous, very great director, Max Reinhardt. I got only small parts. I left after six months and went to small cities, where I got big parts. At the age of twenty, I gave up acting and started directing and founded my own theater in Vienna with another young actor. I eventually took over Max Reinhardt's theater when he retired from it. At the age of twenty-eight, when I was running this theater, I was discovered by a Hollywood motion picture mogul or tycoon, Joseph Schenck, who came to Vienna. I had made a film there. It was lucky, because I came here three years before Hitler. I watched picture-making at Fox, and then directed two pictures for Fox. Then I had an argument with Mr. Zanuck and was thrown out of Fox. I went back to New York and did plays. I came back to Fox acting a Nazi; they were very rare here then.

[Laughter]

Then I made a film in Mr. Zanuck's absence. His assistant, Mr. Goetz, liked me and gave me this film. *Laura* was a big success, and Zanuck and I made up. I stayed here until I became an independent producer and director, and that's what I still am.

Knight: One of the reasons for asking Otto to come up this afternoon is because he is one who has frequently maintained that he doesn't read reviews . . .

Preminger: I have never said that. I read reviews, but I have learned—you know, I'm older than all of you—I have learned that it serves no purpose. A reviewer does not work for me; a reviewer works for his publication. He doesn't owe me anything. As a reader, I have the right to criticize him.

What would be an interesting question for me to ask is: your [Art Murphy] reviews appear in a Hollywood trade paper [*Variety*]; yours [Charles Champlin] appear in a daily [*Los Angeles Times*]; yours [Arthur Knight] appear in the *Saturday Review*. Now, if you three could exchange your jobs, would you still write the same reviews? It would be very interesting to know.

Knight: That's one of the things that I wanted to develop this afternoon: to find out if there really is a difference in approach between someone who writes for a daily, someone who writes for a trade, and someone who writes for a national middle-brow weekly. What would you say about that, Charles?

Charles Champlin: Well, I think that your final assessment of a film is not going to change, whatever medium you're writing in, but I think that the content of your review is certainly dictated to an extent by the medium, which is to say your audience. I'm writing for a daily generalized newspaper audience of 800,000 or whatever it is, and a non-trade audience, although I think it's a little different here because I *am* in the midst of the industry, and I know that a certain number of my readers are going to be people in the industry. However, I have to write for the general reader, so that I, for the most part, either go easier on the technical credits of a film, and I have to be somewhat careful about even talking about techniques, and I have to be somewhat more explicit if I want to talk about, let's say, jump cuts or something like that, because I'm presuming to talk to an audience which in general does not know that much about the making of films. I certainly don't write down to the audience.

Preminger: What is a successful critic? Isn't a successful critic a critic that has a following? You want your readers to believe you. If they read in your review that you like a film, you want them to go and see it.

Champlin: Yes.

Preminger: So you have to consider that you might, with your background and education, like many films that the majority of the six million people who probably read your reviews, or have the opportunity to read them—I hope they don't all read them all the time . . .

[Laughter]

But I mean, you are only successful if these people believe you. This was the reason for my question. For instance, if Arthur would ever write a review where he would express dislike for any arty, foreign film, the whole *Saturday Review* would go up in flames.

Now, it would be interesting to find out if we could take two recent films. Let's say *The Detective* and a similar film, *The Thomas Crown Affair*.

Knight: Can we go into that a little bit later? I would like Arthur to discuss the same film, *The Detective*, because I think I have another angle on it altogether.

Preminger: About his readers?

Knight: Yeah.

Preminger: There is an accusation against the honesty of trade papers. But part of the idea of a trade paper [e.g., *Variety*] is that it considers itself part of what you call the [American film] industry. A trade paper at least says that it wants to help films, and usually does. In other words, you, Mr. Murphy, would never, just because you personally like a foreign art film, when you review it say that this is the greatest film in the world, because you know that this is not the purpose of your paper. Your paper is an American trade paper. It is not here to support this trend of grading down every American film and grading up every foreign film. The mere existence of the *Saturday Review* is basically to do this.

Knight: You've only been reading our reviews of your pictures.

[Laughter]

Preminger: It is not true. I read, for instance, recently a review of yours about a film which I haven't seen but am anxious to see called *Boom* with Elizabeth Taylor and Richard Burton . . .

Knight: You'd better hurry.

[Laughter]

Preminger: The strange thing is that, of all places, in the *Saturday Review*, under the byline of our friend Arthur Knight, because it is directed by a man called [Joseph] Losey and only because of this reason—who is a very good director, who shoots through any flower that he can find . . .

[Laughter]

. . . that Mr. Knight, of all people, I was never so surprised, *liked* that film. I am sure that you couldn't have liked this film, but I haven't seen it. I am sure that you couldn't have written a rave about it, because only when you write for the readers of the *Saturday Review* have you an obligation to love whatever Losey does.

Art Murphy: Before Arthur gets around to commenting on the reason why *Saturday Review* content is different from *Women's Wear Daily* . . .

Preminger: Not so different.

Murphy: A trade paper does fulfill a function of informing the potential buyers of a film what the reviewer for this trade paper figures is in the film both artistically and commercially. For a simplification, say that every film is either artistically good or bad, and commercially good or bad. And there are all four combinations. There are some films which are artistically bad and will lose money. There are films which are artistically bad, in the opinion of the person who is reviewing it, which are very commercial. *The Detective* falls in that category of artistic junk but very commercial.

Preminger: I must tell you that I saw *The Detective* last night. I think that to call *The Detective* "junk" is absolutely wrong. *The Detective* is, in a way, a melodrama. There are two performances that are far above everything that I have seen during the last months. I think Sinatra has never given a better performance. When you say that it is very commercial but not artistic, I don't know what commercial is for you. What do you call commercial? And Lee Remick gives a great characterization.

I'm afraid I haven't seen *Boom*. I appreciate that, because it is Losey, you say—if I remember right—that every shot is beautifully framed. Among people who make films, there could be no more disdain or contempt expressed than saying that the shots are beautifully framed. Shots should never be framed; they should not *look* as though they were framed.

Murphy: As far as *The Detective* goes, Frank Sinatra and Lee Remick are fine. Lee Remick is fine in a totally unnecessary, extraneous, badly written—by Abby Mann, world's greatest screenwriter—screenplay.

Preminger: Why is it badly written?

Murphy: In its literary form. It's melodramatic junk. It's just sprawling.

Preminger: It is not junk. In this melodramatic form, it shows us more truths than many films I've seen. It shows the brutality of the New York police department. It shows the life of homosexuals in New York in a very, very strong and very good way. I agree that it is not artsy. But there is more truth in it than in many, many films. Films are a mass entertainment [form]. Why do most critics have this tremendous contempt for films that are trying to be popular? *The Detective* turned out to be a tremendous popular success. I think it got bad reviews almost everywhere. These pictures are made for these people. Do you have contempt for all these people?

Murphy: No, I just have contempt for what I think is a poorly laid-out film story.

Preminger: How did *you* like *The Detective*?

Champlin: I didn't like it. I said that Sinatra was good, and I said that Lee Remick was good. I agree with Art there. I think it's a film that changes tone in midstream. It starts out pretending to be a slice of life, and then it becomes a private-eye melodrama with a completely improbable plot and with a lot of exploitive use of language . . .

Preminger: What is improbable about the plot?

Champlin: You know, a beautiful girl comes in—midway through the picture instead of in the first scene, as it used to be with Philip Marlowe—and says, "There's something rather suspicious about my husband's death, and I want you to investigate it." Sinatra casts aside everything else, and plows on like Philip Marlowe or Sam Spade to track down this thing, and there are secret tape recordings, and suicides, and a whole nefarious plot to take over the city of New York by a bunch of unscrupulous land speculators or something . . .

Preminger: No, it is the same thing that we are reading about, the same kind of board that is now accused in Los Angeles to have been bribed, in every city . . .

Champlin: I agree that there is corruption, but the Los Angeles thing was turned on about six thousand bucks, it was penny-ante. Did you see *Madigan*? The Universal film by Don Siegel?

Preminger: No.

Champlin: Same content exactly, in the sense that it was a slice of precinct life. Widmark is a New York cop, and I thought he was intensely believable. And you had a police captain with an incorruptible past who takes a bribe for about three thousand bucks, which seems to me to have much more reality going for it than . . .

Preminger: But they never say how much bribe the policeman in [*The Detective*] got. How did you like the *Crown* capers? *The Thomas Crown Affair*?

Champlin: Well manufactured. I liked it.

Preminger: You see, this is the great thing about the public. *The Crown Affair*, which is a slick picture, where every scene is not only framed but framed from above . . . two people playing chess, amateurishly, they are photographed from the top.

Murphy: The Busby Berkeley style . . .

Preminger: And it is beautifully photographed. The really consoling thing—it got great reviews almost everywhere—the really comforting thing is that nobody listened. They just didn't go to see it. The film is a weak attempt to imitate Hitchcock, who would have done the same thing with humor, while this is done with tears. The girl at the end cries, instead of following [the hero] to Brazil. It's just horrible. Can you explain why, if you like the *Crown Affair*, the public doesn't; and why you don't like *The Detective*, and the public does?

Champlin: Well, H. L. Mencken once said that nobody ever went broke underestimating the intelligence of the American people.

Murphy: Not intelligence: taste.

Champlin: OK. I understand why *The Detective* is doing well: it's got a lot of shock value in it. The language is marvelous, and in the opening scene Sinatra discovers the mutilation of the guy's body, and so on—which makes, by the way, no logical or plot sense, as you discover ultimately.

Preminger: But why do the people go to see it? The taste of the American people . . . you are very unfair. For instance, I travel a lot, and I like paintings, so I go—wherever I go, in small towns or big towns—to museums. Museums are crowded with people. The same people who go to the movies also go to see art, and good art, modern art. They can't have one good taste and one bad taste, according to your judgment. My question is—I really don't want to attack anybody here, we are friends, I hope, I have a picture coming out . . .

[Laughter]

. . . and I don't want unnecessarily to incur your wrath.

Knight: What did you say the name of it was?

Preminger: The name of it is *Skidoo*. I just wonder: what is the function of the critic? It is quite obvious that when you write an editorial in the *Los Angeles Times*, you want to communicate with your readers. But when you write a review, and you fail to communicate, Mr. Champlin, if they don't listen to you, then the function is not clear. If you write a review, for instance, in the *Saturday Review*, I realize you write for your own pleasure, because what is the circulation?

Murphy: Otto, we're not trying to play God. My profession is, if I'm assigned to a film, to see it and write my opinion on it. If somebody reads it, I have communicated my thoughts. Reviews do not influence a picture.

Preminger: But at the beginning of this thing, you said that reviews *do* exist in order to inform and influence people.

Murphy: Inform and influence either one way or the other. I can read somebody's review and I know that if this guy doesn't like a picture, I will. So I'm part of this guy's following in reverse.

Preminger: But do you think this is good to write and know people read reviews in reverse?

Murphy: If critics didn't exist, people would invent them.

Preminger: I would much rather have bad reviews for my films than no reviews at all. I think the very fact that people are seriously occupying themselves with a medium like movies *lifts* the medium. It is good that the *Saturday Review*, all jokes aside, has an important page for movies. There's no doubt about that. It is amazing, however, how this fluctuates. For instance, there is a similar magazine in France, *Cahiers du cinéma*. Very much the same, except that there the critics eventually fled and became directors. But the funny part is that the French pictures that are adored here by the arty critics are disliked there. I am a hero there. They have retrospectives of my films. It's so amusing . . .

Champlin: Next week, Raoul Walsh.

[Laughter]

Knight: If you expect me to defend the *Cahiers du cinéma* critics, you're wrong.

Preminger: Their influence is bigger than yours, because their circulation is much larger. In English and in French; they have an English edition now.

[. . .]

Murphy: In my review of *The Detective*, I start out by saying, "Let it be said at the outset that *The Detective* is going to do hot B.O., having compromised its story to an exploitation style."

Preminger: Why should the *Los Angeles Times* not inform their readers that while the critic probably doesn't like the film himself, he believes that the readers may like it? That, I think, is very honest. Why should the critic of a daily paper not also inform his readers that they might want to see it?

Murphy: With a newspaper or magazine critic, the emphasis is on building up the personality of the man who has the job. In trade papers, on ours [*Variety*], I am identified only by a four-letter italicized slug at the bottom. So it's the *paper's* evaluation, and not mine. If I were working at a newspaper, I would spend more time talking about the good and bad points in a film, and I don't care whether people go to see it or not. I'll tell them enough about it so they can make up their own mind.

Preminger: You said something very true, and I wonder if we could discuss it. Is it right that critics—and it happened more or less recently—would try to build up their personalities and their names by their reviewing? There is a newspaper critic of a defunct New York paper, called Judith Crist. Now, there was one film that I think unanimously everybody disliked, a film with Warren Beatty: *Mickey One*. She came out in her review the next Sunday, and said, "This is the first great American picture I have seen in many years." Naturally, everybody talked about it. I even remember it now, four years later. That is a very good way to build up the critic's name.

Murphy: Except I don't think she did it to build up her name.

Preminger: You underrate her; she's a very intelligent woman. A very shrewd woman. And she did it to build up her name, because she *couldn't* have thought it was a good film. You remember the picture. I don't think that any critic could have thought that this is, in any way, a good picture. Or did you?

Murphy: No. The doctrine of critical infallibility is not being espoused here. We can all make mistakes. But I know what you mean. It's easy to be cute in a review, and to build up a reputation for acerbic cuteness. I don't believe in it.

Preminger: I think it is wrong from the point of view of integrity, if I may use this word. I think it is fine that people have an opinion and express it; I think this is very good. But that they should use this position to build up their name, that's a terrible thing. And that's why, for instance, in *Time* magazine and in many magazines—in *Newsweek*, they've changed it now—they did not print the critic's name. I think this made it easier for critics, when they were wrong, to correct themselves. A terrible thing is when critics are wrong, then they become "wronger" by pressing the point. In other words, when a critic once says something really bad about an actor or a director, then he feels it is his duty to prove it in the next review, and the review after next.

Murphy: Well, there are some people who are cute at the expense of what they're writing about. That's an abuse. If you get right down to it, the three of us are writers. What we do is film criticism, but basically we're writers. And the first responsibility of a writer is to be readable, even before we go into how he does his work. So if I believe that to attract attention, which means be readable to the people I want to read me, if I come to the erroneous conclusion that I've got to make puns and so forth, I do it, because I am a writer first. I am a writer of film criticism. Now, I could write a review that might be accurate and intelligent, and it might be dry as dust. So who would ever read it? They'd say, "I can't plow through that." We're all on the dime, just as much as you are when you make a picture, we've got to start off with the first sentence to attract people's attention.

Knight: There's another thing that a real critic does, or tries to do, and that is to indicate to his readers what his standards are. I think that if you were to look at my review of *Boom*, you would find that it's not filled with adjectives saying that I think that Joseph Losey is the greatest director, or that Tennessee Williams is the greatest screenplay writer. No, you try to indicate what your expectations were for that film, how fully they were fulfilled, and where they failed. If the reader can buy your assumptions, perhaps he'll go to see the picture. It doesn't mean, even then, that the reader is going to agree with me after he's seen the picture, but he does have some idea of where I was when I started to see the film and how I felt about it when I came out.

Preminger: Speak about *Boom*. Explain to us why everybody else dislikes *Boom*—even me, who hasn't seen it . . .

[Laughter]

Preminger: . . . and you liked it so much. What is the reason that you like this film?

Knight: All I can say is that I found a number of qualities in the film that I admire . . .

Preminger: For instance?

Knight: Just a minute. I had seen the play and felt that Tennessee Williams had gotten a lot closer to what he was trying to do . . .

Preminger: You say that this film—finally, after he had done two versions of the play—is the fulfillment of what he wanted to display.

Knight: It turns out that Tennessee Williams felt that way too.

Preminger: Yes, it turned out, but apparently you were both wrong, because Tennessee Williams, as we know, is right now very sick, mentally sick.

[Laughter]

Knight: But there is another thing that I think we ought to be aware of: I feel that, ideally, critics should see the picture with an audience.

Preminger: I agree.

Champlin: I disagree.

Preminger: The audience *adds* to a film. I can tell you as a filmmaker: when I cut a film, I see it at least five hundred or six hundred times. It becomes a completely different film, although I know every word, every gesture, every frame by heart, when you go into the theater with an audience; it is different. It takes on a different texture. That is the great miracle of show business. That is the advantage of the theater for the stage actor [versus] the actor in films, because the theater actor is in touch with the audience. And *you* should be in touch.

Champlin: But when you're cutting the film, you come to a certain scene where there may be a laugh, and you hope that people are going to laugh at this. You are supplying your hoped-for audience reaction. As a critic, when I see a film all by myself, I can supply the audience reaction.

Preminger: The audience is an element that you cannot supply yourself. That is the great thing about show business. I can finish a film and think whatever I think of it—I usually think well of my films—and then I show it to an audience and they don't like it. Nobody—I defy anybody . . . all these people in our industry always say, "I can, to the million, tell you how much it's going to gross." Nonsense. Nobody knows this.

Champlin: Not anymore.

Preminger: What do you mean, "not anymore"?

Champlin: They used to be able to . . .

Preminger: They used to be able to when they controlled the theaters.

Champlin: That's right.

Preminger: That's a different kind of gross, because then the theaters lost the money. But you cannot say how much. And a critic should certainly not be away from this audience element. It's too important.

Knight: But, Otto, I'm not trying to cop a plea now, believe me.

Preminger: You said that when you saw the movie, you saw it with an audience that loved it . . .

Knight: No, I didn't. I saw it at ten o'clock on a Monday morning all by myself in a screening room at Universal. And that is the least proper way for a critic to have to judge a film. Since there's nothing else around you, what you're left with, then, is a heightened perception—the kind of thing that *you* have when you're working in your own cutting room—you are more aware of the framing, you are more aware of the lines, you're more aware of the movement of the camera, you're more aware of performance, everything. Really, I'm not recanting on that review [of *Boom*]. Perhaps if everybody could go to Universal on a Monday morning and see it all by himself, he would have a higher opinion of the film too. It just doesn't seem to be a picture that has worked with an audience.

Preminger: I can tell you that I admire very much the critic of *Newsweek* [Joseph Morgenstern], who wrote a review of *Bonnie and Clyde*. He wrote practically a carbon copy of what Mr. Bosley Crowther wrote about seven times. He repeated himself because he hated it so much. He came back a week later and said, "I saw the film again with an audience, and I must say that I was completely wrong. Nobody asked me to do this . . ." And I'm sure nobody did, because there is nobody who can buy the critics of *Newsweek*. And he then explained that the film was a completely different film with an audience. I really think that there should be a rule that critics should make themselves, that they don't want to see the film at ten o'clock in the morning—that they want to see it with the public, the real public. Like a play.

Champlin: It's not always possible, though.

Preminger: Why?

Champlin: Because the studios, more and more, are holding off their product until the last moment.

Preminger: This is where you should be tough against the studios. You should say, "Well, then, you won't get any reviews." I mean, if you feel that you would give a different review if you saw it with the public, then this responsibility should even more make you *insist* that you want to see it with an audience.

Knight: Otto, I'd like to raise another question with you and with the gentlemen by my side. Otto, how important do you think it is that the film critic should know about film technique, what goes on behind the camera, that sort of thing?

Preminger: Well, there are two schools of thought. I really don't think it is necessary. I think that a film critic, as Mr. Murphy says, is a writer. And just like you can take a trip and describe it . . . As a matter of fact, I think it is better that a film critic does not know too much about the various functions. Hopefully, he wouldn't then say, as many critics say, "This was beautifully edited by so and so," because the editor on a film is really just a pair of scissors. He's not an editor. The director, or the producer, tells him what to edit. But it is not necessary to know how the film was made. I doubt that there is any critic who really knows . . . you would have to study the craft to really know how a picture is made. Just a superficial knowledge is even worse than no knowledge. So I think it is not necessary if the critic knows.

A critic should be a man of good taste, and have a feeling of the people—it's a democratic art, if you want to call it an art. In the theater, it should be a more select taste, for the people who go to the theater. It is wonderful to see, for instance, how the theatre in New York has changed. Whatever you see on Broadway is really old-fashioned, and the really exciting theater is Off Broadway. The first-string critics don't go to Off Broadway, so there is a chance for new critics to come along. I was for a week in New York recently, and I saw almost every night an exciting play. But I don't think it is necessary: you don't have to know how to write a play in order to criticize one.

Knight: Charles?

Champlin: I think Mr. Preminger hit on a point that's true: that it's very difficult to know how to assign credit, and I think you're on dangerous ground how you attribute even a performance sometimes—to the actor or to the director. Unless you have been around [the set], or you've gotten some inside information, which I think is usually unreliable, I just think you have to be very careful about your credits. You just say that you like the product or you think it seems to have been photographed well. But you can't, even then, say that it's the cinematographer or the director's work.

Preminger: For instance, in the Academy Awards, very often the director wins the Academy Award and the film doesn't win it. It is impossible for a film to be good if the director didn't do a good job. So the director should automatically win the award if the film wins. But often the directors are not even nominated.

Champlin: If you don't mind, I would like to get to this business of what are the aims of the film critic, because I honestly don't see any contradiction between my not liking *The Detective* and its being a popular success. It's my way of thinking that you *are* making subjective judgments, and you are communicating those subjective judgements. But in writing, for instance, for the *Los Angeles Times*, I think that I have got to give the reader not simply my opinion of "like" or "don't like," although that's where it all begins; I've got to give him a body of information so that he can make an independent judgment as to whether, whatever I've said—pro or con—he wants to go see that film. Now, I suspect that my review of *The Detective* did not deter the people who wanted to go see *The Detective*. It wasn't intended to. I mean, I'm on record as thinking it's a piece of plastic cheese, but I think that people who like Sinatra, who like Lee Remick, who like cops-and-robbers pictures, who like the private eye thing . . . I mean, there are all sorts of clues, with or without subjective loading, in that review to make . . .

Preminger: Sinatra pictures before that didn't attract any people. They got the same bad reviews.

Champlin: *Tony Rome* did well, didn't it?

Preminger: No. No Sinatra picture for a long time did well. It is the beautiful instinct of people that, in spite of bad reviews, and not because some actor is in it—that is really nonsense; no actor attracts people by himself—that they *know*, that they *feel*, that the first day when this picture, *The Detective*, opened in New York, there was a long line [of customers at the theater]. And *Tony Rome* also starred Sinatra, and on the first day [the theatres were] empty. That beautiful instinct of an audience, that's what we love; that's what we like to work for.

Murphy: And that's what we know, that reviews do not influence the public taste. If on a Wednesday, when a film opens in a city, if the local newspaper didn't print a review, if people wanted to see the picture, they'd show up. There's a sixth sense which nobody has put their finger on yet . . .

Preminger: Right.

Murphy: . . . *why* people want to see things. If you shut off the mails and stop the presses, pictures would still perform the way they are. Good reviews of good pictures give them a little extra push; bad reviews of bad pictures accelerate the death. But a good review of a bad picture doesn't help, and a bad review of a good picture doesn't return.

Preminger: I must agree with you. I also want to say that the duty of pictures or television—any mass entertainment—is that no critic can get between the picture maker and the public. Either in a good way or a bad way; by praising or panning. That's why I came here today, because I'm not scared of you.

[Laughter]

Murphy: Otto, I liked *Hurry Sundown*. That was one of my mistakes.

Preminger: It was! The audiences didn't like it. You and all the Negro critics liked it. It's very funny. The white critics all hated it.

Knight: There is one area, though, where there seems to be an agreement, that the critical impotence is not as great as all that . . .

Preminger: Who said critical impotence?

Knight: Well, you are suggesting that the influence of the critics is not that great . . .

Preminger: But impotence would be if you couldn't write. But you are pouring out pages and pages.

[Laughter]

Knight: However, in the field of foreign films, it's generally agreed that a good review in the *New York Times* and a good review in the *New Yorker* . . .

Preminger: It used to be so. Not anymore.

Knight: Why's that?

Preminger: Because the abusing of power hurts the influence of everybody, including critics. When the critics started to praise indiscriminately every imported film, the people who used to read them—the following that the critic has—stopped. For instance, if you take other forms of art: the great credit to art critics that became famous, almost immortal, is when the critic—at a time when everybody laughed at Picasso—started to try to help [Picasso], to explain him, to praise him, when it seemed ridiculous to do so. Or the Cubists or the Dadaists. And *then* the people, by the millions, followed the critics. *That's* the function of a critic, in my opinion. But when it became the trend suddenly to like every movie with foreign dialogue, for a while the people fell for it, but they don't anymore. They don't go because somebody says it's a good picture or an art picture. They make up their own minds now.

Knight: Suddenly we're back at something that we departed from, which I'd like to go into a little bit further: the question of the importance of knowing how pictures are made, for the critic. You said a moment ago that art critics began praising Picasso . . .

Preminger: Not because they knew *how* he painted, but because they were impressed by *what* he painted. And because they were intelligently or instinctively enough in love with art to know that this was going to be a new world where you didn't just paint a tree, but you painted *your* kind of tree. That is what they taught. This is where the leadership of the critic became important. Unfortunately, this leadership does not exist today. In the New York theater, even before my time, Alexander Woollcott was this type of critic. He was a leader. When a play looked like a complete flop, he still kept on writing about how good it is, even after it closed, and it helped that author with his next play.

Knight: Isn't that because he knew something about theater?

Preminger: I don't say that a critic *shouldn't* know about films. I say it is not necessary to know how films are being made, the craft and technique of films—that is not necessary. I feel that every critic, whether I like him or not, I give him the benefit of the doubt that he only writes about films because he likes them. I don't say that you shouldn't know films; I just say that it is not necessary to know the degree of filmmaking. It isn't bad, but it is not necessary.

Knight: Well, not the minute details, but you have to know enough to be able to explain why you like something or don't like something.

Preminger: But that is not the making of the film. That is your impression. For instance, Mr. Champlin said something which I think is very true. I'm a director, and when I saw *Rosemary's Baby* I admired the performance of Mia Farrow. I didn't expect to, mainly because I saw a film—*A Dandy in Aspic*—in which she was very bad. She gave a very bad performance. So, by deduction—I was not on the set—I feel that Mr. Polanski is very much responsible for this performance. That's the only explanation that I have, but I can't say this for sure, I can only [speculate]. If I were a critic, I would have written that: I would say that I think there must be some imprint [by Polanski]. I think that always the performances are influenced by the director. You would have to be there to really know it.

Now, even worse, the functions of the producer and the director overlap very much. It is very difficult to say, unless you have studied their contract, whether the final film is really the credit or the blame of the producer or the director. Whether the producer is simply the figurehead who gets the money and puts the elements together, and then the director makes the film; or whether the producer, as in the case of Selznick, whom I knew very well, and who was a real producer—every detail in *Gone with the Wind*, he is at least as much responsible for it as the director was, perhaps more. But I don't think it matters: when you review a film, you don't necessarily have to review the producer and the director and all the credits; you review the film. The audiences are certainly not interested in who gets the credit.

Audience Member: You made the statement that actors or actresses do not necessarily make or break a movie. Then how can you justify the old star system?

Preminger: I *don't* justify the old star system. The most successful picture running at the moment is a picture called *The Graduate*. This picture has no stars in it. There is one young man who has never acted in a picture before, and in my opinion did a wonderful performance; there is an actress who failed in pictures and went to Broadway and made a name for herself there, and never was so good in pictures before; and there is another young actress, Katharine Ross. And the people go to see them. There is no star who can make a picture. Look at *Boom*. Those are the two unanimously acclaimed greatest stars in the world.

Knight: Certainly the highest priced.

Preminger: Yes, but they also have a very good track record. They have had less flops than anybody else, and they are together in *Boom*, and nobody goes to see it. They made a film, *Who's Afraid of Virginia Woolf?*, just a couple of years ago. It was the biggest box office success. People all over the world went to see it, because the story was interesting.

Audience Member: I wonder, Mr. Preminger, if you feel there has been a change in this respect? I think there is still a name draw. Now, whether it's the actor or not, I think the general audience has become more educated, more sophisticated, to the idea of a director. They are more familiar with the names of directors now, and more concerned with who is directing the picture. Now, where the star name perhaps did not draw people to *The Graduate*, do you think the name of Mike Nichols drew them?

Preminger: No. After *The Graduate* he is a big name, but for the big public who don't live in New York, I'm sure that they didn't even know that he directed *Virginia Woolf*. No, people feel that a film is interesting and that they will be entertained by this picture. I can name you almost every star's flops. It is true . . . for instance, *The Detective*: I have the same objections, in a way, in spite of liking *The Detective*; it is unnecessarily cheap in many areas. But still, it is an entertaining, good, interesting picture, and people learn a lot from it. There is *truth* in this picture. The police departments *do* act like this. I agree that the plot could be handled better, but when you watch it, you cannot say that it is not interesting. It is very difficult, I would think, for a normal viewer to get up and leave *The*

Detective, but it is probably very easy to leave the *Crown Affair*—which I haven't seen, so I can't say. No, word-of-mouth is the strongest factor in the success or failure of a picture.

Audience Member: Mr. Preminger, would you like to see the development in film of the kind of critic that you mentioned in art?

Preminger: I said at the beginning that I have no quarrel with critics. I think it is good that there are critics. I think it would be wonderful if some critics would be interested enough in movies to write in a different way; to awake the people to certain potentials in movies which haven't been [recognized].

[. . .]

Audience Member: Mr. Champlin, you wrote an article recently about the subject of taste, and you were talking about the problem the critic has with making definite decisions sometimes. I was wondering if you were inferring that there are some films where a decision or an agreement can only be in terms of taste. In other words, are there some films where a rational discussion can't follow?

Champlin: Well, I was hassling around in that piece with the question of what are the bases of your judgments on a film. And I was saying that, obviously, a critic has a private stance in some cases which determines the way he goes about a film. I tried to make clear in my review of *Rosemary's Baby* that that's a piece of filmmaking that I thought was very good but intellectually I was appalled by it.

Preminger: Was it intellectual or was it because of your personal beliefs?

Champlin: That's what I'm saying. It's a question of private stance.

Preminger: I mean, what is intellectually wrong with it?

Champlin: Perhaps "intellectually" was the wrong word. I just find it obscene.

Preminger: Obscene or sacrilegious?

Champlin: I found it obscene, really. I think the whole rape scene with the devil, I think that's obscene. Yes, it's sacrilegious . . .

Preminger: I personally—while I liked the film very much—I cannot go for this whole thing of witches. If I had made the film, it would have been a comedy. I could only make fun of it. To me, this whole idea that serious, grown-up people think they can put a curse on some actor so that another actor can get the part—to me, that is childish. But I think this is a personal thing.

Knight: You speak of the public, Mr. Preminger, and the people, and the critics reviewing films the way the people would like it. Do you feel you would make a good critic of the people? Do you feel that your taste is the same as the people?

Preminger: I don't think I have any talent to be a critic. It would never occur to me to be a critic. Not only here but in private, if I like something I become almost unconditionally enthusiastic, and if I don't like it I usually don't discuss it. I rarely say it is awful. I sometimes say it is boring or old-fashioned. I saw a picture the other day called *Interlude*; it just wasn't very successful.

Champlin: I think there's a basic misassumption about the role of the critic. I don't think, and I can't stress this strongly enough, that the effort is to reach some kind of consensus in film criticism.

Preminger: No, but I do think that there should be, ideally, a communication between the critic and his readers, so that the readers of that publication have somebody to believe. That they say, "Well, Champlin didn't like *The Detective*, so I'm not going to go." That would be the ideal position of a critic. That is why I say that the critic should really write for the readers. In the long run, if you are too often disappointing to your readers, the readers will stop reading reviews, and that is not in the interest of the publication, because, at least theoretically, a number of people buy that publication because they are interested in the reviews. Now, ideally, in my opinion, the really successful critic *leads* his readers.

Audience Member: Mr. Preminger, don't you think the critic really contributes perceptions about how the film is working or not working? Very frequently, it's really less important whether you agree with a critic about whether he likes or dislikes a film if he's able to really give you reasons that talk about how the film is working. A good example of this is Stanley Kauffmann's review of *Bonnie and Clyde*. He happened to really put the film down, but in the process of putting it down he was really describing a lot of qualities about how it was working, which could be very useful to people who really like the film.

Preminger: The same thing happened with *Bonnie and Clyde* and Bosley Crowther. If you want to judge Bosley Crowther as a critic, and if you read his tirade against excessive violence in *Bonnie and Clyde*, if anybody has any sense of humor, he must realize that this is all done with tongue in cheek. You cannot possibly have two characters shoot their way out of five hundred policemen successfully and then say these poor policemen died a horrible, violent death. Then you must say, if you are a reader, not a director—Mr. Crowther, unlike many other critics, likes some of my films very much—but I would still say he has no sense of humor, he doesn't understand the very successfully executed intentions of the picture makers of this film to do a satire. *Bonnie and Clyde* is a satire.

The young lady said something very interesting. I didn't read Stanley Kauffmann's review of *Bonnie and Clyde*. You said he wanted to put the film down, in other words, he wanted to write a bad review of the film. He did not accomplish his purpose. He tried to put it down, and in doing so he pointed out how many good things were in it.

Murphy: But when he pointed out what he didn't like about the film, it meant, to the reader, that he didn't like this, this, and this. The reader thinks: "My kind of picture." So he communicated . . .

Preminger: No. He didn't want that. You only communicate if you *intend* to say something to somebody and the person understands. If you intend to say,

"This is a terrible picture because of such-and-such," and the people who read it say, "No, it's wonderful because I *like* such-and-such," then you are not a very good critic.

Murphy: No, Otto. Stanley did make his position clear about the film.

Preminger: Even the *New York Times* let him go after a year of writing reviews for the paper. If ever pomposity was invented, it was invented by him. He is the most pompous, pretentious man in the world. Have you ever seen him on television on Channel 13? It's worthwhile seeing!

Audience Member: Do you think, Mr. Preminger, that the purpose of the review or the critique—whatever you want to call it—is to either make you or not make you go to the film?

Preminger: No. But it is to *convince* you, when you read it, of your opinion. I mean, if you write a review or a critique, and you say something is bad and you point out *why* it is bad, and then the people that read it, because of the very reasons that you say it is bad go to see it, then you have not fulfilled your purpose in writing the review.

Champlin: The purpose is not to dragoon an audience into or out of the theater.

Preminger: But you're not going to tell them, "I hate this film, go in." You say, "I hate this film, don't waste your time."

Champlin: Mr. Preminger mentioned something called the instinct of the audience. There's been a sudden growth in film art, and there's been, to my mind, a corresponding diminution of the value of the critic. Critics seem to be commenting on certain vibrations that come out of these films which seem to emerge from the underground. They don't emerge full blown. You sense them coming: a big Preminger film, a big Kubrick film. They're coming. The whole business of film reviewing seems to be a part of a much larger communications media.

Preminger: May I ask one thing, because you brought up the Kubrick film. Have you seen *2001: A Space Odyssey*? How did you like it?

Champlin: I liked it quite a lot, but with severe reservations.

Preminger: I want to make this point. You cannot say that there is excessive violence in it, or that there is excessive sex in it. When the executives of Metro-Goldwyn-Mayer saw the film, they almost committed mass suicide. The reviews generally, around the country, were at least 90 percent negative. This is *the* biggest success of any film ever. It is impossible to get near the theater. I saw it, and because I didn't understand certain things, I went to see it again, just to study it. It was on a Wednesday afternoon, when people don't go [to] the movies, and it was completely sold out; it was difficult to get in. But there must be something about the instinct of the public that they chose to see the film. There are no stars—just two young actors who most people don't know. While Kubrick is a

very well-known director, he has not done a film for five or six years. What is
it, that instinct, that makes people go? They went through word of mouth. And
there is also a generation gap. Strangely enough, this is a film that if you take a
poll, almost everybody over thirty years old dislikes it, and the younger people
between sixteen and twenty-four all love it. It's a wonderful thing about film, this
is so great: that people, just when they feel they want to see something, go to see it.

Champlin: I'm not surprised by the success of *2001* . . .

Preminger: I must say honestly: if I had seen it *before* I knew it was successful, I would not have guessed for one minute that it could be that successful.
I'm fascinated by many technical things [achieved by the film], but I would not
have guessed.

Champlin: I think that the film picks up on what Ray Bradbury said: space
has become the new focus of idealism for a generation . . .

Preminger: Why did most critics try to destroy the film?

Champlin: The reviews I saw were mostly positive . . .

Preminger: No. They said it was dull and overlong. You see, the critics also
have learned, when they really want to hurt the film, they don't say it has excessive violence or excessive sex; they say it is dull.

Champlin: Now, you said something there, that we try and *hurt* the film . . .

Preminger: I didn't say *you.*

Champlin: Well . . .

Preminger: You don't think that Mr. Crowther wrote that *Bonnie and Clyde*
is dull, which he did several times, because he wanted to *help* the film. When
you say something is dull, then you really want to stop people from going. And
the people who say that the *Space Odyssey* is overlong and dull, that is the worst
thing you can say about a film.

Audience Member: Would you care to comment upon the issue of violence
in film?

Preminger: The issue of violence, the issue of sex, the issue of language
has nothing to do with films. The truth is that society has developed in these
directions, and films—like books, like theater—reflect it. If you do a film like
The Detective about the New York police and you want to be truthful, you must
show that they beat up people. I doubt very much that it influences people who
see it. I think that juvenile delinquents don't go to movies. They have no time
for it; they steal and fight. I think we are much freer now. Certain words—I'm
not speaking about the words in *The Detective*—but let's say, a word like "sex":
when I was young, you couldn't say "sex" in mixed company. And certainly you
couldn't say it on the radio, forget films. Today on radio and television, you can
say "sex," you can say "perversion," you can say everything. That is because our
society has changed, not the media. I think the media reflects society.

Murphy: I also would like to add that we have a tendency these days to say that sex is bad in the films, that there's too much violence in the films, without making the distinction between motivated sex, motivated violence . . .

Preminger: Whatever you put into the film, if it is not motivated, the film is bad. But certainly in *The Detective*, the violence and the sex are motivated. It's about homosexuals and New York and violence in the police department.

Murphy: But you can't say that putting violence in a film has no influence, when the whole purpose of making the film is to influence an audience in the story and in the points you're making . . .

Preminger: Do you really believe that all the people who see *The Detective* become homosexuals? That they go out right away and try it?

Murphy: No.

Preminger: I saw a play in New York, it was one of the most amusing plays that I've seen. It is ten times more outspoken than any film I've ever seen. It is called *The Boys in the Band*—one of the funniest plays I've ever seen.

Audience Member: Almost all the discussion has been around the mass audience, and I'm wondering: there are a lot of young filmmakers today who do not regard film as a mass entertainment medium. What type of critic do they deserve? What should be the preparation of the critic for criticizing this type of film?

Murphy: Well, I think it should be someone who is sympathetic to what they're viewing; not antipathetic or apathetic. At the same time, I feel that this field, more than any other at the moment, needs people who are not willing to lower standards. People who are not willing to say, "I know it's all grainy and out-of-focus, but, gee, at least you got the job done." That kind of criticism I think we have all too much of in this underground film field today, where people are being encouraged to make films who really shouldn't be even allowed to go to see them.

[Laughter]

And it's doing more harm to the field than anything I can imagine.

Preminger: I must say that I, as an older man, give advice to younger filmmakers not to worry. Critics should be the worry of the editors and publishers of publications. The people who make films should only worry about making films. I will tell you as an older and, let's say, established filmmaker, that I look at as many of these films as possible, because I can learn from them. These films help experimentation. They do things which we who are saddled with tremendous money responsibilities don't dare to do. They can experiment, and that helps the older filmmaker very much. For instance, the fact that the Nouvelle Vague had no money for opticals for dissolves got rid of most opticals everywhere. And it is wonderful: who wants those dull dissolves and fades? But nobody dared to do it. It was a convention, and it is very difficult to get rid of conventions when you are a part of what people call the establishment. Because when you are successful and everything goes well, why touch it? Why suddenly take a risk, when you have a two-, three-, five-million-dollar investment, by leaving out opticals? Not only opticals but many things: for instance, the way time is now handled in films— that all comes from the young filmmakers. The people are intelligent enough to know that you go back [in flashback] without having all these explanations and voiceovers and so on. And that comes from the younger filmmakers. Why worry what the critics think? Let the publications worry about that.

Knight: I trust we have you all thoroughly confused. I just want to say, in closing, since Mr. Crowther and *Bonnie and Clyde* came up so many times this afternoon, that these days, when anybody asks me whether a film critic can affect the success of a film, I say: "Yes, of course: look at Bosley Crowther and *Bonnie and Clyde*."

I want to thank Art Murphy, Charles Champlin, and especially Otto Preminger for being here.

Otto Preminger Speaking at UCLA

Robert Kirsch / 1968

Recorded on December 4, 1968. Reprinted by permission of UCLA Department of Communication Studies.

Robert Kirsch: There is absolutely no truth to the rumor that Mr. Preminger will succeed Dr. Hayakawa at San Francisco State.

[Audience laughter]

Although *Dr.* Preminger—he really *is* a doctor; he's the right kind of doctor, a doctor of laws—*was* up there at San Francisco State, probing around, trying to find out whether or not he could accommodate student unrest and anomie to a new picture.

I'm very pleased to be able to introduce Otto Preminger, because I have been among those associated with him in a continuing battle for increased candor and freedom of expression. Otto Preminger was a lawyer, an unwilling lawyer; he was an actor—some people thought a very fine actor—but he wanted to be a director; and he has directed many films. Some of those films were films which did anticipate the extended freedom of expression which we have now. I think most of you know about *The Moon Is Blue*, which at the time of its release was denied a seal. Ten years later it received a seal. *The Court-Martial of Billy Mitchell* was a controversial film made against the opposition of the army and the navy, which felt upset about it. *The Man with the Golden Arm* was a film which, I think, began the serious penetration of the drug issue by motion pictures. Mr. Preminger is, I think, not as authoritarian or dictatorial as his press agents would have us believe. I find him a very humane man, an interesting man, an unpretentious man who confronts each day the practical problem of entertaining and informing people.

We in the academic community, students and professors, have a tendency—and perhaps this part of our function—to assume that this task is an easy one, or that the failures which we sometimes see are the result of some kind of intent. I think we have an opportunity here today to examine candidly through our questions and comments the making of a picture, *Skidoo*, the effect of that picture, and such intent and motivation as Mr. Preminger will undoubtedly reveal to us. So, with great pleasure I introduce Otto Preminger.

[Applause]

Preminger: Whenever I am introduced, it is at once a nice, flattering thing and I feel very happy, but it also makes me a little uncomfortable, because I get, perhaps, a little more credit than I deserve. And there is one thing, because I think it is important to you and important to me, that I would like to correct or at least explain. I had several run-ins with censors: our own censors in the motion picture industry, which really are not censors, but it's a code administration where we have a code of self-restraint, and also with all kinds of censors [such as] the police in Chicago. I always fought these censors. I never anticipated—for instance, when I made *The Moon Is Blue*, which I had directed and produced on Broadway as a play, and it ran three years—that when I put it on film that there would be so much noise about it. Because the difference between the film version and the theatrical version was only that people could see it now for, at that time, one dollar and twenty-five cents instead of paying six dollars in New York. And the reason I defended my right of free expression was never because I felt pretentious enough and silly enough about my work to feel that a little comedy like *The Moon Is Blue* would suffer so much, or that it would be sacrilegious to cut a few lines. That is not the point. My point is that all of us, whether we are movie producers or writers or stage producers or whatever we do—or students—that in our area, in our jurisdiction, we not only have the right but the duty to defend this most precious right that we have, and that we have in the United States perhaps more guaranteed by the Constitution than any other country. [Our rights are] still more alive than in any other country, because I don't think there *is* another country that would permit dissidents—in a case where the country were at war—to come out and express opinions against the war. In other countries these dissidents would probably be treated as traitors. It is very important, no matter on which side you are, and what your beliefs are, to defend this right of free expression, because the minute these rights start to shrink and eventually to disappear, the free government, the democracy as we know it, is in danger.

No totalitarian government, whether from the Right or from the Left, can exist without thought control. And censorship *is* nothing else but controlling your thoughts and the expression of these thoughts, because it starts with people telling you what you can say and what you can write and what you can put in a movie, and those might be very frivolous and little things. But it then continues until you have the same thought control that you had in Germany during the Hitler regime or in Russia—I was in both countries, and I saw it in both. This leads to fear and to injustice and to totalitarian government, which I think none of us wants. It is not a special credit that I deserve for having fought censorship. It is something that I think is my duty and the duty of anybody who has a chance to do it.

Now, I don't like to give lectures, as I announced before, because I don't know what you might be interested in, but I'll be—to the best of my ability—happy to answer any questions that you pose.

Q: What do you think are your best films?

Preminger: This is something that I cannot answer. I want to explain to you that when I make a film, I concentrate on my work because it's my life. I love my work and I do nothing else but think of this film. When the film is finished and I have seen it several times with audiences—and an audience adds something to the film which nobody can really anticipate while he makes a film—two things happen: (a) I then feel invariably, in every case, that I could have done much better—if I had the chance to do it over, I could do it better; and (b) I then detach myself from the film. I don't even think of it anymore, because I couldn't go on working if I would think of my old films.

Q: How do you feel about the motion picture ratings system?

Preminger: Well, this is not censorship. It would be too long and too technical to explain, because I feel two ways about it. But one thing: it is really a means for the producers—for us—to warn parents. You see, I have two children who are eight years old, they are twins, and I let them see anything. I feel that if I succeed to explain to them, to educate them, what is good and bad, what is wrong and right, what is good taste and bad taste, they don't need any protection by anyone; they can see anything. And if I don't succeed, I don't think that *any* protection . . . any group that would say, "Don't let children go to this film until they are at least sixteen," is useless. I think that all this outcry against sex and violence in pictures is ridiculous, because I think that motion pictures and television reflect society. I think our society has become more violent and the cure for it, you know, should be looked at at the roots. Certainly, it's not by hitting people over the head, because that is more violence. As far as sex goes, we are just freer. If you checked with your older friends or parents, you would find that twenty years ago certain things were just not mentioned in mixed society. I think it is much better now. I don't see why there should be any secret about anything. You can still feel that perhaps homosexuality is not an ideal thing, you know, but there is no reason why a film or a drama or a book or your conversation should not deal with it. It certainly doesn't necessarily mean that you recruit more homosexuals. And even if that were the case, I think in a free society, people should certainly be able to discuss and think and see—on films and everywhere—anything they want to. What good is this freedom if we can't use it?

I think that pointless violence and pointless nudity or pointless sex is boring. I was here last week for a couple of days, and I walked on the Sunset Strip. They were playing there at the 16 mm Cinematheque a film by Andy Warhol. Maybe some of you have seen it; it's called *The Naked Restaurant* [*sic*]. And I went in to see it. I sat there for an hour and a half. I saw three completely nude people; a nude woman and three nude men. It was obviously like he usually does it, ad lib: they just talked and walked around and touched each other sometimes. In one scene, a woman and a man were together in a bathtub. After some time, it became terribly boring to me, you know, because it was pointless. After some time, I had time to see that this girl, who originally was quite attractive, she became less and less attractive to me. I had so many chances to study the faults in her body. And the men, you know, became more and more charmless. I'm not particularly interested in nude men anyway.

[Laughter]

But I mean the way they carried themselves seemed so pointless, and I left after an hour and a half because I was bored. I was not shocked. I just think that the experiment didn't work. I think that if there had been one scene where it had made a story point—where the girl undressed or the men undressed—that would be interesting and, I think, very right. But to just walk around nude for the sake of being nude . . . It's just like if we all undressed here, at first it might be a shock, but after half an hour we would be—at least *I* would be—pretty disinterested in all of you nude. On the other hand, when I look around here and see some of you dressed, I might be curious.

[Laughter]

Q: You mentioned that you were at San Francisco State. What were your reasons for going there?

Preminger: Well, I didn't talk; this was also a mistake [in Kirsch's introduction]. I *was* in San Francisco yesterday. Originally, I was supposed to talk at San Francisco State. But it was switched to the City College, because San Francisco State is not very much interested in me at this point. However, I had a chance to discuss it there, you know, with many people: I had a press conference, I had several dinners and luncheons. You see, I feel that big mistakes have been made there. This is only my opinion, and I say it without any prejudice. I think, for instance, no matter whether you agree with the way Mr. Hayakawa, the acting president, acts—whether you agree with him or not—I think that he was rendered completely useless when the governor, who is known for being a very conservative and perhaps even reactionary man, came out and praised him, because the students must at this moment feel that the president, in his actions, which should be impartial, is not impartial anymore, that he is practically on the staff of the government. See, I think by praising him, the governor made a mistake. I come from Europe. In Europe these student demonstrations and the participation of students in the administrations of universities is an old thing. It happens very peacefully and without any trouble. In these discussions, and I don't want to go into it, somebody told me: "You can't let the students decide who should teach them or not." Strangely enough, this is a thing which is a matter of course in big universities in Europe, which are all really not state but federal universities. What they do there, they have many professors [teaching] the same subject, and the students can choose [among them]. But to say that a student at this level should just be told, "You've got to go and take lessons from one particular man," that is not the idea of a university. That is really a contradiction to the freedom of learning, because at a certain age young people should have the right to choose from whom they learn. They should be wise enough.

Anyway, I feel that all the violence could easily be avoided if the police were not used and if an appeal would be made to the students to, for instance, have arbitration, where the university would get some people who are generally known as fair, and the students [would select representatives among themselves], and they would form a panel, and grievances would be discussed, if possible, publicly, and I think it all can be straightened out. One thing in my mind is clear: you don't go to university just to cause trouble. You go to university to learn, basically. I don't think that anybody would waste four or five years of his life in order to just picket or demonstrate. And on the other hand, the administration also must basically be of good will and good faith if politicians don't come into it. The minute the police comes in, unfortunately, things become passionate in the wrong way. That is my opinion, but don't go by it.

Q: What was your reaction to the *Sunday Times* article on the making of a new star? How do you feel in general about the public relations aspect of star making?

Preminger: The making of a new star? You mean, Alexandra Hay? Well, I mean this is the kind of thing that goes with all goods, you know. This is a sales point, and you can't take this too seriously. The people at the *Sunday Times*, whether it is here or any newspaper, need for the entertainment section certain features, and they choose them. They called me up—at that time, we were still shooting *Skidoo*—and said: "We want to do a story on Alexandra Hay." I didn't ask them *what* story. They took twenty photographs of me and used one, and one of John Phillip Law who was here with her, I think. This is not in any way serious except for selling. It's really just like critics are really the problem of the papers and not of the people who make movies; in the same way, these articles are a problem of the papers. I made a movie and they sent a man who spent a week with me and was very friendly, in the South, called Rex Reed. He was not very well known. I contributed somehow to his fame that he has now, because six weeks later in the *New York Times*, he wrote an article with not one true word in it. It was funny. I didn't take the trouble to correct it or anything. I didn't care. That is the problem of the *New York Times*; if they want to dish up to their readers a story which is completely untrue and pretends to be a true picture of what happens on the set, you know . . . there was not one true word. Many of the actors and the cameramen whom Reed said I fired, which I didn't, *did* protest to the *Times*. I mean, these are things that happen. It's like anything that you read in the newspaper, it is always slanted (a) toward the editorial policy of the newspaper and (b) slanted in order to entertain or be amusing.

Q: How do you feel about *2001: A Space Odyssey*?

Preminger: Well, *A Space Odyssey* I liked very much. I say this as an audience member; I'm not a critic, and I like the film very much. I admire, first of all, technically, the incredible perfection that Mr. Kubrick reached. This was very difficult. He worked really for five years, day and night, only on this film. I also found the film fascinating. As a matter of fact, I saw it twice. I have, like everybody probably has, certain questions; I mean, you never like anything 100 percent, but I think it is a very, very superior movie. It might interest you that when this movie was shown to the executives of MGM for the first time, at least a majority of them very seriously thought of committing suicide.

[Laughter]

A few of them walked out because they really hated it. When the picture opened in New York and got a majority of bad reviews, they felt even worse about it. The picture didn't do too well in the beginning. But then eventually, through word of mouth, and through the fact that people liked it—mostly young people liked it—it became one of the biggest hits in the history of movies. Now the MGM people like it very much.

[Laughter]

Q: Are you still trying to make a film of *Too Far to Walk*?

Preminger: Well, I don't know. *Too Far to Walk* is a book that I bought in manuscript a long time ago. As I worked on the screenplay and did research—I did very much research, including at one point taking LSD—I felt that it became more and more obsolete. In other words, the times and the various activities of young people moved far ahead of the book. I'm still trying to update the story as I work on it, but so far I have not succeeded in getting the right screenplay. It is one of my principles in working: I don't start a movie until I am satisfied with the screenplay. Even when I'm satisfied, it doesn't always turn out to be the biggest hit, but at least I want to be satisfied.

Q: Did you have any problems working with Groucho Marx on *Skidoo*?

Preminger: Well, I mean, no, not really. First of all, his whole part was done in three days. He has problems in remembering lines by now. He's much older than he looks. When you are patient with him, it works.

Q: Do you believe that anything can be shown in films that are pornographic?

Preminger: I would like to explain the difference between censorship and committing an act of obscenity. Censorship means—basically, simplified—that a group of people, a state board, the federal government, tells you what you can put into a film, into a book, a newspaper, a magazine, before you do it. In other words, it really should be called prior censorship or pre-censorship. Pornography—the word means something obscene in writing, or visually, that is against the law. We have a law in this country, like in any other country no matter how free the society is: obscenity is something that the laws don't tolerate. Now, obscenity is also something that changes with the times, and changes with society as society moves. Sometimes we go backward. Also, what might be obscene in Los Angeles might not be considered obscene in New York. What might not be considered obscene in Los Angeles might be considered obscene in Burbank, or in smaller places. The smaller communities usually are behind. Although this is also not true, because when you read of all the things that happen in country clubs in small towns, you know, between couples who swap wives, et cetera, and then they get terribly outraged when they see a picture that shows a slightly nude woman's breast, you wonder if they are sincere or hypocritical. But obscenity is something that you commit: you can commit an act of obscenity right here, and then the police would come in, would arrest you, and would put you before a judge. And the judge would then decide—it would be his judgment, or a jury—whether it *is* obscene. The same thing is true of pornography. If you write something, or photograph something, that is obscene, then the police would prosecute you, and you would have to answer in court. That is not censorship.

Q: Do you think these judgments by society are valid?

Preminger: Well, naturally, the whole idea of our living in a democracy is that we don't submit to judgments by individuals or by a small group. The society, or the majority of society, decides on everything. And it *is* valid.

Q: Do you consider yourself an artist or a businessman?

Preminger: Well, I hope that I'm not a businessman. I have all my life followed the principle that I like to do what I think I want to do at that moment. I've succeeded with it. I never worry about money too much and I have made enough money so far to live very, very comfortably. So, I don't worry about it. And to speak about myself as an artist also seems pretentious. If you mean as a moviemaker, I must tell you that I cannot calculate—and I don't try to calculate—the success of a film that I make. I make a film the way I feel. I choose the story because *I'm* interested. I choose the actors because *I* think they are right. It's all very subjective. Therefore, you might—if you want to be generous—say that it is an art, that it is artistic. But I do this with the hope that my enthusiasm would eventually become contagious through my medium, on the screen, and get other people enthusiastic, and they would like what I have done. Sometimes my judgment is right, and sometimes I'm wrong, and I have either a success or a failure. That is the excitement of my profession. I don't believe that anybody can say, "We are going to take now a few parts of sex, and a few parts of violence, and a love story, and a star, and when we mix this all up, it will become a success." As a matter of fact, I can't tell you now that *Skidoo* is finished whether people will come to see it or not. I hope they will see it. But it is something that is impossible for me to judge, and therefore I don't worry about it.

I worry about my next film, which is based on a book that I bought six months ago in manuscript. These are the small compensations, or the small dividends, that you get. When I bought this book, everybody thought I was crazy. It is called *Tell Me That You Love Me, Junie Moon*. It is the first book by a young woman called Marjorie Kellogg. It is a very strange story about three handicapped people who meet in a hospital—a girl and two men—and decide to make a life together. They decide not to mix in society, where they expect, at best, pity and charitable or tactful avoidance, because they are all crippled. They want to try to make their own life. It shows courage. I liked it very much. The book was published about four weeks ago and received unanimously rave reviews from every book critic in the country. It is selling very well, which nobody expected. You feel justified in your judgment: now people don't think I'm crazy anymore.

Q: How did you get started in Hollywood films?

Preminger: A man from Hollywood came to Vienna; he had heard about me, and then met me, and hired me to come here. I started to learn how to make films at Twentieth Century-Fox. The man's name was Joseph Schenck. I also directed—I don't want to tell you my whole life story—some plays on Broadway, and I even taught in Yale at the Drama School when I worked in New York. I then acted again, playing a few Nazis—at that time, it was very difficult to find Nazis in the United States; I wouldn't have to struggle now, so I don't act anymore.

[Laughter]

When I came here to Los Angeles for the first time, I was interested to see things. I wanted to see young people. I was then only twenty-seven, but it was always interesting to me how young people learn. I enlisted here at UCLA into a drama course that was conducted by an actor. I still remember his name: Antrim. Naturally, I just sat in back and didn't do much, and somehow, through publicity one day, he had found out who I was. He came into class and was raging mad. He thought I was a spy or something, and he threw me out. He said, how could I do this? So that was the end of my academic career at UCLA.

Q: How much preproduction planning do you allow yourself?

Preminger: Preproduction planning is, in my way of making pictures, very important. I do first the script. I don't even start to talk to actors until the script is finished. Then I cast it, and while I cast it, I usually have first an art director go out—I make most of my films now on location—and find the right locations. He gives me choices, and I travel with him. And when this is all finished, only then do I really determine the starting date of shooting. Then I shoot, I make the film, I edit it, and there it is. I preview it and I forget it.

[Laughter]

Q: Do you do your own editing?

Preminger: This is a very good question, and I'm often asked this question. I would like to make it clear that editing is part of the director's job. The editor is only there to execute what the director tells him. First of all, the director edits as he shoots; he edits in his mind. He knows exactly what he wants to use. Or maybe he gives himself a choice, and when he looks at the film, he tells the editor: "Use this angle" or "Use this part of the scene here and there." The editor naturally also has an important function, like the cameraman. The more sensitive and the more attuned he is to the director's wishes, the better an editor he is. And also, physically, there are differences in using two or three more frames, or two or three less frames. But the director is the editor. Then, according to different contracts, it is possible that the studio or the distributor comes in and makes changes. In my contract, I have the final cut—nobody can cut anything in my films against my will, at least not legally. It is just like photography. The director tells the cameraman exactly what he wants to see on the screen. The cameraman's main function is to create the mood that the director wanted. But what you see, the way that the camera is set up, is the director's and not the cameraman's job to decide.

Q: What do you think is the future of avant-garde or underground films?

Preminger: Well, I can't discuss the future of anything, because I'm not a prophet or astrologer. I think that avant-garde films, or Off-Broadway or Off-Off-Broadway plays, or student films are very good and very useful. First of all, I think that film has become more or less *the* way of expression for young people. Many young people—not necessarily young people who wanted to become film-makers—would perhaps in another age have written stories, but are now doing it visually with cameras, with 8 mm, Super 8, 16 mm . . . I think this is very good. It's interesting for us, and I think that everything that you see—like when I told you about this Andy Warhol film—everything that you see as a picture maker that is experimental, whether it is good or bad, helps you to decide what you want to do. So, every experiment is great, in my opinion. I'm for it. Where it is going, some of these avant-garde filmmakers might become the greatest directors and filmmakers in the world, and some might disappear—I mean, that is difficult for me to foresee or to foretell.

Q: Do you do a great deal of ad-libbing?

Preminger: No. I make changes. But this is maybe a limitation that I have. I don't feel that it serves any purpose to let the actor go beyond interpreting the part that is given to him. Not because I underrate necessarily the actor's talent, but the only thing is, if you start it, then there is no ending it. If you let an actor change his lines once, and then two weeks later when he wants to change his lines you say, "No, stop," then he will pout, because he will feel he contributed something and that you shouldn't stop him. But you might feel that if he contributes more, he will ruin your film. I don't do ad-libbing, but there can also be made a case for it.

Q: Is it harder to do a film in color than in black-and-white?

Preminger: Well, it is more difficult in color to get the cameraman to shoot it realistically. Color is an inducement to the cameraman to make things too sweet. But generally, the actual photography is easier in color than in black-and-white. It is more difficult to do a good job on a black-and-white picture photographically than in color.

Q: Are there any actors or actresses that you particularly enjoyed working with?

Preminger: Well, I like actors. Some directors, like Hitchcock—he calls actors "cattle"—and many, many directors don't like actors. I don't think he means it either. But I like actors. Actors have a kind of open nature, you know, and I don't say this against them. Because they are extroverts they have a certain charm, an almost childlike charm, which I enjoy and like. Most actors with whom I work are my friends after we work together.

Q: What do you do if you have a serious disagreement with an actor?

Preminger: Well, it really happens very rarely. I first try to persuade him. It depends on the actor. The director is like a teacher. Many actors are best accessible if you persuade them and if you are kind to them, which is difficult for me. Other actors need to be a little shaken up. I have never had it happen, but if this disagreement should really be very basic and important, I would have to recast the part. There is one thing about directing: it must be the *director's* interpretation, the director's picture. The picture must be made, for better or worse, the way the director sees it. It is not a medium which has room for committee decisions.

Q: What is your position on casting unknown actors?

Preminger: I would like to tell you that I don't even live in Hollywood. Since 1952, when the independent producer came into being, pictures are really made by individuals mainly, with some exceptions of cheaper pictures. I really believe that today there is very little gamble in using unknowns. I think it is just as much a gamble to use a star in a part that he cannot play well, that he is not right for, because he will not only hurt the part and the picture but also himself and his future. As you can often see: to just use people because of their name rather than to use a new actor who is right for the part. The important thing for me in casting is to find the people who in my opinion, at least, could do the best job in the part. I don't worry too much about names. For instance, somebody asked me why I use all these names in *Skidoo*. It was a joke—to take all these former stars and line them up, and they all play small parts. It's like seeing old films on television. They were very right for these parts. I don't know how many of you saw *Skidoo*, but when George Raft plays a captain on a gangster's boat, it is naturally a reflection on his past when he played many gangsters.

Q: Is it really true that the field of moviemaking is overrun with good actors and actresses?

Preminger: This is absolutely untrue. Let me tell you this: there are never enough talented writers, actors, people who want to direct, produce—anything that needs talent is always rare. Talent is rare. As a matter of fact, you hear always people saying, "My God, in the good old times there were more good plays." I mean, how many good plays do you see on Broadway? There is never enough talent. So don't let anybody tell you that there are too many good actors or too many good writers in any field. That is nonsense. As a matter of fact, as the communications expand and we have now in addition to films and theater also so much material—and actors—eaten up by television, we always need more and more actors, writers, and talent in movies.

Q: Do you think that some films are really actors' films?

Preminger: Well, it is not true that movies are known because of their actors, but this again is a question of selling, not of who really does it. If somebody has a big name, it's like a brand name in any goods, like Kellogg's breakfast food. The people who make the breakfast food are not necessarily the family Kellogg, you know, but they have established this brand name. If Steve McQueen is in a picture and the director is not a very famous director, Steve McQueen's name is being printed bigger and used more in publicity because they think it will sell the film. It is not always true, you know. Some McQueen pictures attract many people, and others don't. But that has nothing to do with the importance, and Mr. McQueen still doesn't *make* the pictures that he's in. He only acts in them. And if he has a director who is really a director, he does exactly what the director tells him to do.

Thank you very much. It was nice to see you. Good luck.

The Great Otto

Deac Rossell / 1969

From *Boston After Dark*, February 12, 1969, 22–23; 27. Reprinted by permission.

Otto Preminger is a man to be reckoned with in the film industry. He has the reputation of being a single-minded, intelligent producer-director who has left broken barriers and broken actors behind him. He single-handedly broke down the hypocrisy of the old Motion Picture Code (not to be confused with a newly instituted system of voluntary self-regulation) by producing a film which dealt seriously with drug addiction, *The Man with the Golden Arm* (1955), and had an earlier film, *The Moon Is Blue* (1953), condemned by the Legion of Decency (now the National Catholic Office for Motion Pictures) because the word "virgin" appeared in dialogue. Small steps they seem to us now, in an almost grown-up film world, but it was Otto Preminger who took the first halting steps in redefining the styles and themes of the postwar American film.

I first met Preminger, a man whose instant temper, Germanic perfectionism, and almost dictatorial control on the set has become legend, at a private appointment that quickly turned into a circus. Tim Hunter and I had an appointment to meet with him at the Ritz-Carlton, just before he was due at a faculty dinner at Boston University, where he delivered a lecture later that night. Hunter is a critic (*The Crimson*) and filmmaker who knows more about Preminger than Preminger himself (self-admittedly on the director's part), and I had hoped to bring some of his astute questions to bear on the tough-but-gregarious producer-director. No such luck. By the time Preminger arrived, tired and disheveled after grabbing a last-minute train to Boston when all flights from La Guardia Field were cancelled, his suite was filled with an assortment of press agents, miscellaneous friends of the producer, two immaculate young gentlemen from BU awed by their first contact with screen royalty, and our two intrepid critics. Boston University got in the first question as one of the upstanding young men inexplicably asked: "Do you like to talk about television?"

We were off and running. Preminger is hesitant about discussing the specifics of his films but will make sensible and incisive comments on almost any other subject, from censorship to Hollywood to hippies to student demonstrations. Even while he is on a publicity trip to create news stories about his latest film (*Skidoo*, a comedy starring Jackie Gleason, Carol Channing, and Groucho Marx, among others), he is already deeply involved in his next picture, [*Tell Me That You Love Me,*] *Junie Moon*, and reluctant to look back to *Skidoo*.

After brushing off my first questions about the style of comedy in *Skidoo*, he finally gave an answer: "Comedy, the way I see it . . . as long as you make me discuss it, is the variance in values. Jackie Gleason in *Skidoo* is a criminal who is called back from retirement by the gang to do another job, and he is put into prison to hit this other prisoner. In prison he meets a young man who is a draft-card burner, a boy who has courage and sincerity, even going to prison for what he believes. Yet Gleason and the others in the prison look down on him. The whole prison—a microcosm of society—looks down at the kid. Comedy doesn't have to be laughable, it is a comedic counterpoint, and it is funny to me that Gleason has to depend on the kid to get himself out of prison. And even Gleason himself comes to realize, after his LSD trip, that you should not go around killing people."

Preminger made a comedy about LSD and the establishment because he feels that it is easier to make a funny picture about things like LSD and marijuana. To be serious would require a depth that Preminger feels is almost impossible in the movies. In the course of researching the film, Preminger himself took a dose of LSD, after consulting with Dr. Sidney Cohen, a well-known researcher who has legal access to the drug through a government grant. Preminger's trip, however, followed an evening meal with Dr. Timothy Leary.

"I had Dr. Timothy Leary for dinner one night, and my wife and I each took a capsule. I had only one thing on my mind: we live in a private house, a brownstone in New York City, and in the back of my mind is always the question 'What happens if there is a fire? Will the children be able to get out?' Leary brought a candle to me, he wanted to be our guru, but he dropped the candle. This disturbed me very much, and I said: 'You must leave.'

"After he left, the effects of the drug began to take hold. *Skidoo* is what happened to me then. I looked at my wife, and she became very small, about six inches high, although she talked in a normal voice. So the same things happen to Gleason in the prison, when the cellmates get very small.

"It is hard to describe the effects of the drug. All the time you are up with the drug you are standing beside yourself, you know that what you see is an illusion. The senses are not dulled, as they are with alcohol, and you have a strange feeling of triumph, a feeling that you are somehow right—especially if you have a pleasant experience like I did, a good trip."

After settling down in the Ritz suite, finally getting everyone a drink from room service and getting Preminger rolling about his film, one of the BU people stood up and boldly announced to the assembled company that it was getting late and we had all best start for dinner. A couple of press agents almost dropped their glasses, but Preminger stood up and began to leave, as Tim Hunter asked why there was so much crosscutting in his recent films. I sat and wrote Preminger's answer—typically a divergent comment on style in films—while a dozen people milled around and sorted out their coats.

"What is style?" the director asked in reply. "Style is not something you work on, not something mechanical, not whether you do more cutting or less. There is an old countryman of mine, who I knew in Hollywood because he had come from Vienna, named Hans Brahm. He made a bunch of low-budget pictures at Fox (*Hangover Square, The Mad Magician*, etc.), mostly suspense pictures, while I was also there. He would always cut holes in the floor, so he could put his camera in and shoot up at his actors. He would also build his sets on platforms. It was his trademark; he thought the public would like to see all those angle shots. They were the mark of his pictures. But was that style? No! All it means was that he had a lot of low set-ups. That does not make a style.

"Style . . . everybody concedes that Ingmar Bergman has a style, he is a great director, and every film that comes along you say, 'Here is another Bergman masterpiece.' But he does not have a style as a strictly mechanical way, his style is not a matter of set-ups. Style is how you treat the whole idea, the whole story. In my opinion, the less a director is noticed, the better the film is."

The Preminger I saw that night was not at all the Preminger of tyrannical temper. He was affable, speaking readily on a number of subjects, even though he was obviously tired from his day-long expeditions. The next day, at a luncheon at the Algonquin Club, he proved that his despotic legend was really only one side of his personality. As the members of the press sat in a corner to ask questions once again, one of my colleagues managed to pour the entire contents of her highball glass into Preminger's left-hand pocket and down his leg. He started from his chair like a wounded rhinoceros but was instantly back under control as another interviewer, Alta Maloney of the *Herald Traveler*, quipped: "Well, there's more than one way of making a critical comment."

In this generally older (post-fifty) audience, Preminger was still at ease but pointed many of his comments at today's youth with an almost messianic zeal. Speaking in his Viennese accent with the broad-minded reason of sixty-three years of experience as a human being, and with a mind that has remained agile and contemporary, Preminger seemed eager to give his views on students, hippies, drugs, and demonstrations.

"I think that young people want to be heard," he said, twisting his bald head at the assembled press. "They want dialogue—if these demonstrations are handled with patience, like the president of Brandeis handled them, there is no reason to call the police. If you call the police to beat and arrest them, then violence becomes stronger. Like what is going on in San Francisco State College—it is shameful. It is probably true that some demonstrators are misused by radicals and communists, but this too could be solved by patience. To us, the reasons might be wrong, but young people are very sincere, they are honest. Young people don't care to compromise—children from affluent homes choose not to live in luxury—they want time to examine things thoroughly, to think about themselves. I have never met a young person who does things just for kicks—they are all searching for something, and we must realize, us old people, that we have not done so well—there is one war after another . . ."

As we moved from a small circle of interviewers to lunch—with my colleague once again upsetting a glass of scotch-and-soda, Preminger loosened up and gave some of his random views on various subjects. Here, we had a glimpse of his audacity, of the Preminger who broke the old conventions, of the Preminger who thinks for himself:

On nudity in theater and films: "If people would only realize that nudity is another kind of costume."

On the popularity of films on TV: "The television networks have failed to produce enough top-rate entertainment of their own, this is why motion pictures are the hottest commodity on TV."

On acting: "My acting career stopped at the age of twenty in Vienna. I played a few Nazis during the war, because there were no Nazis available. I did one episode of *Batman*, because my two children were fans of the show."

On directors: "All directors are great. Directors are a superior kind of people."

On Hollywood: "Hollywood is a suburb of Los Angeles—and not a very pretty suburb."

On Hollywood again: "There is no such thing as the film industry—not since 1951. Industry is something to make automobiles or shoes. Do you talk about the book industry? No. You talk about the writer and the book. The painting industry? No. You talk about Picasso."

On violence on the screen: "Our society has become so violent that movies just reflect this—does anyone really believe that the alleged assassin of Dr. Martin Luther King was sitting in prison watching TV to learn how to shoot?"

On censorship: "I have so often talked about censorship, but I will have one statement: the problem is that censorship is evil, because censorship without any doubt leads directly to totalitarian government. No dictator has even been able to live with free expression, a freedom of expression which is still great in the US."

As the luncheon ended, after a toast to the director by his long-standing Viennese friend, Dr. Leo Alexander, Preminger had one more arrow to loose. "I personally believe that the whole idea of dividing films into American films and foreign films is wrong—there are good films and there are bad films. A new group of American films, like *Star!*, *Bullitt*, and *The Killing of Sister George* couldn't be more different from one another."

He went on to mention the current public concern with violence in the film: "Motion pictures do not change society. It is an element in society which naturally has some influence, but motion pictures mostly reflect their society. People like senators and other politicians get a lot of publicity saying pictures have more sex, more violence; but that is all nonsense. Our society has gotten franker and that is reflected in films. If you look at things objectively, it is not movies who are ahead, it is society. When we were young, you wouldn't have mentioned the word "homosexuality" in mixed company. All society is freer now."

It was a pleasant return to Boston for the director who had made parts of *The Cardinal* here in 1963. That film had followed a series of successful ventures, beginning with *Anatomy of a Murder* (1959) and including *Exodus* (1960) and *Advise & Consent* (1962). One sure thing about Preminger is that his work fits no easy category. Some films, like the above, have been taken from best-selling novels; others, like *Skidoo*, are original screenplays. He continues to make about one picture a year, *Bunny Lake Is Missing* (1965) and *Hurry Sundown* (1967) immediately preceding *Skidoo*, and a project from a first novel by Marjorie Kellogg, *Tell Me That You Love Me, Junie Moon*, is already in preparation.

The luncheon was beginning to break up, as newsmen dashed back to their papers to make deadlines, and guests finished their desserts. Impeccable waiters from the Algonquin Club hovered in the background refilling coffee cups for the die-hards, and Preminger said polite good-byes to old friends and new acquaintances. Suddenly, out of the corner of his eye, Preminger saw the scotch-and-soda bearer trundling down the side of the long table on her way to speak to one of the press agents, with yet another full highball glass. Jerking forward in his seat, and swiveling his thick neck deeper into his collar, he murmured as she went past: "Will someone please disarm that woman?"

Otto Preminger on *The Dick Cavett Show*

Dick Cavett / 1969

From *The Dick Cavett Show*, New York, June 24, 1969. Courtesy of Daphne Productions / Global Imageworks.

Dick Cavett: Otto Preminger is a distinguished movie director. I never know what he does between jobs. He happens to be in New York, between engagements, and he's always in demand on talk shows. I don't know where he goes in New York, where he eats, what he does here. I've often wondered: what does Otto Preminger do when he isn't actually directing a movie? He samples sandwiches in well-known restaurants or something, I don't know; I'll find out what it is. Here is the lovable Otto "Bubbles" Preminger.

Preminger: Well, I'm glad to see you again. I want you to know that I live in New York, I vote in New York, my main office is in New York, my house is in New York, my children go to school in New York—I'm a New Yorker.

Cavett: Well, what are you doing here?

Preminger: At the moment, I'm rehearsing for my next film here. On Sunday I'm leaving here to make my next film in and around Boston.

[Light applause]

Cavett: A smattering of applause for Boston there. I *didn't* wonder what you did in New York, but I had an idea for a joke, and I couldn't get it formed in my head. Does that ever happen to you?

Preminger: I never have an idea for a joke. What is the joke?

Cavett: I never could get it; it was something to do with what you do between jobs, and I never worked it out.

Preminger: I'm rehearsing at the moment. And when I'm not actually shooting or rehearsing, I work on the script.

Cavett: Actually shooting with a camera.

Preminger: Yes, naturally.

Cavett: Well, I clear that up, because you have a reputation for being tough . . .

Preminger: But never for shooting. Sometimes for shouting, but not for shooting.

[Laughter]

That must have been the joke.

Cavett: Somehow I doubt it.

Preminger: Your modesty speaks for you. I must tell you that I have watched your shows, and they're wonderful.

Cavett: You have sat in front of a set and watched me on the screen?

Preminger: Yes, yes.

Cavett: Gee, you've stuck with me . . . you've been on here several times with me . . .

Preminger: I love to be on with you.

Cavett: And you gave Jean Seberg a second chance after she did that one movie that was such a bomb. You've stuck with all the losers, Mr. Preminger.

Preminger: It doesn't apply to you. You're a winner, a great winner.

Cavett: I hope you're right about that. Say, I saw *Stalag 17* again—you know they show it occasionally on the late show—in which you play a German or a Nazi—there is a difference . . .

Preminger: Hardly. Slightly.

[Laughter]

Cavett: Can we forward the mail with the eagles on it to you? [Laughs] I heard that on the set of that movie, it was hard for you to get out of character, because it's a very strong character that you were playing, and there were jokes that off camera, as well as on, you were the character. Is that just a slander?

Preminger: One of the oldest jokes Billy Wilder said, "I must be nice to you because I still have family in Germany."

Cavett: Billy Wilder said that originally? He may have started that.

Preminger: He said it originally.

Cavett: I read something that intrigues me about you—I was looking back over all the things you've done: this may be wrong, by the way, because it was in one of those bios that are frequently not factual . . .

Preminger: I forgive you.

Cavett: But you directed John Barrymore in *My Dear Children*?

Preminger: Yes. On the stage.

Cavett: That's amazing. That's the play right at the end of his career.

Preminger: His last play. It was a wonderful experience, not because the play was particularly good, but [because] he was one of the brightest and wisest men about the theater. He knew more about acting and about the theater than most people that I've ever met, and I've worked with many great actors. He was a wonderful man. He was just tired. At the time I worked with him, I remember

I came once to St. Louis to inspect the show—it was on the road—and the show [should have ended at] eleven o'clock p.m., but he ad-libbed until one in the morning. It was awful. He just was tired; he sat down, he didn't get up. After the show, we were in a restaurant, and he said, "Well, professor, how did you like it?" I said: "Terrible. It is beneath human dignity." Everybody thought there would be a fight. He was very quiet. And he said: "Tomorrow. Come tomorrow." And I went the next day, and he did it perfectly, like we rehearsed it—every position, every line; he knew everything. So I went to his dressing room. I said, "Jack, why don't you do this every night like this?" He said: "Bored, dear boy. Bored." You see, he was just bored. He was too bright to do the whole silly play every night the same way.

Cavett: What profession should he have gone in if he was bored with acting?

Preminger: No, he should have been an actor, but [he was bored with] the repetition . . .

Cavett: . . . of the play, yeah.

Preminger: You see, this is why many actors—in spite of the fact that the contact with the audience *is* gratifying—prefer working in films and on television, because you don't have to do it so often. If you go on doing the same thing every night . . . like, if *you* did the same show every night, it would be terrible. This way, because you don't know what your guests are going to say, there's suspense in the air. What am I going to say?

Cavett: I hate to think. [Laughs] You also worked with . . . these are sort of tragic figures: Barrymore and Marilyn Monroe. Did you make a film with Marilyn Monroe?

Preminger: I made a film called *River of No Return*. But the greatest actress I ever worked with was Laurette Taylor. I did a play with her called *Outward Bound*, and it was a terrific experience.

Cavett: Somebody should do a study of alcoholism in the theater. I believe she was also, was she not, an alcoholic?

Preminger: Yes, but she was completely cured when I did this play with her. As a matter of fact, the play was invited to play in Washington for Roosevelt's birthday; we were invited to the White House. This was a great experience, so great for her that she was tongue-tied. She had prepared maybe twenty questions to ask him, and we sat at the same table next to the president, and she couldn't open her mouth she was so excited. He was a wonderful man. It was really a wonderful experience to meet him.

Cavett: Have you seen the new book on Marilyn Monroe? I haven't read it yet.

Preminger: It was sent to me. When I started to read it, there were so many inaccuracies in it . . . They asked me for an advance blurb, and I called them and I said, "If I give you an advance blurb, you won't print it." It's very difficult with

Marilyn Monroe. She was really a very nice, poor girl, who tried very hard and was very unhappy. Whatever you read, there's so much gossip and inaccuracy that it doesn't make sense.

Cavett: Mm-hm. Do you know Tiny Tim?

Preminger: I met him several times, and I met him just now outside. He is wearing all the hair that I lost.

[Laughter]

Cavett: When he comes out here, he'll be sitting next to you—or you'll be sitting next to him—and it'll look like some weird sort of before-and-after, won't it?

Preminger: As a matter of fact, I bought today—for Liza Minnelli, who plays the lead in my film that we are rehearsing now, *Tell Me That You Love Me, Junie Moon*—a wig for one scene, and it looks exactly like Tiny Tim's hair.

Cavett: Gee, I wonder if it is. We have to pause, we'll be back.

Otto Preminger on *The Dick Cavett Show*

Dick Cavett / 1970

From *The Dick Cavett Show*, New York, July 1, 1970. Courtesy of Daphne Productions / Global Imageworks.

Dick Cavett: My first guest is without a doubt the prettiest . . . bald-headed, German-speaking film director that I know. Will you welcome, please, Otto Preminger.

[Applause]

How do you do, sir?

Preminger: I'm glad to be back, sir.

Cavett: It's nice to see you. How's your brother, Ingo?

Preminger: My brother Ingo is in Salzburg, Austria.

Cavett: And how are Groucho, Chico, and Zeppo? (Laughs)

Preminger: Groucho I saw on Park Avenue. He's getting old.

Cavett: Well, which of us isn't?

Preminger: You're not getting old. You look younger and younger.

Cavett: Well, the lift did wonders for my face.

Preminger: What lift?

Cavett: That was just a joke.

Preminger: A joke?

Cavett: That was non-Teutonic humor.

Preminger: [Laughs] If that's non-Teutonic humor, then I must say it's not very funny.

Cavett: Otto's a true friend; he'll point out when I'm not funny.

Preminger: Do you know that I am working day and night on your play? The rise-and-fall of practically nobody. You forgot.

Cavett: My play?

Preminger: Don't you remember when I was here before, I offered you a part, and you accepted it in front of twenty million viewers?

Cavett: Yeah, but I didn't take that seriously, because you find it very hard *not* to offer people parts.

Preminger: What are you talking about?

Cavett: Well, you were offering half the people in the waiting room parts, I overheard you . . .

Preminger: No, I only told Jane Fonda that I am making a film with Frank Sinatra in the middle of January, and that there is a part for her, and I'd like her to read the script. You're not in bad company with Jane Fonda.

Cavett: But you do offer people parts. I do know that you offer people things. I mean, Merv Griffin is still waiting to play the cardinal in the movie that you did . . .

[Laughter]

Preminger: No, one moment. That is not true. Merv Griffin *had* a part in *The Cardinal*, and at that time they didn't permit him to leave New York. He did a radio show at that time—it was before he did television—and they didn't permit him to do the show from Boston. I needed him in Boston. I couldn't move Boston here.

Cavett: No, that's true. Although I don't know very many people who would try, and you might. You've moved heaven and earth to get things done. Well, earth.

Preminger: Do you know that, while I am sitting here, my film is opening today? *Tell Me That You Love Me, Junie Moon.* It's right now playing at the Beekman Theatre. And I just got the reviews. Something unheard of, for me, happened: I got a good review. Four stars in the *News*—tomorrow morning, you can read it.

Cavett: It must be a typo.

[Laughter]

Preminger: I never get good reviews. People don't like me.

Cavett: Why, now, why?

Preminger: I don't know. I'm charming and nice. I do my best.

Cavett: [To the audience:] He isn't in public; he *is* charming and nice . . .

Preminger: What do you mean "in public"? Have you ever seen me in private?

Cavett: No, but I have spoke to them as has.

Preminger: Yes, who? Give me one.

Cavett: Well, various actors. This is the constant enigma of you, Otto. You come on and you're as charming as a little elfin . . .

Preminger: It's only because I played a few Nazis, everybody calls me Teutonic, and naturally I'm not Teutonic. And because I have no hair, people make fun of me and use me as a target for their jokes. Like you. I don't mind; I'm not sorry for myself. I feel very good. I'm glad to be here.

Cavett: Okay [Laughs]. I heard that you and Frank Sinatra were going into a venture.

Preminger: We're going to make a film together, after fifteen years.

Cavett: Oh, it *is* a film. I didn't know what it was, I just heard you are joining together . . .

Preminger: Last time he played in my film *The Man with the Golden Arm*. And we always wanted to find something, and we found a film. It's called *Where the Dark Streets Go*. We are going to do it together, and do it in kind of a new way, which I don't want to go into . . .

Cavett: Too boring for the average person?

Preminger: Not to them, to you. The average person might be interested. [Laughter] You are easily bored. We are going to start shooting here in New York in the middle of January. And I'm *not* offering you a part. I want to make this crystal clear.

Cavett: That's crystal clear and right off the top of your head, is it?

[Laughter]

We'll be back after this message of interest.

[Interval]

Cavett: I was talking to Mr. Preminger during the break, during which a fly landed on my head, and you were nice enough to point it out. Has it gone?

Preminger: Gone. A fly wouldn't dare to come here. [Points to his own head.] It's too slippery.

Cavett: It would be fun to see a fly skid. You were talking about people who always talk about you. I tried to defend you one night recently, on this show. I don't know if you were watching, but Rex Reed was on.

Preminger: I wasn't watching. Who is Rex Reed?

[Laughter]

Cavett: I think you've answered him. He's a film critic for *Holiday* magazine, and he had some kind of negative things to say about a recent project of yours, and yourself . . .

Preminger: Look, I believe in free expression. I like to express myself, and whoever he is, whatever he wants to say, is fine with me.

Cavett: "Whoever he is"—he says he knows you very well.

Preminger: No. He might know me very well, I don't know him.

Cavett: Do critics kind of lay for you, though? Like Judith Crist?

Preminger: I usually get bad reviews, but I don't mind. Judith Crist is not a friend of mine. She has never liked anything I have done. And I must say, when I get up sometimes in the morning and see her face on the *Today* show, I leave the room.

[Laughter]

It spoils my day just to look at these wrinkles. She looks unhappy.

Cavett: She has wrinkles?

Preminger: On my television set, she has wrinkles; I don't know about yours. She's like a field that a plow had gone through. A very unhappy-looking woman.

Cavett: Every time you come on, we have to have five people on after you to defend them.

Preminger: No, you brought it up. I didn't know that this—what is his name, Reed Rexes? I didn't know that he attacked me in my absence. He wouldn't dare when I'm around.

Cavett: Say, we have a piece of your film.

Preminger: Yes.

Cavett: I don't know why it's distributed in pieces. [Laughs] But we have a [clip] . . .

Preminger: It is not distributed in pieces, but if you get it for free you can only get a small piece. And this piece is a scene in which Liza Minnelli, who had a fight with her lover—who is played by Ken Howard—sits on a pier, and he comes and she sees him. During the scene you will see the kind of makeup . . .

Cavett: Oh, she's had a bad accident.

Preminger: She has an acid-scarred face, but believe me, when you see the film, after some time there are so many laughs that you forget that. Seriously speaking, I'd like to say this on the air: as a trooper, as an actress, as a disciplined woman, as a charming girl, and, I think, as a future great star, I have never known anybody that impressed me more than Liza Minnelli.

Cavett: That's very nice.

[. . .]

My next guest is the prettiest member of the Flying Fonda Family—it sounds like a circus act, really. She's an outspoken lady, as you may know if you've ever seen Jane Fonda. I remember when she was just a movie star. Lately she's been in the news pages, being arrested for things . . . Will you welcome Jane Fonda.

[Applause]

Preminger: I love Jane.

Cavett: Yes, you made a film together . . .

Preminger: *Hurry Sundown.*

Jane Fonda: We worked together and I love him. Contrary to many actors. [Laughs]

Cavett: So you're one of the actors who will actually make a pro-Preminger statement?

Fonda: Oh yes. I loved working with Otto.

Cavett: What is it about him that is so appealing?

Fonda: Otto is a happy person. And a charming person.

Cavett: How's the movie business treating you otherwise? Are you doing another film now?

Fonda: Not at the moment. I'm starting in a couple of weeks a picture in New York, with Donald Sutherland and Alan Pakula.

Cavett: Donald Sutherland of *M*A*S*H* fame.

Fonda: That's right, yes. He's a fine actor.

Cavett: Now listen, Jane—I've seen you on pages other than the entertainment pages lately . . .

Preminger: [To Fonda:] If you need any help, just call on me. If he wants to attack you for your [activism] . . . Because many people think that actresses should not do anything but read the parts that they are given. Actresses are citizens like anybody else, and Jane has the right to do whatever she feels like doing.

Fonda: That's right. It's very important to break through the classification . . .

Preminger: Right.

Fonda: My identity is not fulfilled by just being an actress. No one should be put into a category.

[. . .]

Cavett: Otto has to leave for his premiere. Thank you, Otto, we'll see you.

Preminger: Thank you very much.

On Joseph L. Mankiewicz

Kenneth Geist / 1972

From the Joseph L. Mankiewicz Collection © 1972, used courtesy of American Film Institute.

Otto Preminger: I came to Twentieth Century-Fox from Vienna after a three-month stay in New York, where I directed a play for Gilbert Miller, in the beginning of January 1936. I met Mankiewicz, I think, very soon after; I'm not good on dates. While we were never really very, very close friends, we always when we meet—which is to me the proof of real friendship—we just continue, even if it is after a year or two years, we just talk as though we had seen each other yesterday. He never wanted anything from me; I never wanted anything from him. Since he's not only a very good writer but also a very first-rate director, there is no way for me, for instance, to ask him to write a script for me. I think he's a brilliant man. Also, there was one connection between us: I discovered in Vienna a young actress who later came to California. Her name was Rose Stradner, and she, as you know, married Joe Mankiewicz. I liked this girl in Vienna, she was very talented, and she was very, very gay; you know, she loved life. It was very difficult for me to understand . . . I was very shocked when I learned that she had committed suicide. I feel that she must have been somehow out of her mind, because it was not in her whole nature. Instinctively, you have a feeling about some people who might be inclined to depressions that might lead to suicide, though you cannot predict it, of course. Of all the people I knew, she would be one of the least probable candidates. That's why I was very shocked. And also Chris and . . . what is the name of the other son?

Kenneth Geist: Tom.

Preminger: . . . and Tom Mankiewicz, are very bright people. I know also Mankiewicz's present wife. Mankiewicz was a very great ladies' man before he met Rose Stradner. He was married before her; I knew also his first wife. But after he divorced her, there was a time in his life when he used to go out with every star in Hollywood. If I remember right, there were two great love affairs: one was with Judy Garland, which I think was very serious, and then there was one, I think, with Joan Crawford, which was less serious, because Joan Crawford was kind of like a man: she would take a man for as long as she wants him, and would wander to another one. Those two things I remember. He was always a very attractive man. He was known for his close friendship with Louis B. Mayer; he was Louis B. Mayer's favorite for a long time. He had tremendous influence. That's how he became trusted. He was originally a writer when they met, then he became a producer, and then eventually a very, very good director.

Geist: When you say that you discovered Rose Stradner, does that mean that you signed her for the company?

Preminger: No. I had a theater in Vienna. I started in Vienna, first as an actor when I was seventeen. I was an assistant and an apprentice actor to Max Reinhardt, who at that time—with the help of a very rich man, Camillo Castiglioni—rebuilt an old theater which is still, in my opinion, the most beautiful theater in the world. It's called the Theater in der Josefstadt. Josefstadt is like Manhattan; it's one of the eight districts of Vienna. He spent a fortune. Then I left him, and I went and started, with another actor, a theater which also still exists in Vienna called Die Komödie. Then I left that, and still with another actor, we opened a very huge, popular theater. After a season and a half or two seasons, I went back to Reinhardt, now as a director. I had given up acting. And eventually, when Reinhardt withdrew, I took his place. I took the theater over. The theater was in very bad financial straits, and this man Castiglioni and I became great friends. He was also a client of my father's, who was one of the top lawyers in Vienna. While I was there, I also took over Reinhardt's school called Reinhardt's Seminar, which was a theater that the government gave him in the summer residence of the Schönbrunn. A beautiful little theater.

At any rate, that leads to Rose Stradner. When I say I discovered her, that is maybe too much. I don't remember whether she went to the school or not. I do remember that she played one part in another theater, and from this part I hired her then to this theater, the Theater [in] der Josefstadt. She worked there for me for a while. Then I think I went first to California. There was no connection between us: my going to California had nothing to do with her going to America. But I think she came after me. She had no reason to go. I left also before Hitler, but I'm Jewish. But Rose Stradner was not Jewish; she could have just as well stayed there. She had a contract with Metro [MGM], but she never made it in Hollywood.

What else can I tell you about Joe?

Geist: I was interested in his first production there with Lubitsch as producer, who took his name off the film—*Dragonwyck*.

Preminger: I don't know about it. You see, Lubitsch at a certain time stopped directing. He was really a great director. He always saw a doctor, and there were times when he couldn't direct, and then he selected somebody at Fox . . . Was Joe at Fox at that time?

Geist: Yes.

Preminger: I remember, for instance, Lubitsch had worked on a script for Tallulah Bankhead called *A Royal Scandal*. He asked me to direct it, and I directed it. We had a very good relationship. I respected him. He had a terrible hatred for Tallulah. I think it was because Lubitsch was a very erratic man in many ways. First of all, he was terribly scared after his first heart attack, which really influenced his whole life. He would, for instance, come to my house for dinner, and in the middle of dinner he would get up and ask me to take him home—he lived very close to me—because he felt [a heart attack] was coming again, but it was not true; he was just scared. And he hated Tallulah because after she was signed, he had dinner with Garbo, and he told her the story [of *A Royal Scandal*], and Garbo was willing to do the part. He went to Zanuck, and Zanuck said, "No, I'm not going to pay Tallulah $100,000 and not use her." He hated Tallulah after that.

He might have had some conflict with Joe. It's easily possible. I wouldn't necessarily blame Joe. Lubitsch had a great sense of humor and an amazing instinct for humorous situations, to twist situations for humor. But in *life*, you know, he was not that humorous. He was very—I wouldn't say opinionated, but he didn't like people . . . he felt like an elder statesman, you know, he was older than all of us and also much more famous. Lubitsch was a tremendous name; you might not appreciate it today as much as it was when he was still alive. And he might have had an argument with Joe. Joe, I think, probably wrote *Dragonwyck*, and Lubitsch might have asked for some changes and Joe didn't do it or something. And that could make Lubitsch incredibly mad. He was very passionate that way.

Geist: I wondered, whether, since you worked with Lubitsch, you ever discussed Joe, since Joe speaks of being his protégé?

Preminger: Well, I didn't know much about it. I didn't know that Joe directed *Dragonwyck*; I even forgot that Joe worked at Fox. I remember him mainly at Metro. But I remember now that he really directed only at Fox. He left Metro. This is when he had, I think, a falling-out with Louis B. Mayer. I remember that now.

Geist: So you had little contact with him, then, at Fox?

Preminger: I can't tell, you know, this is so long ago. Like everybody's life, there are periods. When I first came to California, I came with a contract to Fox. Then I had a fight with Zanuck, and I left Fox. Then I went back to Fox when Zanuck was not there. Then I made a very big hit—*Laura*—and Zanuck loved me. I saw him last night, as a matter of fact, at 21. He looks awful.

Geist: Both you and Joe came to New York at the same period.

Preminger: Well, I moved here permanently in 1951. I was always attracted to New York. I get lazy in California—the open car and the sun—and I find New

York much more stimulating. Maybe too much now, with the horrible crime and everything, it's really awful. I have two small children who, when they leave for school, I'm worried. If I give them two dollars, I say, "If somebody mugs you, just give them the money and run." It's sad, you know, it's terrible. But still I prefer to live in New York.

Geist: Did you have any involvement at this time with the friction between DeMille and Mankiewicz over the loyalty oaths, those two factions?

Preminger: That was the only time that I ever went to a meeting of the Directors Guild. You know, I am not a joiner; I hate all these things. But he invited everybody, and I went because of him, because he was attacked by DeMille, and I think I even spoke up there. The funniest thing is that of all the people, Joe was a Republican. He was always a Republican. He was never really, like many people in Hollywood, very liberal. I was always considered liberal, but I never really mixed professionally in politics. The only liberal thing that I did, I did it because I had nothing in my past that anybody could attack. Nobody could say that I was ever a member of the Communist Party or anything. So during these times, I remained friendly with men like Ring Lardner, who had worked for me and who then was fired at a story conference. We were sitting at my office and an executive said, "Mr. Zanuck would like to see Mr. Lardner." And I said, "Does he want me to come too?" I didn't know what it was about. And Lardner left and three minutes later he came back and said, "I've just been fired." I couldn't believe it, you know. I must say that later on I also learned that it was not completely without foundation: they did have an underground power base, not necessarily Communist but very leftist. I gave Dalton Trumbo credit before anybody else because I had nothing to be afraid of.

It was really foolish to attack Mankiewicz, which DeMille did, for Communist or leftist leanings, because he was always a Republican. I remember I was one of the people who spoke up [at the meeting]. Joe won overwhelmingly, because DeMille . . . I didn't know DeMille well, mainly from this incident. I don't know if the Birch Society existed then, but he was really more than a reactionary—he was a fighting reactionary.

Geist: Do you remember any of the events of that era?

Preminger: I only remember this one meeting. Mankiewicz was the president of the Screen Directors Guild, he asked everybody to be sure to come, and we gave him a great vote of confidence.

Geist: Do you have any knowledge or understanding of why a week after that resounding vote of confidence that ousted DeMille, Mankiewicz wrote a letter asking every member to sign a loyalty oath?

Preminger: That I don't remember. I don't even remember that the loyalty oath was the point. In what way?

Geist: That was what apparently started the recall against Joe.

Preminger: He didn't want to sign the loyalty oath?

Geist: He *had* signed it, because he had to as an officer of the guild. There were many members who were opposed to this open loyalty oath.

Preminger: It is very difficult today to even remember the fears and the pressures that were really rampant then. Like I told you how Ring Lardner was dismissed. To give you an example: people say that there was no blacklist. I made a contract with Twentieth Century-Fox in 1953, I think, to do an independent picture—*Carmen Jones*. I still remember how clever it was. I had complete authority over casting, writing, everything. But it said in the contract that I had to notify the legal department of Fox what writer or what actor I wanted to sign before I made a contract. The legal department—not the artistic people—had the right, without giving me any reason, to object to anybody I wanted to sign. Obviously, they couldn't legally say that they were doing this because of the blacklist; it would be against the law. But there was a blacklist, without any doubt. And maybe Joe was pressured, with this loyalty oath, to change his position.

Otto Preminger: An Interview

George E. Wellwarth and Alfred G. Brooks / 1973

From *Max Reinhardt, 1873–1973: A Centennial Festschrift of Memorial Essays and Interviews on the One Hundredth Anniversary of His Birth*, edited by George E. Wellwarth and Alfred G. Brooks. Reprinted by permission of Binghamton University Libraries' Special Collections and University Archives, Binghamton University.

Preminger: It's very difficult to imagine today what the name Max Reinhardt meant when I grew up in Vienna. Particularly to a young person as I was then, who had chosen the career of acting, which I did at a very early age—I was nine years old. When I was somewhere between sixteen and seventeen, I decided to take a decisive step. At that time, Max Reinhardt had, with the help of a very rich man named Camillo Castiglione, acquired the Theater in der Josefstadt. This is an old theater that must by now be more than two hundred years old. Reinhardt, with his great taste and his unerring instinct, was spending tremendous sums of money putting the theater into shape. He worked with a Viennese architect, whose name escapes me now, and together they did a tremendous job in redecorating and renovating the theater. He did not change its style (it's a beautiful baroque theatre); instead, he added things like a beautiful crystal chandelier with eight hundred candles—electric candles—which, at the beginning of the performance, rose to the ceiling as the candles faded and created a wonderful mood for the play. He also had the original wallpaper, which had become old and shabby, re-created in silk. The chandelier was made in Venice, the silk was woven in Belgium. Reinhardt also redecorated the so-called Sträusselsäle, where the audience could eat and enjoy themselves after the performances and during the intermissions. He had Canaletto copies on the iron curtain. It is really an incredibly beautiful theater.

I last saw the Josefstadt in the early sixties when I was in Vienna making a few scenes for *The Cardinal*. After seeing theaters all over the world, it is still, in my opinion, the most beautiful and has the greatest acoustics of any I know.

During the period that the theater was being renovated, I wrote a letter to Max Reinhardt asking for an audition. I didn't give my parents' address but asked that the answer be sent to the post office. I wanted to keep this secret from my parents, since they were not in favor of my becoming an actor. My father, who was originally the prosecuting attorney for the whole Austrian Empire and then later, during the days when the empire had disappeared, became a prominent lawyer in Vienna, felt that I, as eventually my brother did, should become a lawyer rather than an actor. My father was very understanding, but he considered the entire matter a passing whim.

Instead of going to school, I went to the post office three times a day to see if the answer had arrived. Finally, after six or seven weeks, without an answer, I gave up. Only by accident, a week later, did I go by the post office and found a letter from Max Reinhardt setting a date for me to come to his office, but the appointed day had passed. Still, I went to his office, but he had left. He had gone to Berlin or Salzburg, I forget where, and I finally had an audition with his assistant, Dr. Hock. Dr. Hock thought that I was very talented and promised to notify me when Reinhardt came back to Vienna. He did, and I auditioned for Reinhardt, and he engaged me as an apprentice actor for the first ensemble of the Schauspieler in der Josefstadt—its official title, an ensemble composed for the biggest German stars.

My first role for him was in the premiere performance in the redecorated theater. It was Goldoni's *The Servant of Two Masters*. There, I and the other apprentice actors (I think that there were between five and eight altogether) began our careers. It was a neutral set, and he didn't use the curtain. The scene changes were effected by just changing the furniture; and the furniture was changed by us young actors carrying out little tables and chairs in a dance step. Anyway, this was my beginning with Reinhardt.

I then left and became an actor in various provincial theaters in Germany and Austria. Eventually, I gave up acting, and very soon—at the age of nineteen—became a director. When I was twenty, I started a theatre in Vienna with another director. When I was twenty-two or twenty-three, I returned to Max Reinhardt's theater as a director and directed several plays which were very successful. Reinhardt eventually retired as the head of the theater, I think in 1932. He only came back once a year to direct one play. I took over the management of the theater until in 1935 I left for the United States in order to make pictures in Hollywood and to direct a few plays on Broadway.

But what I really want to say about Reinhardt is that he was truly an actor's director. He was most effective when he liked an actor, and perhaps *only* when he liked him. There were very many great actors whom he directed; and I was present, I watched when I was first in his theater, and even when I was a full-fledged director, as I felt I could learn a lot by watching Reinhardt direct. If he felt the slightest resistance in an actor, he let him go his own way. He told him a few things, of course. But, if he felt that the actor really wanted to be directed by him, then his imagination, the variety of advice, the way he worked the actor in the scene and *for* the scene, was just fantastic. Maybe it was because he was an actor originally and that's why, for instance, most of the opening nights of plays Reinhardt directed ran overly long, because he was not a play's director; he was a very good director for the play as well, of course, but this was not what he cared about. When he liked actors, he let them vary the scenes and do them in so many ways that it often became overly long. Obviously, he cut it for practical reasons after opening night.

To see Reinhardt work with people like Max Pallenberg or with his wife Helene Thimig, or with Dagny Servaes—all the actors who were really Reinhardt actors—was a delight. On the other hand, there were certain actors, great actors where the situation was different. For example, my very great friend Anton Ethofer, probably the greatest Viennese actor—he died only a few years ago. Now this man and Reinhardt had a very strange relationship of great respect for each other. But Reinhardt felt that Ethofer could not be directed in his manner because Reinhardt directed every detail, every step, every word, every breath of an actor. Ethofer gave very good performances in Reinhardt's productions, but he let him go. On the other hand, Hermann Thimig, who was one of his favorite actors, or Hans Thimig, the brothers of Mrs. Reinhardt, that was really wonderful to see, because you could learn. The great thing about Reinhardt is that he did not direct actors in one way; rather, in every possible way the scene could be played.

People ask me if I have learned from Reinhardt. Certainly. I adored him and I admired him. I did not really learn detail from him. That is to say, I did not imitate him, but nobody who watched him direct and became a director could escape his influence. I don't know anybody I have seen—to be sure, I haven't seen so many people direct before or after, because I became a director myself, and then you don't see other directors—but I cannot imagine there was ever any director like him. If you go to the other systems of directing, like the famous Stanislavski system (I never met Stanislavski), it's a different kind of analytical direction, where the director goes into the characters and explains. But Reinhardt's way of directing was a kind of very happy, Renaissance way of directing. He loved to show the actor what to do. He loved, particularly in certain plays of Shakespeare, in the play I mentioned earlier by Goldoni, the rich opportunity for actors, and while he would never permit an actor to overact, he also did not make them underact. He didn't believe in it: he wanted it *rich*. In Reinhardt's film of *A Midsummer Night's Dream*, you can also see his incredible ability at discovering talent. In this one picture, he discovered Olivia de Havilland and Mickey Rooney. Eventually, on another occasion, in a theater in New York, he discovered Gregory Peck. Reinhardt knew more about actors and about the nature of acting talent than anybody in the history of the theater.

Penthouse Interview: Otto Preminger

Jack Parks / 1973

From *Penthouse*, vol. 4, no. 5, January 1973, 52–56.
Reprinted by permission.

When, twenty years ago, the fearful words "sex" and "virgin" were actually pronounced out loud in a film comedy called *The Moon Is Blue*, the Catholic Legion of Decency rose up and pronounced it "condemned." Whether that was the reason for its success can never be known, but *The Moon Is Blue* became an instant hit, and Otto Preminger's reputation as a director was made. He went on to turn out *The Man with the Golden Arm*, *Saint Joan* (launching Jean Seberg), *Anatomy of a Murder*, *Exodus*, *Advise & Consent*, *The Cardinal*, and others. Along the way, not only the Legion of Decency but the American Legion and various other groups concerned with hoarding the nation's morals snapped at his ankles. As late as 1967, the Decency people called down fire and brimstone on the film *Hurry Sundown* for "suggestive love scenes." It was "condemned" (which is certainly a more imaginative way of putting it than the motion picture industry's flat and pallid "X" rating). Though Preminger has traded punches with many such groups, his films are really not all that controversial. True, an independent Catholic film critic, Moira Walsh, did write: "We are in Mr. Preminger's debt for the part he played in shaking the film world loose from some of its ill-considered pious assumptions." Yet many critics have accused him of mediocrity in his treatment of potential controversies ranging from sex through drugs to race and back to sex.

It is in his private life that Preminger has struck the most sparks. There was his public disclosure a few years ago that he was the father of Gypsy Rose Lee's illegitimate son (now grown up). He was named by the late J. Edgar Hoover as one of those contributing to the Black Panthers' Legal Defense Fund (and was roundly reviled). Recently he tangled with the Congress on Soviet Jewry, accusing them of irresponsibility in refusing to let activist Rabbi Meir Kahane address their meeting. Then there was the time an angry agent hit him with a waterglass in a New York night club, which is hardly worth mentioning, since that happens to all directors eventually. But Preminger appears to thrive on dissension. Asked about his penchant for getting into arguments, he smiles. "I don't know. Wherever I go, there is always something."

Preminger was born in what used to be the Austro-Hungarian Empire. His father held the rank of attorney general. Otto obtained a doctor of law degree, but he never went into practice. By the time he finished school, he was already deeply involved with the theater, first as an actor under the famed Max Reinhardt and later as a director. In 1934 Joseph Schenck, then head of Twentieth Century-Fox, brought him to America, where he did a workmanlike job but attracted no great crowds until *The Moon Is Blue*. Now, at sixty-six, he can look back on a directing record of thirty-six films and thirty-one plays. Preminger lives in New York City with his wife, Hope, and their twelve-year-old twins. This exclusive *Penthouse* interview was conducted there by Jack Parks in a room filled with some of Preminger's extensive collection of twentieth-century paintings. In person Preminger displays the sly charm, the accent, and the dislocations of English grammar familiar to millions of Americans through his frequent TV appearances.

Penthouse: Nineteen years after Julius and Ethel Rosenberg were executed under the Espionage Act of 1917, you are making a movie about them. What are you trying to say about this controversial case?

Preminger: I think that if anything the film will be an argument against the death sentence. I'm against death sentences. Why should a jury of twelve people, or a judge, have the right to say: "This man or this woman should be killed." I think this is wrong. Anyway, in the film we leave it to the audience, and that makes it also more interesting. The original title indicated this. I was going to call it *Open Question*. But it is now retitled *The Implosion Conspiracy*. "Implosion" is a term used in describing the workings of the atomic bomb. An explosion gets all the energies out. Implosion first pulls them in, and this detonates an explosion and triggers the destructive forces, which expand outward. I had the idea for the film and first asked my lawyer about whether I needed releases from living people if I based the whole film on the trial. Since the trial was public, I felt that I should not need anything. So I had dinner with an old friend of mine, Louis Nizer, who is the famous trial lawyer. I asked him, and he said: "Absolutely not. Anything in a trial record you can use." As we talked during dinner, I said: "Louie, why don't you write the screenplay?" And he said: "You're kidding." But the idea seemed so right to me. We talked about the case—he already knew something about it. Finally, after working on the trial record, which is three bound volumes, for maybe a week or two, he started to write the screenplay. And while he was writing it with me, Doubleday made him an offer to first write a book about it. So now the book is finished, and we're close to finishing the screenplay.

Penthouse: There was a 1970 stage play *Inquest*, which was also based on the Rosenberg trial.

Preminger: Yes, I saw the play in Cleveland, and then I saw the play also here. Like most of the books written about the Rosenbergs—and I read them all—this play assumes they were innocent. *We* cannot assume this. I want to leave this to the audience. I'm being very impartial. In my opinion, drama is to show both sides. I really don't have a firm conviction about whether they were innocent or not. Certainly it is not like this play describes it. If you read the trial, there's quite a lot of testimony and also circumstantial evidence that pointed to them. I mean it is not that simple, you know. I'm not going to take sides. I don't think anybody can prove today whether they were guilty or innocent. They were *found* guilty, and when you read the trial record, you are inclined to believe that they possibly were guilty. But you also feel that if they had not been executed, that is if it were possible to reopen the case, it might be proven one way or the other more conclusively.

For instance, Mrs. Rosenberg's brother confessed and told everything about himself and about them and his wife. Yet *his* wife was not even indicted, and he got away with seven years. And the Rosenbergs got executed. My French lawyer sent me a French play about it, which was quite successful, though I never heard of it before. It is called, in translation, something like "They Shouldn't Have Died." And it is incredible—so vitriolic, so anti-American. There are two FBI agents in the play who go around investigating. There was never any portrayal of the Gestapo as vicious as the way this play portrays these FBI agents. They beat the Rosenbergs in the play, and, as we know, this is not true.

Anyway, the Rosenbergs' trial did take place, and I will try to show this in the film. We will also try to show the atmosphere of the times, which we've almost forgotten. You see, during the Korean War and the McCarthy investigations, there was really such fear here. Everybody was so afraid to be suspected that people bent backwards. I think for instance that the judge bent backwards. I don't say that he was not fair, but he did everything in the world to avoid any appearance of helping them or making it easy for them, particularly because he is Jewish and they were Jewish. I remember this time very well.

Penthouse: You mean the atmosphere of the McCarthy era?

Preminger: Yes. I remember I was working with a writer in Hollywood by the name of Ring Lardner Jr. He was under contract to Twentieth Century-Fox. We were sitting in my office when my secretary called and said Mr. Zanuck, who was the head of the studio, would like to see Mr. Lardner. We were working on the same script at the time. So I said, "Does he want me to come, too?" "No," she said, "only Mr. Lardner." He left and five minutes later he came back, and said, "I was just fired." I said, "What?" Well, he *was* fired because he was one of the people suspected of being a Communist. Now, you see, there's always a grain of truth in everything. It was true that the Screen Writers Guild, at that time, was maybe not dominated by the Left, but the left liberals had a lot of power. However, they were not necessarily Communists. I asked Lardner—and this is very amusing—I said to him, "Why didn't you ever ask me? Maybe I would've wanted to join." You know they had these meetings where they recruited new people. He said: "Because we knew that you would never join." You see, in a way, I'm very independent. I was never a member of any party.

Penthouse: How did the blacklist affect you?

Preminger: Hollywood exploited these people after they went to prison. When they came out, they were still not employable. They didn't say it was a blacklist, because that's illegal. But that's what it was. Producers would go to men like Dalton Trumbo, a top writer and one of the so-called Hollywood Ten who lived in Mexico then, and gave him $1,000 for a whole script. So I gave him a fair salary, and he wrote *Exodus*. When it was finished, he had no rights, and I said to him: "I'm going to give you credit as the writer." He said, "You're crazy if you do this." I said, "You'll see." I went to lunch with Mr. Krim and Mr. Benjamin, president and chairman of the board of United Artists, and I told them what I wanted to do. The board said: We're not going to stop you. You have the right—as an independent producer—to do whatever you like. So he got credit, and nothing happened, and since then he has gotten screen credit ever since. You see, blacklisting is completely against our system and our law. Even if they were guilty, they paid for it in prison, and so they must have the right to come back and pursue their profession.

Penthouse: Does a blacklist still exist?

Preminger: No. Not anymore. It could come back, but I don't think so. You see, I could do that because I was completely clean. I wasn't even president of anything.

Penthouse: You ran into criticism from the American Legion in 1963 when you hired Ring Lardner Jr. to work on one of your screenplays.

Preminger: Yes, but Ring Lardner Jr. is now working. He did the script for *M.A.S.H*, which was very successful. Look, this is another thing. The American Legion has the right to say to their members, Don't go to see a film that Ring Lardner writes, or Dalton Trumbo. You see? Just like the Catholic Legion of Decency. I mean, I don't recognize them—I'm not Catholic—but if they tell their members not to go to see a film, I mean, that is their right. Sometimes the members go even more.

Penthouse: Then you think this type of censorship works in reverse?

Preminger: Not really. Not always. You see, in small towns it hurts, because people know each other and they don't care to be seen going. In New York, who cares? I remember when I made *The Moon Is Blue*, a very harmless little comedy, Cardinal Spellman spoke against it in St. Patrick's Cathedral. But the film did tremendous business. Whether Catholics went or not, I don't know.

Penthouse: What do you have to say about the motion picture code?

Preminger: People always mix up censorship with obscenity. If you commit an obscenity by taking your pants off on Fifth Avenue, they will arrest you. If you do the same thing in a film, they may arrest you. Censorship should really be called *pre-censorship*—when somebody tells you in advance what you may and may not do. This is against our Constitution. I feel we should fight, because if we don't protect this right of free expression, it deteriorates. If people, like our vice president, assume the right to tell commentators on television what they may and may not say, then we slowly move toward a totalitarian government. And a totalitarian government, regardless of whether it is the czars, or Stalin, or Krushchev, or Hitler, cannot coexist with free speech.

Penthouse: Do you agree with Jane Fonda?

Preminger: I don't agree with Jane Fonda. I think she goes much too far, and she's used by a few people, and she pays for all these things. But that she can go to Hanoi and then come back and say on television, "President Nixon is a traitor," is a wonderful thing. I don't agree with her, but the very fact that she *can* say it and they don't beat her up or throw her in jail, like in other countries, gives me hope. When my film *Advise & Consent* was shown in France at a retrospective of my work, students from the Sorbonne asked me questions. They could not understand how I could make this film. They could not understand that I was permitted to shoot in government buildings, and that the government never asked me to show them the script. Now, these students asked this in France, a free country, not a totalitarian one. The freedom that we have here we must preserve. I don't mind that Mr. Agnew attacks the press. He must have that right, too, as long as he has no right to stop them.

Penthouse: Could you shoot *Advise & Consent* today?

Preminger: Yes.

Penthouse: Violence in films is an issue just now, but most of your problems with film codes have been over the portrayal of sex.

Preminger: Well, I will tell you something. I think that sex is healthy. I don't think that any child will be spoiled by seeing sex, or by having sex explained, as early as possible. We explained sex to our children as early as possible, when they were seven or eight years old, and whatever questions they ask we answer. It is old-fashioned to keep sex a secret. But violence, when shown to an immature mind and usually executed in films by stars whom these young people adore, unfortunately, invites imitation. If they see hitting and killing and the like, it is bad. So I am against it, and I don't use it. I would not tell other people not to do it, because I am still not for censorship, but, don't misunderstand me, I do personally think that too much violence is bad. I was in Spain many years ago, and some motion picture representative there introduced me to a beautiful young Spanish actress. She was so shy she wouldn't open her mouth. She was a sweet little girl. Now I wanted to see a bullfight—the only time in my life—and I went with her. Suddenly this shy little girl jumped up on the bench next to me and started to shout! I think that any kind of fight where people hurt each other is unnecessary. I don't think that our civilization or any civilization needs this.

Penthouse: It was reported last year that the Rosenberg film, *The Implosion Conspiracy*, would be presented for an exclusive first showing on network television. Will that happen?

Preminger: No. I had an offer from television, but then, you know, when I talked to ABC—and this is very amusing—they said that I can't mention the names of the Rosenbergs. I said: "Why not?" And now you will hear why! If I mention their names, they said, then this department that made me the offer—which is called Circle Films—cannot handle it. It would have to be handled by the current events and news department. And so instead of waiting for all this bureaucracy, I called my very good friend Leonard Goldenson and said, "Let's forget the whole thing and make it into a picture for theaters, and then maybe I'll sell it to television."

Penthouse: You've had difficulties in the past with showing your films on television.

Preminger: Well, for instance, I had a lawsuit against Columbia at one point, because they sold *Anatomy of a Murder* and made it a leader, as they call it, of a package. They sold it to 105 stations without protecting it against cutting. I did not quite win my suit. The judge said, in spite of the fact that my contract gives me final cut, that final cut is only for the theaters. The judge said that it's customary to make cuts—small cuts. He said that they have the right to make minor cuts. *But*, as he did not define minor cuts, nobody ever cut it. It was played uncut, as most of my films were. Because they're scared. But when I sell my own pictures, I make a contract that says that they cannot cut anything—not one line—and it also says that I determine in advance the number and the places where they can insert commercials, and only two commercials at a time, because usually they have four commercials at a time. They figure now that they make commercials much better than we make films. Yet really the networks, particularly, have learned that they only lose by it. Because in order to sell, you want to give your audience pleasure. Right? Now if there are too many commercials, they make the audience impatient. If you disturb the viewer, then you hurt yourself. So they're not really tough about it, and I don't have trouble. You must permit commercials if you want money; if I gave them the film free, it would be different.

Penthouse: Are you in favor of pay-TV?

Preminger: Absolutely. I think in our competitive, capitalistic society, people should pay for everything. It is an illusion to say, or believe, that you don't pay when you turn on your television set, because they advertise, say, aspirin, and when you buy it you pay for it. The advertisers pay only indirectly. Wouldn't it be much fairer if you sold the film itself, and the customers paid, directly? And it would be a tremendous market. Right now, a TV film maker gets only a small part, but make a film that interests, let's say, four million people, and each of them pays $1.00, then you can in one night gross $4,000,000. Naturally, you would have to pay the network. You know, any show that is being seen by 12 million—15, 16, 40 million people—that would make a great deal. I feel that television, because of these various obstacles and limitations, has never reached its potential. It's a tremendous medium, much greater than theaters or anything.

Penthouse: But doesn't the small size of the TV screen do harm to many productions?

Preminger: I don't know if you remember, but when television started, there was one particular television set which could project on the wall a film in any size you wanted. This will come back again, and eventually you will be able to show television as large as you want. It doesn't have to be in a small box. You can project it from the box. And the possibilities for specials . . . you could do ballet and opera for television. You might spend a million dollars on a ballet, and that's a lot of money. But it would easily come back, and it could be played over and over again. I think that there are unlimited possibilities. It's very similar to the way motion pictures were produced by six or seven or eight major companies with one boss to each company. His word counted. He decided what picture you could make, who directed, who acted, etc. But they couldn't keep this up, and they had to go to independent producers where the producer could devote himself to one project with all his talent for maybe twelve or eighteen months. The same thing will happen on television. Now there is one boss at NBC, for the films, and one at CBS, and at ABC. And they say: "You do this and you do that." And they always take the easy way out, and they say, "We don't spend more than $750,000 for a film." If free competition sets in, that will all change.

Penthouse: Has this lack of free competition hurt television in other ways?

Preminger: Yes. It's difficult for young people to get in. But even forgetting that, the very fact that these three networks—perhaps there's four with the Westinghouse Network—decide what two out of three Americans can see on television is unfair. They already have difficulties and they go to independent producers. Only they don't give them the same freedom as theatrical film producers do. TV hasn't the same freedom yet as the movies have. But it will come. And if it can be done on pay-television, it will be terrific. You take a risk. If you make something bad, you lose your money. But if you make something good, you can make a lot of money—which is our way of life.

Penthouse: Did you find any of the old-time movie moguls helpful? Did you learn from them?

Preminger: Well, I think that Zanuck—with whom I've had many run-ins and fights, and sometimes he threw me out, though we are good friends now—was a terrific executive. He was a picture maker *and* an executive. But it's difficult to say you learn something—you learn from everything. You also learn negatively. When I see an approach that I don't like, I learn. But I can't say I learned *from* so-and-so. Naturally, when I see a film, I learn from the director whether I like it or not, because I see things that I like and I don't like, and probably, without imitating it, I will pick up some elements and I will reject some.

Penthouse: John Ford has said that he had to make two mediocre films for every film he really desired to make in order to get along with the studio. Have you found this to be true?

Preminger: I don't know. I often, you know, don't understand why I made a picture. When I make it, I really make it only because I want to. Even when I was under contract with Fox, it happened a few times. For instance, I remember they had already started *Forever Amber*, and they were shooting for two months, and Zanuck invited me to Palm Springs to his house for the weekend. The first thing at breakfast, he said, "You've got to take over." He had hired the new cast, and he had a new script, which was also written by Ring Lardner. I didn't want to do it. I said, "Look, I read the book, you know, and I wrote you a report." And he said: "You are a member of a team, and you've got to do it. I need it. I won't hold it against you. You can't say no." Even so, I always find something in my work that I love—I'm never disinterested. I think Ford is so much older than I, and he is basically a director, you know, not a producer. So maybe that is what is different. But he is a wonderful director. I don't know Ford that well. I have met him a few times. We have a different way of life. He lives on a boat; I live on the ground.

Penthouse: You seem to borrow your stories from other media, especially from novels. Why?

Preminger: A novel is a richer material, you see. In a novel you can select, and the characters are worked out. But some of my other material has come from plays, and some is original. I am preparing a film in Israel called *Genesis '48*, based on a book by an American newspaperman named Dan Kurtzman. This concerns the first Arab-Israeli war, the War of Independence in 1948. I'm also preparing another one, the story of a famous Canadian surgeon, Dr. Norman Bethune. Few people in America have heard of him, but in Canada everybody knows his name. I'm waiting now for my visa to go to China, because in the last year and a half of Dr. Bethune's life, he helped the Chinese. He set up blood banks for them in the war against the Japanese, and he got infected during an operation because he didn't have gloves. He died in 1939 at the age of forty-nine. He was a fabulous man, in every way. Also his love life was interesting. He married the same woman twice and divorced her, twice. Wherever he went, women were after him. It's an ideal motion picture story. The truth.

Penthouse: Will you be shooting it in China?

Preminger: I will shoot it in Canada, and I'll *try* to get permission to shoot it in China. But it's slow. They didn't say no, but they also didn't say yes. I even talked at one time to a cameraman who was in China with Mr. Nixon and Mr. Kissinger. This cameraman came to me when he heard about this project. He became so friendly with the Chinese that he has a permanent visa to go back and forth. He was in Washington, and he arranged a three-way conversation. He talked to the director of information in Peking. The man in Peking speaks English better than I do, but when it was all finished, he had said the same thing as the man at the embassy and the ambassador to the United Nations. He said to apply for my visa right away. You have to have patience. They don't move as fast as we do.

Penthouse: What is your attitude to changing a novel's plot for filming?

Preminger: I don't feel that I have any obligation to keep faithful to the story. The writer has consented to sell, and my buying the novel implies that the writer gives up the rights and I acquire them. It then has to filter through my brain, and it becomes my way, you know, and not the writer's way. Sometimes the writer doesn't want it this way, and I have been attacked for my most successful pictures by writers. About *The Man with the Golden Arm*, for instance, the writer complained that he didn't get enough money, and Leon Uris made statements that I ruined his *Exodus*. The truth is that he wrote a bad screenplay, and I threw it out. I paid him. But it hurt his vanity. However, those things are part of life.

Penthouse: The last stage play you did was in 1960—*Critic's Choice* with Henry Fonda. If you enjoy the live stage, why has it been so long since you last directed?

Preminger: Because it is very difficult for me to find plays I like. But now I am preparing a musical which I will direct and produce. I just acquired the rights—for Broadway—on my film *Man with the Golden Arm*. I don't even have a composer. But I think that today the theme of drug addiction lends itself very well to a serious musical. It's also a love story, you know.

Penthouse: Have *you* ever taken drugs?

Preminger: One time, when I prepared a film on drugs, I talked first to a doctor who wrote a famous book about psychedelic drugs. He told me that if I wanted to try LSD, he would give it to me if I felt reasonably balanced. His theory is that it brings out only things that are really in you. But I didn't take it. Then one evening, Timothy Leary was in my house for dinner together with some others, and after dinner we were sitting in my projection room, where I was supposed to show them a film. I saw one of my guests, a young lady, take a pill, break it in half, give half to Leary, and eat the other half herself. I said, "What is this?" She said, "LSD." And I said, "I want to try it, too." So they gave me a pill. And something very funny happened. Leary asked my wife to bring him a candle. He wanted to be my guru. He looked at the candle and looked at me and started to talk. And then he dropped the candle. Now, there's one thing I'm scared of, and that is fire. I live in a private house, a brownstone with several floors, and I have a fire extinguisher on every floor. When he dropped the candle, the LSD was just starting to take hold of me. I said, "Please leave." But my wife, who knew by this time that I had taken LSD, asked him to stay because she was scared of what might happen. I said, "No, I will only have peace if you leave," and I took him to the door and let them out. Then I went to bed and had a very pleasant experience. Across from my bed I have a huge drawing. It is as big as a door. It is a drawing by Degas of a woman, and you see her back as she bends over a basin and washes her hair. As I looked, I suddenly saw every bone in her back. You know, the whole spine. But I said to myself—and remember this because to me this is the most characteristic thing about this LSD—I said to myself: "I only see this because I took LSD. It is not really there. I can see it only because Degas was a great painter and even though he didn't paint in the spine, the anatomy is right." It was very pleasant. My wife appeared very, very small, very suddenly. I told her, "You are so little, so charming." I talked most of the night, according to my wife, and she was scared. But nothing happened. When I woke next day I said to my wife: "You had better call the office. I have an eleven o'clock appointment. You must cancel it because I won't be able to go." It does not block out awareness. On the contrary, somehow you become brighter, more aware. My wife said, "We cancelled this long ago, because it is now four o'clock in the afternoon." That was the only thing bad. Time had gone by faster. The whole thing lasted eighteen hours. Then it was gone, and I was completely normal. I would never take it again or want to. I took it really as an experiment.

And also, I don't smoke. I tried pot, with two friends in California, two famous directors who were smoking pot. I tried it but I can't smoke, you see. It only burned me here, in my chest. Then somebody brought me some marijuana cookies here in the office, and unfortunately I ate three. When I went home I started to get all dizzy, but that was all. I would never take it again. I don't need it. Apart from the dangers, I am against this whole system. I think to make narcotics a crime only helps the real criminal. If we treated it as an illness, doctors would be able to give their patients enough methadone or heroin to take them off. And heroin would not be so difficult to get and so expensive. Then all the pushers, the criminals who go to the park and give it to children so they get hooked and have to buy it, they would be out of business. Practically every doctor tells us that pot is not dangerous and is not as bad as alcohol, yet there are states where you can have thirty years in prison for the possession of it. This is crazy. We never learn. This is worse than Prohibition. But I think it is changing.

Penthouse: Living in New York, far from Hollywood, do you feel isolated?

Preminger: No. You see you don't need Hollywood. I moved to New York in 1951. It's a question of personality. I love it there in Hollywood, but I also get lazy. That open car, and the sun. But I don't find the same stimulation. It might be only in my imagination, but when I walk on Fifth Avenue, I feel life is going. On Wilshire Boulevard all seems placid and slow. Also I think it is good not to be only with people in the same business. I have enough friends in the theater, but I also meet doctors and lawyers and everybody. I feel that New York is, has been for a long time, and will be for a long time, the center of the world. I'm worried about New York like a father or a brother is, because of the violence. You know I have twins who are twelve years old. Every day they go to school, and I am worried because of what you hear and read. The fact that I don't dare to go when it is dark to Central Park is sad. You cannot tell me that if they employed five hundred more policemen that they couldn't make Central Park and the nights safe. I said this to our mayor once. People laugh at me and say it's a dream. Why? Why shouldn't it be possible to have a few hundred more policemen and keep the city safe. But I still love New York. From the moment I arrived, I fell in love with it.

I must stop. If I tell you all this, I won't have anything to write in my autobiography.

Penthouse: Mr. Preminger, thank you.

Interview with Otto Preminger

Robert Porfirio / 1975

Preminger: I must tell you, quite frankly, that people ask me frequently if I have a style, and my answer is always, when I'm dead I hope some people are interested enough in my films to examine this. I personally don't look at my films from that point of view. I don't think of my old films. As a matter of fact, I usually forget them after I've seen them, once, twice, maybe thrice with an audience, which is an additional thrill. I go on to my next film because I can never make new films if I would always think of the old ones. I leave it to other people to judge them. In my opinion, the trouble with film schools in the United States is we do not have a film school. We have at the various colleges and universities film departments, and these film departments are usually run by people who have never made a film, who can talk about it from having seen films, from having read about films, from having listened to theories like that which you have just explained to me about film noir, but to teach film, we have no school. I was in 1962 in Moscow, and I was the guest of the Russian filmmakers, the Union of Russian Filmmakers. And among other things, I saw their school. It was the only thing that really impressed me tremendously. They had an academy of film where they had at that time about eight hundred students, and the teachers. At this academy were or are the foremost directors, actors, cameramen, who between film assignments go there and teach, so that the young people can really learn from masters the craft of film, and how to make films.

The other thing that you tell me about my old films, about other films, you see I know and I admire Fritz Lang and Hitchcock, but I don't really see much similarity between them and myself. For instance, if you take *Laura*, which was my first successful film: while Hitchcock has a brilliant technique to create suspense, I still remember that for much of *Laura* I deliberately told the story very simply. I didn't use any tricks, any suspense tricks that would make it so.

If I have a style, you can only find it out once I'm dead if someone is interested enough; somebody like you who studies style, he might look at somebody's pictures and might find something that all my pictures visually have in common, and that might then be called a style. By the way, you can't develop a style. I don't think that most of the great painters who certainly have style deliberately had a style.

Whoever you want to take, Miro, for instance. People talk about Miro paintings and very often they say, like children's play. But when you really look at them, there is an incredible vision and style in it. But he doesn't do it deliberately. You see if you try to develop a style, then some horrible thing happens like this wallpaper, that we look at here, in this hotel. This man who designed it probably thought he had a style. Now I don't say necessarily that I'm right, this is my personal attitude about these things, and maybe I'm completely wrong. But for me personally, the idea that I would always shoot from right to left or move the camera in a certain way or shoot from up-down, or from down-up in order to create, this is not style.

Porfirio: You mentioned trying to avoid a great deal of camera gimmicks or trickery. Let me ask you, then, what you think are some of the important influences on you as a filmmaker?

Preminger: I have no idea. You see, I live and probably every film I see influences me one way or another. And I have this judgment that there have been these very successful films which I didn't like at all, and less successful films that I liked very much. I am a great admirer of Hitchcock, and mainly because Hitchcock, too, you can't say that he has a style. Oh, sure he has a style, but a deliberate style he hasn't. In every picture he tries new things, you see, no Hitchcock picture is like another. He takes risks, you see. Hitchcock, you're probably not aware, has made many unsuccessful pictures, and there's also something about him which I like very much, a complete lack of pomposity. He has a humorous attitude about everything, including himself, which you can see, when you know him. I don't know him very well, but we used to meet when I lived out here, and he's a wonderful man. A great sense of humor, and he has a sense of humor about himself too. He's not pompous. While I adore Fritz Lang, and he was a very good friend of mine, Fritz Lang has this thing that you could call Germanic, to take himself and his work and everything he has done and his schooling very seriously. Maybe a little too seriously. That is not a mistake, that is fine, that is his character. But his character hasn't got that lightness or that humor that Hitchcock has. Now, you see, Hitchcock is aware, and I hope I always will be aware, that making a film, as important as it is to me, is not really an earth-shaking event. And that good or bad, it won't change anything really in the world. You see, I believe for instance, and I wish it were different, but people accuse films of having ruined the morality of people, and that there's too much sex and too much violence, and they have accused the films as though the films have created the violence or the sex. They forget that this is only a reflection of our times. The violence and the sex, the openness, the frankness about sex is something that we have. Now, I think that this frankness about sex is very good. You see, I don't think sex is something that you should make secrets about, and I am very much against excessive violence. You will not find in my films that if somebody stabs somebody, that suddenly two hundred liters of blood flood out.

Porfirio: You don't like the movies of Sam Peckinpah, then?

Preminger: No. Because it isn't true, you know, what you see on screen, it isn't true. I think he's a good director, but you see, his trademark, he likes that exaggeration. I do believe that this is the only point where films can have a bad influence on young people. I don't think it's bad for young people to see sex; sex is a very healthy thing. And to know about sex. I saw *Chinatown*, a very good film, by the way, and also a very good director. But it was very violent, and unnecessarily violent. It is not necessary.

Porfirio: *Chinatown* was an attempt to recapture film noir; an important aspect of that is the private eye, who comes out of the tradition of Dashiel Hammett, Sam Spade, Philip Marlowe, etc.

Preminger: You are a historian of film, and I am not. So you call it film noir if you want, fine. I think that [Roman] Polanski, all his films, including *Chinatown*, have a certain thing in common. They are rather violent, and strong. I liked the film very much. But we speak about style. Now, will you tell me if you saw scenes from various films, if I showed you fifty scenes, from various films, from various directors—not enough that you would be able to tell what film it is—would you really be able to say that this is a Hitchcock film, this is a Polanski film, this is a film by Fritz Lang?

Porfirio: I'm not sure that I could, although I have met people who have done that, at least with directors that have a pronounced style, like Max Ophuls, who tended to use certain camera moves.

Preminger: Ophuls is a typical director like the one that I told you. He tried to create something which he thought was a style, and you can't create a style. Either you have it and it comes out of nature. He tried to move the camera in such a manner that people superficially looking at it would say, "Ah." And you would also recognize an Ophuls film, probably, if you saw them all, because he did this.

Porfirio: Von Sternberg often did his own photography, and he certainly had a visual style, particularly in the films with Marlene Dietrich.

Preminger: No, no, they were not effective. I think that von Sternberg was a very good director, but he didn't quite fulfil himself because of Dietrich. You see,

I try always to have new people. It is very easy, you see. I made the first picture with George C. Scott, *Anatomy of a Murder*. We loved each other, we worked very well together, and if I had wanted, I could have put him under contract and made ten successful pictures with him, because he's a really first-rate actor. But I tried to avoid it. Because you see, this marriage between a star like Marlene Dietrich and a director like Sternberg, there stands the question: who is stronger? And because of her looks and because she was stronger, she made him do things. He did things because of her, which stopped his development, as an independent director, if he had made pictures with other people. And he was a very unhappy man, and partly because of that. Because he was one of the people that felt that people didn't give him enough credit. That disgusted him about it. I said, "What do you care, you have enough to eat, you make a lot of money, why do you worry about what people think of you?" You see, this is one of the first things that a man, no matter what his profession is, should learn. To only satisfy himself with his work, and not other people. I'm very happy that other people like my films. But to work for them, to try hard for it, to be unhappy if they don't, it's very dangerous.

Porfirio: You're saying you can't make a film for the critics, but you do try to make a film that's successful in the marketplace, right?

Preminger: It has to be a success, of course, but I also can't think like that. I must tell you that maybe this accounts for many of my failures. I am not able to select a story because I feel this story has elements of sex, a little element of violence, and love, and a beautiful woman star, and a strong male star, so it will be a success. I can only do a story because it excites me, because I find it exciting, and then I try to project through the screen this excitement on the public, on the audience. Sometimes I succeed and sometimes they don't agree with me. But it is only an all-around question. I mean the picture is finished. Look, the film that I just finished, I had a preview of it, I have the final cut, and everything. I still cannot tell if people will like the film, whether people will go and see it, and nobody can. The people who tell you it will be a great success are only guessing, and the people who tell you it won't be a success are only guessing, and it is always colored by their own interests.

Porfirio: Is there a type of thing that draws you toward one book or some type of material over another?

Preminger: Also, this has to do with the different time of your life. I mean, I am not sure that today I would read the story of *Laura*, which I liked very much and I practically forced Darryl Zanuck to buy, that I would get that excited about it. At that time it worked very well for me. You grow, you get older, you develop.

Porfirio: But you could have kept making more versions of *Laura*. You mentioned the director who could wed himself to the star, a director could wed himself to the same story, too.

Preminger: That's exactly what I try to avoid. That is why I like Hitchcock so much, because if you look at the stories, they are all different. They might all be the same genre, suspense-thrillers, but they are all different.

Porfirio: Let me ask you about expressionism, when it is applied to film. Do you think that by the control of mise-en-scène, settings or light and shadow, you reveal a state of mind?

Preminger: There is one picture that I remember, *The Cabinet of Dr. Caligari*. Now there you could say that this movie had deliberately created an expressionistic style. But otherwise it's very seldom, because basically the camera demands realism. For instance, in this film that I saw, *Earthquake*. In this picture, you see, the picture is really, up to the point where the special effects start, unbelievably bad. It is badly written, badly acted, but when the special effects start, the sound, you really have the feeling you're in the middle of an earthquake. But then this is several times interrupted during the earthquake when you see that these buildings that you see collapse are badly made sets. That disturbs you, because the camera wants, basically, to see realism. This is, for instance, why I make all my films not in sets but in real places, where the story takes place. There's not one set in my last film. Good or bad, but it's real. It is really an office.

It's an absolutely realistic medium. And I think that the more real you can make the film, the more people will believe it, because the camera, it is photography, it is not painting. You see, when you paint you make things expressionistic, or impressionistic, or whatever you want. But when you shoot with a camera, then it must be real. Photography is real. What is photography? It is a completely real picture of reality.

Porfirio: Let me bring you back to your own personal experience, because I think this is an interesting avenue to pursue. You started as an actor with Max Reinhardt, at the Reinhardt Theater, with an impresario who was renowned, at least in histories, for bringing expressionism to the stage.

Preminger: This is nonsense. What are you talking about? Where did he bring expressionism?

Porfirio: During World War I, when the sets couldn't be grandiose, so he began to throw certain lights onto the stage so that actors would walk in and out.

Preminger: Who told you this nonsense?

Porfirio: It's in most books on German theater.

Preminger: Well, that's nonsense. That has nothing to do with the sets. He had various ways, if anything it was impressionistic, not expressionistic. When he did the *Midsummer Night's Dream*, he used perfume to make it smell like perfume, like the woods, and he was very realistic, he was really not a director for plays so much, but probably the greatest director ever for working with actors, when an actor accepted him, when an actor wanted to be directed by him.

I learned by watching, and then I was his assistant, and took over his theater. But you see it is also wrong if you try to mix up films and the stage. Because as great as Reinhardt was on the stage, he never could make it in film. Because he didn't understand the medium. When he tried to make a film, it became photographed theater. You see, when you feel the theater, when actors act right in the theater, then the camera doesn't accept it. Laurence Olivier is one of the greatest actors ever. That is, in the theater. He is, or at least he was when he was younger, a very, very handsome man. He played more leading parts, he never became a star of films. He never became the man with whom audiences identified or against whom audiences identified. He never became a star like Gable, or a star like Bogart. Never. And he knows it. I made a film with him, and he knows all this that I tell you now, but he can't help it. Because the greatest actors of the stage develop a style, that is their personality. On the other hand, the film actor has the camera photograph his or her personality. I made a picture [*River of No Return*] with Marilyn Monroe; now, she was very ambitious, she wanted to be an actress, but she wasn't. The thing that you got from her was this personality that called for mothering, for protecting. It was not sexy, she was not sexy. It's all nonsense. She was a very poor little girl, and people felt that and identified with her, and wanted to protect her and to help her. But it was there. It was she. She couldn't act it. She couldn't act from here to the door. I don't say that against her. She was a very great star.

I made a film with Gary Cooper [*The Court-Martial of Billy Mitchell*]. Gary Cooper had this personality, but he was a wonderful actor. Everything that he did, he did deliberately. He knew what he was doing. That slow talk, that looking down, that was all deliberate. But he had this personality, also, you know, that at least exuded realism and reality. But he was also a very good actor. See, he was not like Marilyn Monroe. I made a film with him, and he was a very good friend of mine. On the other hand, I made a film, the last film, with Charles Laughton. And Charles Laughton was a great actor. And as a character actor he was so great that people even believed him. Because the characters that he played were kind of theatrical, and the way he studied them, you know, he played a southerner in my film *Advise & Consent*, and he went to a real southerner, and he took his part and he said, will you read a part with me? And he taped it, because he wanted to get used to really effortlessly being able to talk with a southern accent, and he did. You see, there are two things, in other words, you can be a great actor and still be a star if you really know how to handle it. But you can also be a star without being able to do that.

Porfirio: Do you think there was a marked change or movement in the mid-1940s, where people wanted, even though it might be more expensive, to leave studios?

Preminger: The change started first of all by the fact that film became more sensitive. There was a time when you could not shoot a room like this unless you had no ceiling and you had big lights up there. Now you don't need this. You can just have two lights here and it is enough. Because film is more sensitive. I mean, I like to shoot only in real places; in twelve years I haven't had a set, except, for instance, I had a set in *The Cardinal* where I needed a projection room, I had to have a projection room in order to project. But it was my only set.

Porfirio: But so much location work does seem to be done now, do you think the audiences have changed?

Preminger: No, the directors have changed. Sure they've learned. It's much better. You look at these old pictures that you admire so much. What you call expressionism are lousy sets.

Porfirio: The backdrops and so on.

Preminger: Hitchcock uses a lot of locations; at that time it was unheard of. He did *Lifeboat* mostly outside on location. He did not use back projection except for a few places where he needed close-ups, etc.

Porfirio: Once again, maybe I'm relying too much on histories of the era, but the usual assertion is that location work was easier and created a higher degree of realism after the war. Do you think that technological developments during World War II had . . . ?

Preminger: That's nothing to do with it. It's just that it happened then, but I don't think the war had anything to do with it. It has to do with the fact that film became more sensitive. You must realize that in the beginning, for instance, of color film you needed so much light to shoot in color. This was also one of the reasons that you shot back projection. Outside, you know, it was dark in the street.

Porfirio: How about the new, lighter cameras that were manufactured? The Mitchell was a pretty heavy camera . . .

Preminger: People still use big cameras. Sure, it is better to have light equipment. There is now a camera that you can lift with one hand. I used it in my last film. It is called the Panaflex. But I mean, those are things that you would discuss with me whether it is better to write with a blue fountain pen or a black fountain pen. We are not covering or discussing or bringing up the real questions of filmmaking. You are talking like a man who is interested in manufacturing cameras, or lights, or films, or sets. That is all not important.

I am not doing the interviewing, but when you speak about film noir, why are you interested in lumping people together? I feel very honored to be mentioned in the same breath as Fritz Lang or Hitchcock; but as I said I don't think we had anything in common.

Porfirio: Well, besides being entertainment, movies are cultural artifacts; and when you look at them over a period of time certain tendencies of style or story emerge.

Preminger: Okay, that may be. But I don't think of myself as a small page in history. Maybe this is why it sounds funny.

Porfirio: I think your comments were pertinent, in any case.

Preminger: I hope they were. You will have a much better time with Fritz Lang. Give him my best.

OTTOcratic PREMINGER

Vincent Firth / 1975

From *Film Review*, vol. 25, no. 6, June 1975, 26–27. Reprinted by permission of *Film Review* magazine, FilmReviewOnline.com

On my way to meet Otto Preminger, I couldn't help wondering what sort of mood I might find him in—argumentative? aggressive? even explosive? In the event, it was a charming cultured man who welcomed me to his suite at the Dorchester Hotel, where he always stays when he visits London. "They look after me very well here," he confided. "They always manage to give me this suite, and they always remember my likes and dislikes without ever making a mistake." Mr. Preminger will certainly appreciate that, for he has been a stickler for efficiency in every film he has made. In fact it has been his endless search for perfection that has often caused a rumpus on the set either with the actors, the technicians, or both. We each chose a Coke out of his fridge and settled down to chat.

"Are you tired of journalists asking you if you are tired of people asking you if all the stories about your belligerency with actors are true?" I began. He laughed outright and then his mobile, expressive features assumed a look of innocent surprise that would have done credit to the late Fernandel.

"I am never actually belligerent," he said. "True we have—er—differences of opinion sometimes, though not very often. After all, it's a director's job to direct and that's what I try to do—without belligerency."

He finished with a deprecating gesture that signaled I should get no more out of him on that tack, so I turned to his current film, *Rosebud*. The basic plot centers on the kidnapping of five pretty girls from wealthy families who are then held hostage by a unit of the Palestine Liberation Army. I asked him if he hadn't been a little apprehensive about tackling a subject which is so potentially explosive in view of the present tense situation in the Middle East.

"Not at all," he answered with another grimace of innocence. "Why should I? It is all in the book, and I have simply translated to the screen what the two authors had written in their book."

I remarked on what I considered to be an excellent screenplay for *Rosebud* which had been written by Erik Lee Preminger, Otto's son by the famous Gypsy Rose Lee. This pleased him very much, as he is a great family man.

"I was very proud of Erik when he put that screenplay into my hands," he said. "It was a shooting script that made my work very much easier. Erik had previously been my story scout and casting director, but I think he will be concentrating on writing in the future."

I also congratulated him on the exciting, colorful locations in *Rosebud*, which he assured me were all authentic, from Corsica to Nepal. I asked him how he had fared with the two British stars, Peter O'Toole and Richard Attenborough.

"Peter is a first-class professional, and he and I got on wonderfully well together. I am completely satisfied with his performance, and I am convinced we couldn't have found a better actor for the part. As for Dickie Attenborough, I don't think it's possible to meet a more charming fellow—but of course you know all about that yourself."

I certainly agreed that the majority of film writers put Richard among the top three "gentlemen of the screen." Just then a fresh-faced youth of thirteen came in to say that O.P. was wanted on the phone.

"This is my son Mark," said his father proudly, as he introduced us. Later on he told me that neither Mark nor his twin sister Victoria intended following him into films, Mark being keen to be a doctor, while Victoria seems set on reading law and also doing some writing. Leaving aside *Rosebud*, I asked him if any one of his films had pleased him more than the others—if there was one, for example, that he'd like to be remembered for.

"No," he answered simply. "Each of my films—the unsuccessful no less than the successful—was at the time I made it an important part of my life. I lived with it, worked on it, met stars and technicians perhaps for the first time, made new friends, strengthened older friendships. So you see I can't sort one or two out and say these are the best, because I know I would be unfair to the others."

I asked him about some of the stars with whom he has worked during his long career in films (he's been making films since 1932), and he certainly appears to have kept on friendly terms with most of them in spite of rumors to the contrary. He spoke in glowing terms of James Stewart and Lee Remick (he directed them both in *Anatomy of a Murder*) and Henry Fonda, the mention of whom prompted me to ask him what he thought of Henry's daughter Jane, who starred in Preminger's *Hurry Sundown*.

"Jane has an enormous talent as an actress," he said. "But more than that she has a rich personality, which makes her a most interesting girl to talk to. I like her very much, as indeed most people do who really know her."

Speaking of *Hurry Sundown* naturally brought us to Jane's costar Michael Caine, for whom Otto has both a liking and a respect. Willi Frischauer in his "unauthorized biography" of Preminger recounts the story of Caine telling the press that "O.P. is only happy if everybody else is miserable. Still, if you can keep his paranoia from beating you down, you can learn a lot from the guy." Frischauer says that when Michael read in cold print what he might or might not have said to the press, he penned a cable to Preminger: "Dear Otto, I have looked the word up in the dictionary. Paranoiac you are not."

"Michael and I soon got to understand each other," he laughed. "He's an actor of both power and style. I hope we'll make another picture together one day."

I asked him how he'd coped with those two superstars, John Wayne and Kirk Douglas, who costarred in his famous war film, *In Harm's Way*.

"There were no difficulties at all," he replied. "Duke and I shook hands on a 'No Politics' compact, and both of us observed it to the letter. With Kirk there was never any problem." John Wayne is, of course, well known for his right-wing views, which he never tries to conceal. Kirk Douglas, on the other hand, is liberal in outlook like Preminger himself.

He gave me to understand that all was sweetness and light 'twixt himself and Frank Sinatra when they made *The Man with the Golden Arm*. Each knew the explosive potential of the other, and they were careful not to provoke each other. Preminger did not deny that Sinatra teased him by calling him Ludwig (O.P.'s long-discarded middle name), nor that he retaliated by calling Sinatra Anatole. One day Sinatra said to the director, "Ludwig, if I were you, I'd fire that cameraman. He's no good." "Anatole," replied Preminger, "when you're a producer you can do as you please, but on my pictures I do the hiring and firing." The cameraman stayed and Ludwig and Anatole remain friends to this day.

When I mentioned censorship I touched him on a very raw nerve. "As you know, I have had several fights with censors," he said. "But please remember this—I do not think, nor have I ever thought of, any of my films as sacred. A line here or a bit of action there that is of no great consequence and might hurt someone's feelings unnecessarily, then I will go along with the censor. Yet as a citizen of the United States, I claim my right to express myself freely through the medium of my films—just like a painter with his pictures, a musician through his music, and a poet or novelist through the printed word. The very term 'censorship' is wrong," he continued. "What we are talking about is *pre-censorship*. If you commit an obscene act, the law is there to punish you. But censors claim the right to tell you in advance that what you *propose* to do is wrong, without any legal authority or safeguards." Preminger was now really roused, and he was an impressive figure as he hammered home his points with his fist on the arm of the settee. "Censorship is an evil thing," he said vehemently. "Every authoritarian government this world has ever known, be it of the Right or of the Left, has introduced censorship as its very first act. We must all fight censorship in our own way—I as a film director, you as a writer—because censorship always poses a sinister threat to human freedom."

He was obviously incensed, and I shouldn't be a true member of my profession if I didn't wholeheartedly agree with him. Gently steering him away from that subject, I told him about my colleague who had recently interviewed Peter Bogdanovich and had asked him why he never used Scope ratio in his films. Bogdanovich replied that he doesn't like it himself and that Otto Preminger is one of very few directors who can use it successfully.

Preminger, like the majority of artists, was gratified to hear praise for his work from a fellow craftsman. "Peter's a good man," he said. "He began as a film critic, and now he's doing good work as a director. We shall see a good deal more of him in the future."

My time was beginning to run out, as other scribes were waiting to see him, so I asked him if he'd ever thought of retiring. "Making films is my life," he replied. "If I don't make films, what is there left to do?" I reminded him of the answer Cecil B. DeMille used to give to people who asked him towards the end of his life what he proposed to do. He would say, "Another film or another world." Maybe Mr. Preminger felt the same way?

"You can say that with my full authority," he said as we shook hands.

Cult and Controversy

Gordon Gow / 1979

From *Films and Filming*, vol. 26, no. 2, issue 302, 12–16.

However much a spy story taxes one's credulity, it doesn't do to protest. The activities of real spies are so very secret that a novelist and filmmaker can go to almost any extremes in the confident knowledge that hardly any spectator can say for certain that the tale is unlikely. Even a spy might not know everything possible to know about other spies. Nevertheless, some storytellers in the genre are more convincing than others, and one of the most persuasive, when he turns his hand to a spy thriller, is Graham Greene, whose recent book, *The Human Factor*, has been filmed by Otto Preminger.

The feeling of authenticity in this case, Preminger likes to point out, is related to the fact that Graham Greene used to be in the Secret Service himself. "As a matter of fact, he might still be in the Secret Service now, but they don't tell you that. If somebody were in the Secret Service at the present time, he would never say so."

Nicol Williamson plays the lead in *The Human Factor*, and Preminger has surrounded him with a starry cast including John Gielgud, Richard Attenborough, Robert Morley, and Derek Jacobi. It is not the first time he has directed a cast of luminaries, and I asked him if, when they are present in such quantity, he finds it a bit of a problem to handle them.

"No, never," he said. "It is never a problem for me to handle them. It is always their problem to handle me."

The roguish twinkle lets you know how well aware he is that his image as a martinet of the movie set is no bad thing to cultivate. It lends him a certain air, a trace of grandeur in a world where movie names are on the whole less grand than they used to be.

While I had been traveling high in the lift of his London hotel for the interview, I thought of how typical it was for Preminger to have taken a penthouse suite. I recalled the set of rooms he occupied in a Vienna hotel in 1963: I'd gone over there to visit some of his locations for *The Cardinal* and to interview him, and people remarked that Preminger's hotel suite was the one that Hitler had occupied, which they all said, mostly with laughter, was apt.

If, however, he can turn on some Teutonic moods on occasion, I have no personal knowledge of them. Having encountered him numerous times over the years, I have always found him a man of easy charm—a charm that seemed to me boundless; and although any movie man who grants a journalist an interview is virtually bound to put a good face on it, I must say the charm has never appeared to be costing Preminger the slightest effort.

Perhaps he hasn't always preserved it on the set, where things, as we know, can at times be trying. He got along very well, he says, with Frank Sinatra, who took the lead in one of the strongest Preminger movies, *The Man with the Golden Arm* (1955, an intelligent study of heroin addiction), but, as Preminger tells it, the shooting was not without its problems.

"Sinatra was most helpful. It was a comeback part for him, and he was wonderful. Kim Novak played the feminine part, and it was the first time that her actual dialogue spoken on the soundstage during filming was used, because I didn't like to have it dubbed in later, as they'd done in her previous pictures. We sometimes had to make thirty-five and forty takes. And Sinatra was most patient and helpful."

And how, one wondered, was Marilyn Monroe when he directed her in *River of No Return* (1954)? "Well, she tried very hard. But she always had a coach, and her coach on that picture was a German woman who taught her to speak in the most affected way, moving her lips in an odd manner. But my great help there was Bob Mitchum, who played the lead. Every time I said, "Now let's shoot," after she'd rehearsed like the coach had told her, Bob would hit her on the behind and say, 'Now come on, act like a human being.' And she got so scared that she immediately spoke normally."

Preminger began his career as an actor, of course. That was in Vienna, of which he is a native, when he was seventeen: "A learner, an apprentice to the famous Max Reinhardt, an Austrian who had made his big success in Berlin, which was a main center of the theater, but he'd come back to Vienna and bought a theater of his own."

Reinhardt was famous for producing *A Midsummer Night's Dream* (later, in Hollywood in 1935, he joined forces with William Dieterle on the famous star-laden Warner Brothers movie of it), and Preminger, in his Viennese teens, played one of the lovers, Lysander, for Reinhardt. But by the time he was nineteen, Preminger took over a theater himself in Vienna, and virtually gave up acting in favor of directing. Eventually this earned him a Hollywood offer, which he accepted, although, as things turned out, his initial American experience was in the live theater.

"I first did a play in New York for a famous impresario, Gilbert Miller. *Libel*, it was called: a courtroom play. I was the son of a lawyer. And I knew the play: I had done it already in German, which the man who had seen my theater work was a help, because I could hardly speak English when I went to America. Then I went to California, to Twentieth Century-Fox, and I did two pictures for Darryl Zanuck." These were rather trifling, and by now forgotten: *Under Your Spell* (1936) and *Danger, Love at Work* (1937).

"And then he gave me another assignment, and I read the script, but I didn't like it. It was a story that took place in Scotland. Well, Gregory Ratoff was a very good friend of mine, and he was also the go-between for Zanuck and his directors and actors, and I said to Gregory Ratoff, 'Look, I want to tell Zanuck I can't do this: I don't know anything about Scotland.' He said, 'Zanuck is producing it himself, and if you tell him this, he will throw you out.' So I started the film because of this warning, but during the making of it I had various differences with Zanuck, and I quit.

"I wanted to cancel my contract. But in Vienna and [who] subsequently gave me the contract for Hollywood was Joseph Schenck—one of the Schenck brothers. He was the president or chairman of the board at Twentieth Century-Fox. So at this time I wanted to see him, and I couldn't get an appointment for two or three months. I called his secretary every day, and even she laughed over some of the excuses she had to make up.

"Well, several years later I was on the stage again, in a play called *Margin for Error*. It was a very big success in New York. And Katharine Hepburn was playing in the theater next door, so very often after the shows we would have supper together. One night we were sitting upstairs at 21, and in came Joseph Schenck, and he came up to our table right away and embraced me and said, 'Miss Hepburn, I brought this man to the United States, and look what a big success he is now! I'm proud of him.' And then he said to her, 'By the way, Miss Hepburn, how come that in all these years in Hollywood we two never met?' And she said, 'Mr. Schenck, I consider that to be one of the achievements of my life.' And what did he do? He sat down then and there and had supper with us. He couldn't be hurt."

It was back at Fox, however, in 1943 that Preminger both directed and starred in the screen version of *Margin for Error*, a comedy in which he played the menacing Teutonic type which was to typify his few movie assignments as an actor. The following year he directed an inconsequential piece, *In the Meantime, Darling*, and then his first really important movie, *Laura*, a mystery thriller of great style, with a sound psychological basis and a haunting theme tune which is still played quite often today.

"Zanuck had been absent from the studio when I made *Margin for Error*. He was in the army. His successor was Bill Goetz, who was normally his aide. He was very nice, and he bought the rights of that play and asked me to act the same part, and I said I would only do it if I could also direct, because I had not directed any pictures since I had previously left Fox—only plays. And Bill Goetz said, 'Fine.' And then Zanuck came back. And now he and Goetz didn't get along. He fired Goetz. And during the last weeks before he left, Zanuck worked in a house on the beach. He called me to the house and told me he had a story, *Laura*, which I could produce. But, as he said, 'You will never direct as long as I am here.'

"So I had the screenplay written, and it was a very good one. And he offered the job of directing to several people. He offered it to Milestone, who was a friend of mine, and he said to Zanuck, 'Why doesn't Preminger direct it?' Then Zanuck offered it to Rouben Mamoulian, who started to direct it. I didn't like what he did. Well, Zanuck had gone to New York, so I told his new assistant to send the rushes to New York for Zanuck to see, because I thought they were awful. The result of that was a telegram from Zanuck instructing him to have Mamoulian resume work, and also instructing him not to permit me to go on the set.

"In my opinion, the work Mamoulian did then was just as bad, and when Zanuck came back and saw it, he felt that I was right. Zanuck is quite a fair man. There was a dining room away from the main office building at Fox, and he used to eat there with the producers; and one day after lunch he called to me, and as we walked out of there together, he said, 'Monday you can start directing *Laura*.'

"It was a story that appealed to me, although I couldn't tell you why. I don't do pictures on account of any logic: when something appeals to me, I like to do it. But on the other hand, after I've seen the finished picture several times with audiences and made some adjustments, I deliberately detach myself from it, so that I'll come fresh to the next picture and not imitate myself."

Today if *Laura* or any other of his films should turn up on television, his wife might very well watch, but Preminger himself, true to his self-imposed code, will not. *Laura*, of course, has become a cult movie and is one which stands up superbly to repeated viewings. Subtly suggesting decadence amid elegant New York surroundings, it centered upon the rather enigmatic Laura (Gene Tierney), missing [and] presumed dead for a good deal of the film, and seen during this time in flashbacks, while the detective in charge of the case, ferreting for information, falls deeply in love with the evidently deceased subject of his enquiries. A strong cast included Dana Andrews as the detective, Vincent Price and Judith Anderson as mildly sinister acquaintances of Laura, and Clifton Webb as the waspish columnist and broadcaster whose villainy provided a suspenseful climax. Preminger handled with brilliant assurance the two vital passages: when the detective has sunk into a gloom over his dead and unseen love, known to him best through her portrait, his reverie is shattered by the sudden arrival in the room of Laura herself, very much alive; and when later on Laura is alone in her apartment, listening to the Webb character talking on the radio, this villainous columnist is actually infiltrating her room, for the voice on the air is a recording and is to be, he hopes, his alibi when he has murdered her. Far-fetched, to be sure, but carried through with consummate skill.

Because *Laura* is my personal favorite among Preminger's movies, and also because the suspense thriller is so effective in the film medium, I could wish that Preminger had devoted a good part of his career to this genre. But he has chosen to be versatile. At first, no doubt, a range of subjects, not always to his taste, was thrust upon him in those journeyman days when he was under studio contract; but even in his years of independence, it has not been possible to pin him down into very specific categories, except perhaps to note a penchant for melodrama, or at any rate for drama that is pretty high powered.

Occasionally, however, he has also displayed a diverting sense of humor. As far back as 1945, he directed Tallulah Bankhead as Catherine the Great in *A Royal Scandal*, which was considered a sophisticated romp in its day. And one of his biggest successes, of course, was *The Moon Is Blue* (1953), with Maggie McNamara, William Holden, and David Niven. Adapted from a Broadway play of a couple of years before by F. Hugh Herbert, it owed its popularity as a movie to the sensation value, for audiences beyond the Broadway belt, of such words as "seduction" and "virgin," which were never previously used in American cinema. The plot was saucy, but only slightly so even then; and the whole piece seems so exceedingly tame today that anyone encountering it for the first time now would wonder what all the fuss has been about. Nevertheless, when it was new, *The Moon Is Blue* seemed to be deliberately challenging Hollywood's outmoded but still functioning Production Code, and the Legion of Decency as well. Cardinal Spellman spoke against the film. And, as invariably happens when people cry "filth," the public couldn't wait to rush the movie houses. The show was a hit, and Preminger, who had battled to preserve the controversial words, was regarded as a liberator. It must be said that a good many other movies, by other directors, that "benefited" from the liberation thus gained were rather trashy.

Thereafter, from time to time, Preminger scored further hits, and often with artistic success as well, by broaching matters that might be unsensational today but were quite daring when he tackled them: drug addiction in the aforementioned *Man with the Golden Arm* (1955); the clinical and explicit discussion of rape in the trial drama *Anatomy of a Murder* with James Stewart, Lee Remick, and Ben Gazzara (1959); homosexuality in the political melodrama *Advise & Consent*, with Don Murray, Henry Fonda, and Charles Laughton (1961).

"I felt that I, as a motion picture director, must have the same freedom to put on the screen what an author is able to put in his books. And although I hate censorship, I didn't mind if the internal censorship people for the industry classified it R, not good for children, or even X, because I must make a picture the way I feel is right for it, and I cannot start to make changes in advance, anticipating censorship. Additionally, ever since I've been an independent producer, I've had contracts where I have the final say: nobody can cut anything without asking me. I even had a lawsuit at one time, when television cut one of my pictures by ten minutes, and I won."

Twice, untypically but notably, he has directed film versions of famous stage musicals—both, coincidentally, with all-Negro casts—*Carmen Jones* (1954) and *Porgy and Bess* (1959). He used CinemaScope, which was fairly new then, for *Carmen Jones,* and in the course of it he demonstrated that an immobile camera could have its virtue if what was happening on the screen was of intrinsic holding power. The show used fresh lyrics by Oscar Hammerstein but retained the Bizet score for *Carmen,* and during the Flower Song and the Michaela (Cindy Lou) aria he left the performers alone on the screen in medium shot, realizing that the music would sustain such lengthy takes. He also placed Harry Belafonte in the first case, and Olga James in the second, towards the side of the elongated CinemaScope frame, avoiding the conventional center positioning which invariably looks awkward when one person occupies a very wide screen, because this reminds the spectator how empty the space on either side looks. If, on the other hand, the spectator is enticed to look steadily to the left or right of the frame, even for a considerable time, the compositional problem is decreased. Elsewhere in *Carmen Jones,* of course, there was movement enough.

Such things, Preminger says, are not for him the result of long hours of advance thinking. On the set, he is more of an instinctive operator. "When I stage a scene, I never prepare myself. I know the script very well, and I don't have to do what many directors do, which is to get the art director to draw sketches of every single setup. Coming from the live theater, the best way for me is to direct the scene, and then set up the camera and look through it, and at that point get the feeling of the way I want it to look on the screen."

Like all directors, Preminger's career has had its less satisfactory elements from the critical viewpoint, not least in two long films of long novels, *Forever Amber* (1947) and *Exodus* (1960). But sometimes critics have been arguably too harsh with him: there was something to be said, I always thought, for his kidnap melodrama *Bunny Lake Is Missing* (1965), although those who derided it mostly found words of praise for Laurence Olivier's light and persuasive study of a police inspector with a passion for junket. A little of the equivocal flavor of 1968 came over aptly, I also thought, in his heavily savaged *Skidoo,* made that year and depicting a clash of gangsters and hippies, with John Phillip Law, Carol Channing, Jackie Gleason, Groucho Marx, Frankie Avalon, Mickey Rooney, and Frank Gorshin among the talent on view.

Confronting the critics of Preminger movies, and going to another extreme, have been his cult admirers, many of them young, who at one stage tended to find great value in the least of his efforts. Preminger himself recalls one such fan. "When I lived in Hollywood, Lewis Milestone and I were very good friends. But his daughter was torturing him because, on every possible occasion, she would say, 'You know, Otto Preminger's pictures are much better than yours.' I laughed about that—but he didn't like it."

For the benefit of his own children, twins, Preminger made one of his infrequent returns to acting. "The twins were seven or eight then, and every Wednesday and Thursday afternoon they used to look at a television series called *Batman*. So when I ran into the producer of *Batman*, I offered to play Mr. Freeze for him for free, just to see what the children would say. And when my episode came on, I watched it with them, and they said, 'Daddy! Daddy!' That was fun."

Mr. Freeze was a villain, and all of the Preminger acting we have seen in movies has likewise been villainous. He tended to be typed as a Nazi, to best effect perhaps in his role as the prison camp commandant in Billy Wilder's *Stalag 17* (1953). Such excursions have been by the way. Directing is his primary occupation, and one that keeps him on the move a great deal.

"In the days of the big Hollywood studios, they built sets. Nowadays, I make my pictures in real places. If I wanted a room like this room"—he gestured around the luxurious decor of his penthouse domain—"I would shoot it here. I very rarely built sets. In *The Human Factor* there is only one scene that was built on a stage, and the reason was that it takes place in Moscow, and naturally for just one scene you don't go to Moscow. I wanted, through the window, to see something of Moscow, just as through these windows we see London down there, so I used back projection. Otherwise, every scene in the film is shot in the real places, hotel room, dining room, and so forth. Part of the picture I made in Africa, in Nairobi."

The next Preminger movie, *Blood on Wheels*, will be a major location job too. "I have permission to shoot part of it in China. It's about Dr. Norman Bethune, who is today the fifth-most popular man in China's history. He was a Canadian doctor who eventually went to China and helped Mao in the Chinese-Japanese war. When he died Mao wrote a eulogy, which has been published in a booklet.

"I started to work on this film in 1972. I had been in China before, in 1949, but only as a tourist. But in 1972 when I asked for a visa, I couldn't get it. I asked again and again. But only recently, about a year ago, I met by accident two people who have an American-Sino trade corporation, and when I told them what

I'm telling you now, they said, 'We'll get you a visa.' And I got it. And also they found out why I hadn't been able to get it in 1972, because while Mao esteemed Dr. Bethune, Madame Mao hated Dr. Bethune, and she simply said that I was not to be given a visa. She was that powerful. But subsequently, as you know, she fell into disfavor and was no longer able to do anything about it.

"I met an author when I was in China recently who wrote a book which has become a best seller now, but when Madame Mao was still in power she had said that she didn't like it and that it was not to be published. And I met two other people who made a beautiful animated cartoon, two hours long, of an old Chinese tale, *Uproar in Heaven*—beautiful; I have a copy of it in New York. But when Madame Mao saw it, 'No,' she said, 'that won't be shown in China.' Such was her power.

"And a strange thing about totalitarian governments is that even now, when I ask people, 'Where is Madame Mao? Is she in prison? Is she in exile? Is she dead?' they still don't want to commit themselves by saying anything. They're scared that the whole thing might turn again, and she might come back to power. This is the difference between a democracy and a totalitarian government. There they believe that she could possibly become powerful again and take revenge on anybody who had said anything against her.

"Dr. Bethune's great help to Mao was that he had the idea of putting blood banks, for transfusions, on trucks and taking them to the soldiers instead of having the soldiers travel to hospitals, because so many died on the way there. Dr. Bethune reduced mortality among Chinese soldiers by 75 percent.

"He cut himself during an operation, because he didn't have gloves, and he became infected and died at the age of forty-nine."

For Preminger, at seventy-three, the prospect of another location jaunt might be expected to seem a bit daunting. Younger directors than he have been known to complain of the long hours and the brain fatigue of the average shooting schedule. But Preminger merely says, "I like my work and I like to be busy. So far I've had no difficulties. If I should get sick, that would be different. I get up early anyway; that is part of age. I wake up every morning at five-thirty or six. And I go to bed early. My wife doesn't care about going to nightclubs, which many men have to do because their wives like it. Very rarely, when we're invited, we might go to a party."

A cosmopolite on account of work, Preminger lives in New York City and feels at home there: "There are only two cities where I would live if I have the choice: New York is one and the other is London. I would not like to live in Paris, and certainly not in Vienna, where I was born. But I like big cities, and what London and New York have in common for me is that, while the people are quite different, there is in both a feeling of home."

Vot You Mean: Ogre?

Tony Crawley / 1980

From *Films Illustrated* 9:1 January 1980, 196–202.

"I'm not a Catholic, I'm a Jew—but I made *The Cardinal*. I'm not a senator—but I made *Advise & Consent*. I'm not a dope fiend—but I directed *The Man with the Golden Arm*. And I'm not a virgin—but I produced *The Moon Is Blue*."

Since when (San Francisco, 1963, to be precise), Otto Preminger could and most probably has added that he's not a Nazi, either, although everyone loves to think so. "I hear Otto's on holiday," runs the old Billy Wilder jape. "In Auschwitz . . ." Today, Preminger can further testify that he's not a spy (nor, as events turned out, an expert in the current vagaries of film financing), but he's completed his first movie for four years, his friend Graham Greene's espionage drama, *The Human Factor*, which the Rank Organization promptly picked up to prove it's not only into retreads.

Whatever he is not, to the press of the world, he's Otto the Terrible; to the alliterative headline writers, Otto the Ogre. I rather think he enjoys the label, the only one his vast divergence of movies has left him. He plays up to the temperamental imagery with a caustic tongue and theatrical glower beneath the shining, bald head. "Directing Marilyn Monroe is like directing Lassie. You need fourteen takes to get each of them to bark right." Wilder was no less polite about her, but no Nazi nicknames for him.

The Preminger image, fed as much by himself as fellow Viennese Wilder, onscreen and off, has always been Adolf in jackboots—a taller, more guttural Von Stroheim, whipping films and actors into shape, ranting and raving, reducing women and children to hysterical tears and burying the odd star who dares answer back. Remarkably few of them appear to bear witness to such outbursts. Peter Lawford, who is to acting what Woody Allen is to prizefighting, did once agree that "if you fluff a line and stop to do it over before Otto tells you, God help you." Michael Caine, on the other hand, firmly denied Rex Reed's report of him calling Preminger paranoid. "I did not know what the word meant," ran Caine's cable to Reed, "so I looked it up, and I can assure you, paranoid he's not."

Most of his stars, more aware of the image than the man, tend to come out fighting before the first bell. Like Nicol Williamson during *The Human Factor*, they issue the old-time Hollywood threat: Scream at me, buster, and it's the last you'll see of me! Or so it has always been reported down through the ages. It makes good copy, and Preminger is a past master at winning every possible ounce of publicity from any project.

He's no angel, of course. He owns to a certain impatience at work. And with an accent like his, somehow still thick with ja's and vot's, dis's and dat's after some forty-four years in the Americas, any raising of the voice does make one look around, expecting a Panzer division to burst through the door. However, unlike either version of the director's gospel according to St. Hitchcock, Preminger insists he does not treat actors like cattle or feel that they should be treated like cattle. He just cannot and will not abide actors turning up late for work or, worst sin of all to a former theater man, not having learned their lines.

He has, in fact, and more than once, sacked stars from his productions. Lana Turner was bounced, unceremoniously, from *Anatomy of a Murder* (1959) for insisting on a wardrobe flashier and more expensive than he deemed suitable for a lowly GI's wife. (That's how Lee Remick was born.) And Robert Mitchum, with whom few directors mess around and live to tell the tale, was peremptorily dumped for reasons never fully explained—or agreed on in their later statements—from Preminger's last and very lackluster film of *Rosebud* (1975). Since then, Mitchum has made several films and grown, if that's possible, even more so in screen stature, while Preminger all but disappeared from view, working on several ventures, including a long-cherished dream for a film inside China, before making instead this third feature in London during the summer.

Even at seventy-two, or according to his great-grandfather's records, seventy-three, Otto Ludwig Preminger therefore is something of a daunting prospect to spend an afternoon with, high above Knightsbridge in his hotel penthouse suite. With casting almost complete (an actor was waiting to audition as I left), he was about to begin that thirty-seventh film a few days later.

Q: An arduous schedule, I hear?
A: Vot you mean: arduous. For whom?
Q: For you?
A: No. Only for the actors!

The movie has cost him dear: most of his art collection, including a few Picassos, among the much-headlined financial angst both during and after shooting.

At the same time, the project has grown increasingly timely. A month ago, the capsule description would have been "*Tinker, Tailor* . . . revisited." Now, in the light—indeed, the searchlights—cast into the overly protected shadows of British espionage by Andrew Boyle's book *The Climate of Treason*, the new Preminger is proving less Greene fiction (if it ever was) than startlingly reinforced fact.

(The ensuing revelations since Boyle's publication date could mean that Michael Klinger's much-postponed *Philby* film will finally be switching titles instead of proposed stars . . . and it even brings into question Ian Fleming's original description of James Bond as M's *blunt* instrument.)

Preminger says *The Human Factor* intrigued him as much, if not more so, for its love story than its spymaster hunt for a leak in the African Section 6A of our rat-infested Secret Intelligence Service. It's a mole hunt to delight those Le Carré followers who always felt that the mole should turn out to be the rather dull Smiley himself.

While researching my meeting with Preminger, I ran into continual ambivalence towards both the man and his movies. Such a feeling is, perhaps, natural enough considering the mixed bag of his output, musicals to melodrama, history (ancient and modern) to skillful comedies. Rex Reed may know where he stands (compiling his ten best and worst films of 1973, he regretted the absence of a new Preminger for his Rotten classification), but as a friend put it to me, "You never know where you are with Preminger. Every film is different." He would consider that a tribute.

"Let me tell you," he said at one point (he begins most of his declarations with, "Let me tell you"), "I'm afraid of nothing more than to imitate myself. Many people would think that means a style . . . But I don't like to do that. What I do, deliberately, when I finish a film and I've seen it twice or three times with an audience—I forget it! When I say I forget it, I really mean that. It is finished for me! I remember one time I was supposed to be going out with my wife, Hope, and one of my films was on television. I think it was *Fallen Angel* (1945). I started to look at it, and as it went on, of course, I recognized the situations and the scenes, but it was almost like somebody else's picture. Hope was dressed and ready, so we had to leave . . . and I still don't know what the end of the film was. Really!"

Understandable, given his range and longevity. If Preminger pictures lack any common thread, they do adhere to a personal stamp, and one beyond his fierce independence as a filmmaker. His style, his major interest in drama, is the development of character over plot every time.

As always in any interview, the problem is where to begin. For all his sudden fall from power in the seventies, Otto Preminger represents a hefty chapter in Hollywood history. From toiling in the sweated labor of Darryl Zanuck's Fox contract system, "not unlike being a foreman in a sausage factory," to Herculean efforts in battling staid and silly censorship authorities around the world once breaking free of contractual chains with a string of self-generated successes in the late fifties and early sixties.

His background is known too well to question anew. The first of two sons (the other is Altman's *M*A*S*H* producer, Ingo) of a Talmudic scholar, surviving by necessary brilliance in Roman Catholic Austria as the state's chief prosecutor. A doctor of law himself, Otto Preminger preferred the stage very early as a teenage actor, and by twenty stage director of Max Reinhardt, pulling his Theater in der Josefstadt out of a slump. Preminger had also run his own Die Komedie theater, and because his partner and his partner's wife did not take to her, he missed signing a new actress in town: Marlene Dietrich. He didn't make the same error when one Hedwig Kiesler called by his Josefstadt office. "I had never seen a lovelier face. She was seventeen and wanted to act. Reinhardt gave her a small part immediately." Then Gustav Machaty gave her a film, *Extase* (1933), Hollywood blinked and kept her nickname, added a new surname. Hedy Lamarr. In these Vienna days, Preminger also discovered Oscar Homolka.

As Reinhardt's wunderkind, he was offered a contract to head the State Theatre, "the highest theatrical position in the country." Like his father, getting close to his top job years before, he was also asked to convert to Catholicism. Both Premingers refused; Mark got his prosecutor spot; Otto lost his. The times when a Vienna mayor declared, "I determine who is Jewish and who is not," were fast changing. Seeing the writing on the wall, literally in most instances, Preminger *fils* took up one of his innumerable offers to go to America. Tallulah Bankhead, whose uncle was the Speaker in the House of Representatives, helped to bring his family over in 1938. He calls his arrival in New York on October 31, 1935, his second birth. Learning English from scripts, he was acting on Broadway within months and rapidly moved on to Hollywood.

His first Hollywood period included his first Nazi appearance—the villainous consul he had played with distinction in Broadway's *Margin for Error* (1943). He says his acting ambitions were adopted at eight, achieved at seventeen, and abandoned at twenty. In Prague he would be billed as Otto Pretori, as the Preminger name was hardly in favor with the new leaders, "many of whom my father had prosecuted for treason during the First World War." By 1939 he did not intend acting again as Pretori or Preminger. He was, in fact, directing the Clare Boothe Luce play with Sam Levene, Leif Erickson, and, as the consul, a German actor, Rudolf Forster. Preminger took over the role when faced in rehearsals with a note: "Dear Otto, I'm going home to rejoin Adolf. Love, Rudolf." He made the film version as actor, producer, and director, calling in a soldier on leave to assist with the script: Samuel Fuller.

There followed his heady triumph in *Laura* (1944); an ill Lubitsch asking him to take over *Czarina* (US: *A Royal Scandal*; 1945); and a string of Fox sausages with Crawford, Grable, Darnell, Dana Andrews far too often, and, above them all, Gene Tierney—amid rambunctious dealings with Darryl Zanuck and Howard Hughes. Not, he says, the happiest of times in the film industry.

"People always want to call it the industry. It's not an industry now. It was . . . only when Mr. Zanuck had the right to say, 'You make this film or I will fire you.' It was very difficult to extract yourself. The one thing that helped was success. After *Laura* everybody was after me. They want success. They don't examine talent. You can be the most talented man, but unless you've made one big success, they don't believe in you. Even after *Laura*, Zanuck called me in and said John Stahl was making a lousy job of *Forever Amber* (1947), and I must start it over. I disliked the book and wanted Lana Turner instead of Linda Darnell, but I gave in. I had to. It was the worst picture I ever made.

"Then he rented me out to Howard Hughes for *Angel Face* (1952). I didn't like that script either and told him. Hughes would pick me up in his little Chevrolet. He didn't want to admit he was hard of hearing, so he drove this noisy car around, so that people had to speak loud! He said, 'If you don't like the script, hire a writer, five writers, ten writers. Anybody you want as long as they're not Commies. You can rewrite it, recast it. You have complete freedom. You can go in like Hitler. Only thing I want is a test of that bitch . . .' What was her name . . .? Jean Simmons, *ja*! She'd had a fight with him. She knew he hated short hair, so she took nail scissors and cut hers. 'I want to see her in a long, beautiful dark wig,' he said. . . . Those years were really like living under a totalitarian government!"

The next period was all of his own formulation. Feeling too much like Zanuck's puppet, he was among the first directors to take full advantage of the consent decree of 1951, following the US government's antitrust suit against the monopolistic control of the major studios in both production and distribution. The door was opened for independents, and Preminger charged through while his agent, Charlie Feldman, warned him he'd wind up back on Broadway. "His 100 percent Hollywood mind couldn't think of anything lower." Feldman was wrong and wasted too many years agenting before he followed suit as a producer, once Otto paved the way with a return to his Vienna-style autonomy and ten years of independent projects. *The Moon Is Blue* (1953), *Carmen Jones* (1954), *The Man with the Golden Arm* (1955), *Anatomy of a Murder* (1959), *Advise & Consent* (1962) and his biggest financial success, *Exodus* (1960). A runaway schedule flawed only by the critical savaging of *Saint Joan* (1957), *Bonjour Tristesse* (1957) and the largely forgotten *One Man Mutiny* (US: *The Court-Martial of Billy Mitchell*; 1955), with Rod Steiger prosecuting Gary Cooper. In all, Preminger has utilized legal battles four times on stage and screen. "I'm attracted to courtroom drama, possibly because I spent so much of my youth fascinated by the trials my father conducted in Vienna." One of these had Preminger *père* prosecuting the first Czechoslovakian president as an Austrian traitor!

From the mid-sixties onwards, as he reached his own late fifties, and saw most other Hollywood moviemakers following his independent lead, his own films fell fallow, unfurling star-filled packages that worked better on paper than on film. They all lacked his old power punch and point. *The Cardinal* (1963), *In Harm's Way* (1964), *Bunny Lake Is Missing* (1965), *Hurry Sundown* (1966) soon headed him to a spate of utter flops, including the psychedelically awful *Skidoo* (1968). His reputation dropped, perking up only momentarily with the bitter ironics of *Such Good Friends* (1971), his best film for six years.

Hidden among all these titles—the good, the bad, and the wholly undistinguished—are other areas of Preminger lore. His often inspired selection of new movie composers: Elmer Bernstein, Ernest Gold, Jerry Goldsmith. His antitype casting of top names: Laughton's southern senator, Olivier's Scotland Yard cop, Widmark's French dauphin, and Sinatra succeeding to John Garfield's banned plans as the golden-armed junkie. Preminger felt only Brando or Sinatra could play the role; Sinatra agreed before Brando had time to read the script. Sixteen years on, when offered *The Godfather*, Preminger would only accept the job if Sinatra played the lead. "Ludwig, I pass on this," said the singer. Preminger passed, too.

There is, also, his adroit use of non-professionals, a list which has to be headed by Judge Joseph Welch in *Anatomy of a Murder*, and also features John Huston in *The Cardinal* ("'You must be out of your mind,' he told me"), New York's ex-mayor John Lindsay in *Rosebud*, Paramount story editor Lee Sabinson in *Such Good Friends*. He also tried to persuade Dr. Martin Luther King to play a senator from Georgia in *Advise & Consent*. "He was intrigued but decided that the hostility his presence would create in that role would jeopardize his case." While planning *Tell Me That You Love Me, Junie Moon* (1970) for Liza Minnelli, the off-Broadway director of *The Boys in the Band* asked for a small role. Any part. "He wanted to watch me work, he wanted to become a film director." That was Robert Moore, who has since divided his time between directing Neil Simon plays on Broadway or in Hollywood.

There's more, much more. . . . his rows with novelists like Leon Uris, and scriptwriters like the pseudonymous Esther Dale (in reality, Elaine May) on *Such Good Friends*—which has to be measured with his courage in forcing Dalton Trumbo off the blacklist for *Exodus*. Making *The 13th Letter* (1950), said to be Hollywood's first movie made entirely on location—"That was not only I. Many people were doing it. That has to do with the progress of film." His creation of stars from Gene Tierney to the late Jean Seberg, finding Elizabeth Montgomery and Barbara Bouchet along the way. His love affair with Gypsy Rose Lee, resulting in a son, kept secret until her death, when Erik was adopted by Preminger and his third wife, Hope Bryce. You get the picture. Where to start, indeed?

From the outset, Preminger proved a most gracious host. No heels were clicked, and he was far from the Billy Wilder portrait: "He's really Martin Bormann in elevator shoes with a face-lift by a blindfolded plastic surgeon in Luxembourg." He ordered some coffee, waved away all interference from jangling phones to an outer office, apart from "At last!" making contact with José Ferrer in Puerto Vallarta, and sat back, or rather up, firm and straight in his chair. He motioned to his deaf-aid, indeed he demonstrated it, and checked my coffee order, grasped the phone again, and rasped, "The coffee is supposed to be black. Like my soul."

The accent is quite unbelievable, *Stalag 17* all over again, not to mention Mr. Freeze in television's "Batman." His memory is not what it was, but then nor is mine. "You'll have to help me with the name of that film," he said once or twice. "Who was that writer again . . .? I forget who said that, Zanuck or Hughes . . . Vot vas her name?" And franker still on several occasions: "I don't know. I don't remember any more."

So . . . from thirty-seven films in forty-eight years . . . "No!" he rasped, and "rasped" is the only word for the escaping gutturals. "I only started making films when I came to America. I forget that one lousy film in Vienna (*Die grosse Liebe*, 1931). Oh, it was awful! You should see it!"

Having dismissed his debut as quickly as his second marriage ("A forgettable marriage"), I began anew. Right, from thirty-six films in forty-three years, I selected my favorite, *Advise & Consent*. It introduced me, as much as JFK did, to American politics, the whole razzamatazz showmanship of it; to author Allen Drury and his complete trilogy covering the wide and prophetic panoply of Washington and New York-UNO political warfare. The movie, one of Preminger's finest casting sessions, also utilized once more credit titles and logo designs from the acknowledged master, Saul Bass—the director's most influential discovery on old-time Hollywood. I've met Bass a number of times—a fascinating, lovely man. I felt some discussion of him might well break the ice and, more important, delay any ogreness until my feet felt more secure under his office table.

I needn't have trodden so carefully. The only chiding I received all afternoon was very Jewish-motherish—"Your coffee, don't let it get cold!" And more than once came that line which made me grow my beard in the first place—"You're too young to know this." Either I'm getting younger or my interviewees are aging fast. Either way, Otto the Ogre turned out to be Otto the Pussycat.

"You know Bass?" he beamed. "One of the nicest men I know, and that's not just a phrase . . . well, if you met him, you know it. Like Moss Hart, he is a gentle, warm man of great charm and intelligence. I forget how we first met now." (So does Bass.) "I was looking for a graphic designer, and he's one of the greatest artists, designing artists. I kind of discovered him with *The Moon Is Blue*. I don't think you can possibly remember this, but I had lots of censorship problems with that film. People said: You can't say 'virgin' . . . sounds so funny today! I fought it and when it was all settled and they agreed the picture was not pornographic, United Artists submitted a publicity campaign around a girl whose bosoms were sticking out, whose skirts were up high. I told them: Look, after I tell everyone this is not a dirty picture, you want to advertise it like a dirty film! Then I met Bass and he designed that lovely logo—the ideas of the man!—those two little lovebirds behind a blind on a window-sill."

The partnership has continued ever since, with Bass also making an art form of the main title sequence since *Carmen Jones*, while his poster-logo, used on all publicity sheets, notepaper, envelopes, continued to sum up a Preminger movie in a neat, graphic form of shorthand. An identi-hit. The flaming rose of *Carmen Jones*; a segmented corpse for *Anatomy of a Murder*; the flip-top Capitol dome for *Advise & Consent*; all manner of arms—angular with clawing fingers representing *The Man with the Golden Arm*; brandishing a rifle on high for *Exodus*; pointing a finger from a US Navy sleeve for *In Harm's Way*; a sexy switch to Reubenish thighs for *Such Good Friends*.

"We discuss them, you know. He sketches, he wants to do what I like. He's not overbearing. I might suggest a slight change, but the ideas are all his. Did you see the logo for this new picture—his telephone? The idea that they are separated and the phone hangs by a thread. *Ja*, very *gut*! We have the kind of friendship that if we don't see each other for weeks or months—he lives in California now, and I live in New York—we can carry on from where we left off. He has one terrible frustration. He would really love to make films more than anything else. He made one here (*Phase IV*, 1973), and I was sitting with him for nights, cutting and changing it. It didn't turn out so well, and nobody wants him to direct. I'm sure he would eventually make good films."

Despite the legendary temperament, Preminger maintains he also has many friends among the actors he has worked with. He calls most of them the most wonderful human beings, then saves the bowing to cliché by commenting on their wisdom as well. "There is this terrible injustice when people look down on them and say, 'Oh, they're just actors.' That's not true. Charles Laughton, Jimmy Stewart, or George C. Scott, to whom I gave his first part in a picture, or Henry Fonda and Jane, his daughter, the only reason any of them are good actors is that they also must know about human nature. It's not just imitating what the director tells them to do. Much more. It must come from here *und* here." He placed his hand on heart and head. "I learned from Charles Laughton . . . the way he approached the part, the way he did it. When he got sick, I got to learn about him as a human being."

Novelists, though, are something else again. Although most of his movies stem from books, best sellers in the main, he doesn't have the same rapport with authors as with actors—apart, that is, from Graham Greene. "With novelists, I don't *have* to get on well," he thundered slightly. "I buy the rights and then I create, together with another writer, a screenplay. I try usually to get the original author for the screenplay, but I had bad luck in two cases: Leon Uris on *Exodus* and . . . you'll help me with the other name . . . ? *Vot? Ja, ja,* Nelson Algren and *The Man with the Golden Arm* . . .

"When *Exodus* came out, Uris said I ruined his novel. He said this in public after getting a lot of money for the rights. I feel if a novelist wants to have a say about how his book is translated to the screen, he shouldn't sell it! The word 'sell' implies giving up his rights. You cannot get 25,000 or 30,000 dollars or whatever it was, and then tell me what to do! Uris is a great storyteller, but he cannot write dialogue and drama. A dramatic medium is different from just writing or telling a story. I had to pay him off on *Exodus*.

"I wanted Graham Greene to write the screenplay of *The Human Factor*; he wrote *Saint Joan* for me, you might remember. But he said he was too tired of the subject and suggested I get another writer. Several people were mentioned, and I met with them. Tom Stoppard seemed the most enthusiastic. Also, I liked his personality very much, and the things he had done. *Every Good Boy Deserves Favor*, his play for actors and an orchestra, is wonderful. So is the new one, *Night and Day. All* his plays! I chose him above the others, but everything in our profession is partly also luck. You cannot just logically say, 'This is the best writer.' There must also be luck. A writer is not a machine. He might be very good and for some reason or another, he doesn't work out so well. This has worked out very well."

Preminger has known Graham Greene for twenty-three years or more and relates various choice anecdotes about the writer in his recent "ottobiography," including a gem about Greene inviting him to an ultra-exclusive, top house in Paris, extolling the not-inconsiderable virtues of the place, only to be greeted by the madame saying, "Oh, Mr. Preminger, how wonderful to see you again." He does not, however, have any guaranteed first refusal on all Greene's books. "I would not use our friendship in that way. That would not be fair. I found the new book and immediately liked it, perhaps because I expected to like it, because I like Graham. You read something and you cannot—at least, *I* cannot—make always logical decisions. A lot depends on my mood when I'm reading. I might read the same book again and be in a negative mood. I was excited by the book . . . I still am. I made an offer to his agent, we bargained a little and I bought it and paid him the money.

"I have no difficulties with Graham Greene. But I'm sure that no writer can be completely happy with another writer creating the screenplay because the other writer also has a personality and together with me, we are emphasizing the things that are important to us . . ."

It was, I interrupted, a cracking scenario. Preminger looked up with surprise. "*Vot?*" he glowered, well, just a little. "You've read it. You've read it, too! I don't even know how Richard Attenborough got hold of a copy. But his agent called me and said he'd read it and would like to play Colonel Daintry. He selected the part for himself . . . ! But, *ja*, in my opinion, it is probably the best script I have ever read. Stoppard didn't change the book. He dramatized it. For instance, the flashbacks—they are necessary to show how much in love Castle and his wife were, that she told him about her son, that he still came back to her and stayed with her . . . *Ja*, Stoppard did a very good job."

Having, inevitably, strayed into the terrain of *The Human Factor*, it was appropriate to study Preminger's casting methods, very much on a par with previous projects: adventurous. Very British, too, and that is not so obvious as it may sound for a British secret service drama, given Hollywood's often quirky casting ideas. In fact, the casting is so low-key, it appears more suitable for a Graham Greene mini television series to follow that of John Le Carré, rather than a big-budget movie due to compete in the box-office star wars. He matches Attenborough with Derek Jacobi, John Gielgud with Robert Morley, with room for Richard Vernon and Ann Todd, and introduces yet another screen discovery, the Somali-born New York model Iman; and, in the pivotal role of Castle, chased after by Burton and Caine both, Preminger gives Nicol Williamson his first star film role in two years.

"I never go for the box-office draws these days or any days," declared Preminger. "How many are there? People might go to the next Barbra Streisand picture, but they won't see the next Michael Caine or Sean Connery picture. Maybe Robert Redford is a star people want to see . . . Who else? But there are many actors who are stars. I mean, there's no doubt that John Gielgud is a star—in my opinion, the greatest living actor. But I don't flatter myself or him that anybody should be going to *The Human Factor* to see John Gielgud. Or Attenborough, Morley—any one of them. But all together! In our times of communications, when the picture is good, people know very quickly. Therefore, the critics are not so powerful with pictures as they are with theater.

"I must say I thought of Morley right away. Nicol Williamson came later. I was looking for people and considered Michael Caine. He wanted to play Castle but only if I made the picture in Ireland. I cannot change it to Ireland because

Michael Caine doesn't want to pay tax. I understand him, though. The tax here is terrible. I talked with Burton, *ja*, and decided against him because—no, this you must not print . . . I offered him Daintry, but he didn't want it. Attenborough is a great Daintry. Actually, that is the best part in the picture. He's such a tragedy. Whenever I read it or think about it, I'm so sorry for Daintry.

"Let me tell you about Morley . . . When I left Vienna, I had an offer to go to Hollywood; otherwise, I would be dead. If I'd been in Austria when the Nazis arrived, you would not be meeting me today. But at that time, 1935, I saw a play in New York, *Oscar Wilde*. And Morley played a completely serious part. Wilde. And he was unforgettable! I felt, in spite of people telling me how he does the British Airways commercials in the United States, that he'd give a great performance as Dr. Percival. He'll give us the feeling of a dangerous man, capable of killing. I'm very happy I could get him . . . every actor who read the script wanted his part."

Sir John Gielgud, another longtime Preminger friend also dating back to *Saint Joan*, agreed to play any part even before the script was completed. "And he meant it. Then everything was delayed a little, and I nearly lost him. All English actors, important and medium-important, always book themselves up for the future with small bits in television or anything, and when there comes an opportunity to play a big part, they're not available! I cannot possibly change my schedule around even for John. So instead of playing Hargreaves (C, the SIS chief, now played by Richard Vernon), Gielgud has a much smaller part. Frankly, it's tremendous for the picture that a man like Gielgud plays a part that is only one scene . . . He's so funny. He told me the other day, he has an offer for a picture in Poland. The trouble is everybody will speak Polish except him. 'How will I know when to start speaking?' he asked me. I gave him a good idea. I showed him my hearing aid and suggested he use one to have the dialogue translated through. So that's how he was going to do it!"

I was more interested in how Preminger would handle one particularly key scene in the movie, where all the SIS high-ups (Vernon, Attenborough, and Morley) meet in C's country house study after dinner and plot the literal plugging of a leak. "We can't afford an inquest," says Morley's rather evil Dr. Percival. "No. He should die quietly, peacefully . . . without pain if possible. Poor chap."

Had Preminger, like Hitchcock, already shot that scene in his head, or did he wait until hitting the set? "Of course, as I think of the picture, even when we are talking now, things happen in my mind. But I'm not a director who designs, or has somebody design storyboards. For instance, George Stevens, a good friend of mine, has his art director design every single shot. You know, where to put the camera, where to shoot . . . I can't do this, because I came originally from the theater. I only began to watch films in America. Of course, I have something in my mind, a visual idea, but what I do, basically, is rehearse as much as possible. I've had pictures where the whole cast was available, and I rehearsed three or four weeks without shooting. Otherwise, I rehearse them during the day. That develops it for me, in my mind—what I want to see, where to put the camera, how many close-up shots I need. And I cut it while I rehearse. I don't cut away for a close-up. I usually move the people into close-ups, not the camera. And sometimes I'm sorry. Sometimes I need a close-up and I haven't done it."

Caine or no Caine (ironically, he was once slated to be Klinger's Philby), Preminger did threaten to remove his production to Ireland when British Equity attempted to block his choice of the model girl, Iman, as Nicol Williamson's African wife. "That is the difference between your Equity and our Screen Actors Guild," he explained, a mite testily. "If I give you a part in America, regardless of the film or whether you're Chinese, English, Polish or whatever, once you get the job, you automatically become a member of the guild—because I cannot have anybody who is *not* a member. All you have to do then is pay the dues. But the guild has no right to tell me who to take or not take. They cannot say: We don't like his nose or his beard. That's what Equity was trying to do, saying I could not hire her because she's not British. She's Somali, married to an American and due to be an American citizen—not that that would have helped me. Equity do the same thing with Americans." He laughs. "Her husband would have killed Equity. He's 6'8" and one of the most famous basketball players in the world."

The publicity hype says Iman browbeat Preminger for the Sarah Castle role. Not quite; he's not *that* much of a pussycat. "That story is not right. I wanted her. I saw her photograph somewhere and talked to her lawyer-agent. He asked an *incredible* price. 'She's a beginner,' I said. 'I don't pay that.' He said she made $1,000 a day modeling in Manhattan; $2,000 outside New York. I said: 'When she's as successful an actress as a model, she'll probably get the same. But first she has to prove she can act.' And he hung up. The next day or so, she called me and cried on the 'phone. 'I'll do it for free,' she said. 'Don't listen to my stupid lawyer.' So we made a deal—and a test. She's never acted before, but she's very good. She's beautiful with a certain warmth and kindness—my wife said the same thing when she saw the test. There's something warm and modest about her. A built-in modesty which says: I don't need to be flamboyant, because I am flamboyant anyway. She is also probably one of the most beautiful human beings I've ever seen."

Being a new Preminger discovery in the year of the tragic suicide of his most unfortunate find, Jean Seberg, may not have provided much comfort for the statuesque Iman. She is, though, merely the latest in a lengthy line of amateurs he has often used to winning effect in his career. Preminger it was who brought John Huston back to acting in 1963 (just as Preminger himself reverted to actor for Billy Wilder's *Stalag 17* ten years before). His most famous coup in this area was signing Joseph Welch as the judge deliberating on the legal tussle between lawyers James Stewart and George C. Scott in *Anatomy of a Murder*.

"I had difficulty casting that judge," Preminger recalled. "I forget who I offered it to . . . Spencer Tracy, I'm sure. My assistant, Nat Rudich, suggested taking a real judge . . . and I remembered the scene in the McCarthy hearings when Joe Welch faced up to him and became a hero for everyone who saw him on television, saying to McCarthy, 'Have you no decency, sir?' I sent him a script, and about three days later he walked into my office, wandered around, and started looking at all my books for a long time. Finally, I said to him, 'Mr. Welch, did you read the script?' And like a real actor, he replied, 'Only my part.' 'Do you want to do it?' 'Of course!'

"We had so much fun on that picture. He was not only one of the most interesting people I've ever met but became my friend. The greatest difficulty working with someone with no acting experience is for them to coordinate movement and speech. Unless you've trained, to walk and speak is very hard. I took care of that with Joe. I had him seated all the time. And he never missed a line."

As he would obviously not repeat himself with someone like Watergate's Judge John Sirica, I wondered if Preminger might consider Richard Nixon in a film role. "Well, I must tell you frankly that the part I would offer him, he would not take!" He laughed again. "I must also tell you, I'm not a Republican. I don't belong to any party. I always vote Democrat because I am basically liberal. But one day I received an invitation: President and Mrs. Nixon request the pleasure of Mr. and Mrs. Preminger's company at the White House . . . I think obviously somebody is making stupid jokes. But no, it was the eightieth birthday of Duke Ellington, with whom I made *Anatomy of a Murder*. And Duke has put us on the invitation list! We were at Nixon's table, and one thing I would never have believed, Nixon was charming. On television, he has this horrible dark chin. In person, he's nice, normal, relaxed. Not to mention her. She's *really* charming. I still don't like what he stands for. He should have been thrown out at the time of the Checkers speech . . . once the dinner was over, there were so many musicians there, they started to play jazz. At 2:30 a.m. Nixon left and we were there until 4:30 because of the music. I've often been at the White House, with Roosevelt, Johnson, several people, but this was the best party I ever saw there. So Nixon is not all bad!"

In the four years since his last movie, Preminger has been dealing more with the leaders of Red China. While still attempting to set up his long-proposed films about Israel, and the case of the executed American atom spies, Julius and Ethel Rosenberg ("It was never proved beyond a reasonable doubt they were really guilty"), he has been steadfastly preparing the ground for another cherished project: the life story of Dr. Norman Bethune, the Canadian doctor revered as a folk hero by the Chinese for his work during Mao's revolution. Bethune is the only Westerner since then to have been accorded a state burial with ceremonial honors; Mao read his eulogy.

Since playing the role in a television play (which he insisted had to be for Canada only), the Canadian star Donald Sutherland has been similarly trying to arrange a movie version. More recently, Ted Kotcheff has been named for a third Bethune production, with Warner Brothers stumping up the necessary $15 million. Such a sudden spate of Bethune biographies appears to have been stirred, if not by the recent fortieth-anniversary celebrations in Peking of Bethune's death, then by Warren Beatty filming the life of an American hero of the Russian Revolution, John Reed.

"The Bethune story will be my next movie," insisted Preminger, unperturbed by the other projects; and he hinted at a chance of a deal with Sutherland. Furthermore, he has already won the necessary permission to shoot his version inside China. He first visited the country in 1949, thereafter continually being denied any visa, due to the heavy hand of Madame Mao.

Finally he was allowed back in and treated like a highly favored guest for three weeks last year. He visited Chinese film studios, of course, where all work stopped, and actors, electricians, directors, cameramen, and others, would quiz him for hours about Hollywood . . . and the possible distribution of their films to the West. Not, he noted, to Russia. "They hate the Russians. They call them swindlers, phonies, not real socialists." He saw one film being made with the top local star, a woman of about fifty, and he checked on salaries and was told everyone was paid the same. "Later on, I found out this was not true. The stars, just like here, get more money and country houses and everything. They don't want to admit it."

He also viewed the official Chinese tribute film, Chang Chun-Siang's *Dr. Norman Bethune*, later unveiled at the Berlin festival this year. Another victim of the Cultural Revolution, Madame Mao, and the Gang of Four, this began shooting in 1964 and continued until 1977, during which time the American actor playing Bethune—Gerry Tannebaum—was sent packing and replaced by one Tain Nin-Pang. The film includes documentary footage of the guerrilla fighters in Yenan and the border regions, where Bethune, a veteran of the Spanish Civil War, spent the last nine months of his life in 1939.

Preminger feels he'll have little difficulty depicting the good doctor's "terrific love life," alongside his more famous medical success in curing TB (his own, for a start) and developing the first portable surgical operating tables. "The love story of Bethune is a very important element of the picture. He was a *great* ladies' man. He married a young English girl, they got divorced, and he had many affairs with all his nurses. His wife came back, they married again—and divorced again.

She married another man, and she still came back to him. This can be done as a beautiful love story . . . But the Chinese are too prudish for that. So, as they offer me their army, free of charge, for the battle scenes, I offer them a dupe negative, and they can make as many cuts as they want to. For China, I don't care that much, but I will not change anything for the West. So, that is our deal."

And an exceedingly magnanimous deal it is from such a dedicated foe of any kind of censorship. As far back as 1944, he fought—and won—a mighty Hollywood battle to allow a married couple to be seen in the same bed—"*sleepink!*"—during *In the Meantime, Darling*. While Paddy Chayefsky and others were dealing with adult subjects in live television plays, Preminger was single-handedly forcing the growing-up of Hollywood with his bitter tussle of the use of mere words—virgin, pregnant, rape, penetration, climax, contraceptive—in *The Moon Is Blue* and *Anatomy of a Murder*, plus daring not merely to mention drugs but depict addiction in *The Man with the Golden Arm*.

"It was not really so difficult to fight when you had the courage just to adhere to the rights given you in the Constitution of the United States," he told me. "That freedom of expression—particularly to a man who lived in Vienna, which even before the Nazis was not so easy—is the greatest thing about America. And here also you can write anything you want to, unless you attack the queen or something. I felt I had the same rights as a filmmaker. And I won because I was not afraid. Nobody backed me, you know. On *The Moon Is Blue*, United Artists only said, 'He has autonomy. We can't stop him.' Rather a negative statement; they did not want to fight. They said to me, 'Look, what difference does it make if you cut a few lines?' I said, 'It makes a lot of difference. That's my life.'

"Do I have to be just a man who puts some actors together and directs them? That means nothing. That was my position at Fox where I was powerless to cast, to edit, to protect my work in any way. No, you have to understand that freedom of expression is the most powerful defense of democracy. No totalitarian government, right or left, can exist without censorship, firmly controlling the speech and writing of its citizens.

"But you look at those pictures today, and it's so childish. Today they do on screen what those words described . . . Let me tell you about pornography. I, personally, hate it. It doesn't interest me. It doesn't excite me. But I think violence is much more dangerous. Violence excites people, particularly young people, to violence. But you cannot have your cake and eat it, too. If you want to live in a free society, you must take the risk. But I never did and I never will do a violent picture."

And there are, he says, more films to come. "I don't have any definite plans after Bethune, but as long as I live I'll make films. Retirement would be a bore. I don't even need vacations. I'm very relaxed, basically. I enjoy having an interview more than messing about in a greenhouse. I have a Jacuzzi bath, and it's the only thing I miss here from New York. I go in my Jacuzzi for a half-hour, and it massages me and gives me the illusion that this is better than exercise."

A rich life, then, and richly remembered in his recent "autobiography," which he cut far more than any of his films, feeling, if you can believe it, self-conscious. "I always felt when I was writing it, who the hell is interested? Strangely enough, they are . . . I prefer Lauren Bacall's book. She's a really first-rate writer; I'm no writer at all. Only when you're Jewish, like I am, can you understand how good she is when describing her family . . . and the illness of Humphrey Bogart—that is heart-breaking. I cried! How she prepared her son for his daddy's death, how she never cried until one night she started to sob and couldn't stop. So human. I don't know her very well, but I like her as a person. She has guts. Of all the autobiographies, this is the one to buy. I wish mine was as good."

What of Joan Crawford's book by her stepdaughter? "Let me tell you about Joan Crawford. She made a picture for me (*Daisy Kenyon*, 1947). She had just adopted the twins. And she asked me, 'Will you please let me go home at 5 p.m. every day, I'll be back half an hour later and work as long as you want. I want to feed the twins.' Most people say about Crawford, it was all an act. Nonsense! Nobody adopts children as an act . . . The book is not half as bad as it sounds. I'm sure many of the incidents are true, maybe everything. But the motivations are not there. When this Christine describes Joan tying the son to the bed, there are probably reasons for it, or when she hit her. Crawford was, basically, not a very well-educated woman. You know and I know that hitting children is old-fashioned, stupid. Even when I was a little boy, my father in his whole life never hit me or my brother. He felt it was not right. Crawford wasn't like this. She thought this is the way to educate and discipline people. I didn't know her well, but she was not like this book wants to tell us. She was a very decent human being."

How about press writers' view of Otto Preminger? "Let me tell you about Rex Reed. Actually, he's quite an intelligent man. But the bitchiness of what he wrote about me, the lies—well, I couldn't care less. The other day I see in *The Hollywood Reporter*, the columnist who used to be Gertrude Lawrence's secretary . . . *ja, ja,* Radie Harris . . . she wrote something terrible. She says that Tom Tryon, who worked with me on *Exodus*, and I don't speak anymore. Now (a) Tryon was never in *Exodus*; (b) I gave him his only big part in *The Cardinal*; (c) we're great friends! She makes up stories. She's a poor woman, she has a wooden leg, and . . . anybody who writes a column regularly has to use the same old names, just from the memory. You interview me today, and you write it, then you see somebody else. You always have the advantage that some of it comes from your subject. You, in other words, don't have to make it up."

Not with Otto Preminger, I don't.

Key Resources

Journal Articles, Book Chapters, and Interviews

Aiello, Thomas. "*Hurry Sundown*: Otto Preminger, Baton Rouge, and Race, 1966–1967." *Film History: An International Journal* 21.4 (2009): 394–410.

Breaux, Lola. "Otto Preminger's Hand in the Initial Moments of *Bunny Lake Is Missing*." *Movie: A Journal of Film Criticism* 7 (May 2017): 34–38.

Combs, Richard. "Anatomy of a Director." *Sight & Sound* 19.4 (Apr. 2009): 38–41.

D'Arcy, Susan. "The Other Otto." *Films Illustrated* 4.45 (May 1975): 334.

Denby, David. "Balance of Terror: How Otto Preminger Made His Movies." *New Yorker* (Jan. 7, 2008). https://www.newyorker.com/magazine/2008/01/14/balance-of-terror.

Ebert, Roger. "Lunch with Otto." (Jan. 23, 1972) *RogerEbert.com*. https://www.rogerebert.com/interviews/lunch-with-otto.

Ebert, Roger. "On the 'Skidoo' Set with Otto Preminger: 'Mr. Von Stroheim, Do You Hear Noise?'" (June 16, 1968). *RogerEbert.com*. https://www.rogerebert.com/interviews/on-the-skidoo-set-with-otto-preminger-mr-von-stroheim-do-you-hear-noise.

Forshaw, Barry. "Pushing the Boundaries: Preminger the Rebel." *Sex and Film: The Erotic in British, American and World Cinema*. London: Palgrave Macmillan, 2015: 42–51.

Gibbs, John, and Douglas Pye. "Preminger and Peckinpah: Seeing and Shaping Widescreen Worlds." *Widescreen Worldwide*. Ed. John Belton, Sheldon Hall, and Steve Neale. London: John Libbey, 2010: 71–90.

Gibbs, John, and Douglas Pye. "Revisiting Preminger: *Bonjour Tristesse* (1958) and Close Reading." *Style and Meaning: Studies in the Detailed Analysis of Film*. Ed. Gibbs and Pye. Manchester; New York: Manchester UP, 2005: 108–26.

Halamish, Aviva. "*Exodus*, the Movie—Half a Century Later: The Interplay of History, Myth, Memory, and Historiography." *Jewish Film & New Media* 5.2 (Fall 2017): 123–42.

Kauffmann, Stanley. "The Preminger Paradox." *A World on Film: Criticism and Comment*. New York: Dell, 1966. 170–76.

Keating, Patrick. "Otto Preminger." *Fifty Hollywood Directors*. Ed. Yvonne Tasker and Suzanne Leonard. New York: Routledge, 2015. 186–94.

Lippe, Richard. "At the Margins of Film Noir: Preminger's *Angel Face*." *CineAction!* 13/14 (1988): 46–55.

Lyons, Donald. "Otto Preminger: Auteur de Force." *Inter/View* 23 (July 1972): 14–16; 43–44.

Lyons, Donald. "Preminger's Brass." *Film Comment* 26.4 (July 1990): 47–51.

Mayersberg, Paul. "From *Laura* to *Angel Face.*" *Movie Reader.* Ed. Ian Cameron. London: November Books, 1972. 44–46.

Mayersberg, Paul. "Carmen and Bess." *Movie Reader.* Ed. Ian Cameron. London: November Books, 1972. 47–49.

Munby, Jonathan. "*Heimat* Hollywood: Billy Wilder, Otto Preminger, Edgar Ulmer, and the Criminal Cinema of the Austrian-Jewish Diaspora." *From World War to Waldheim: Culture and Politics in Austria and the United States.* Ed. David F. Good and Ruth Wodak. New York; Oxford: Berghahn Books, 1999: 138–62.

Orr, John. "Otto Preminger and the End of Classical Cinema." *Senses of Cinema* 40 (July 2006). http://senses ofcinema.com/2006/three-auteurs/otto-preminger/.

Perkins, V. F. "Why Preminger?" *Movie Reader.* Ed. Ian Cameron. London: November Books, 1972. 43.

Phillips, Gene D. "Both Sides of the Question: Otto Preminger." *Focus on Film* 33 (1979): 22–26.

Poe, G. Tom. "Secrets, Lies, and Cold War Politics: 'Making Sense' of Otto Preminger's *Advise and Consent.*" *Film History* 10.3 (1998): 332–45.

Preminger, Otto. "The Cardinal and I." *Films and Filming* 10 (Nov. 1963): 12.

Preminger, Otto. "Keeping Out of Harm's Way." *Films and Filming* 11.9 (June 1965): 6.

Preminger, Otto. "Your Taste, My Taste . . . and the Censors." *Films and Filming* 6.2 (Nov. 1959): 7.

Rivette, Jacques. "The Essential." *Cahiers du cinéma—The 1950s: Neo-Realism, Hollywood, New Wave.* Ed. Jim Hillier. Cambridge: Harvard UP, 1985. 132–35.

Ross, Lillian. "Anatomy of a Commercial Interruption." *New Yorker* 41.53 (19 Feb. 1966). https://www.new yorker.com/magazine/1966/02/19/anatomy-of-a-commercial-interruption.

Sarris, Andrew. "Preminger's Two Periods: Studio and Solo." *Film Comment* 3.3 (Summer 1965): 12–17.

Schweitzer, Dahlia. "Who Is Missing in *Bunny Lake*?" *Jump Cut* 52 (Summer 2010). https://www.ejumpcut .org/archive/jc52.2010/schweitzerBunnyLake/index.html.

Simmons, Jerold. "Challenging the Production Code: *The Man with the Golden Arm.*" *Journal of Popular Film and Television* 33.1 (Spring 2005): 39–48.

Smith, Jeff. "Black Faces, White Voices: The Politics of Dubbing in *Carmen Jones.*" *Velvet Light Trap* 51 (2003): 29–42.

Smith, Jeffrey P. "A Good Business Proposition": Dalton Trumbo, 'Spartacus,' and the End of the Blacklist." *Velvet Light Trap* 23 (Spring 1989): 75–100.

Sonnet, Esther. "Evelyn Piper's *Bunny Lake Is Missing* (1957): Adaptation, Feminism, and the Politics of the 'Progressive Text.'" *Adaptation* 2.1 (Mar. 2009): 65–86.

Teleky, Richard. "Anatomy of *Anatomy of a Murder.*" *CineAction* 94 (Summer 2014): 62–68.

Thomson, David. "Impulse: Otto Preminger." *Sight & Sound* 15.5 (May 2005): 30–33.

Walker, Michael. "*Daisy Kenyon* (Otto Preminger, 1947)." *Movie: A Journal of Film Criticism* 7 (May 2017): 69.

Wegner, Hart. "From Expressionism to *Film Noir*: Otto Preminger's *Where the Sidewalk Ends.*" *Journal of Popular Film and Television* 11.2 (1983): 56–65.

Wood, Robin. "Attitudes in *Advise and Consent.*" *Movie Reader.* Ed. Ian Cameron. London: November Books, 1972. 53–56.

Books

Frischauer, Willi. *Behind the Scenes of Otto Preminger: An Unauthorised Biography*. London: Michael Joseph, 1973.

Fujiwara, Chris. *The World and Its Double: The Life and Work of Otto Preminger*. New York: Farrar, Straus, and Giroux, 2008.

Grob, Norbert, Rolf Aurich, and Wolfgang Jacobsen. *Otto Preminger*. Berlin: Stiftung Deutsche Kinemathek and Jovis Verlagsburo, 1999.

Hirsch, Foster. *Otto Preminger: The Man Who Would Be King*. New York: Alfred A. Knopf, 2007.

Lourcelles, Jacques. *Otto Preminger*. Paris: Éditions Seghers, 1965.

Pratley, Gerald. *The Cinema of Otto Preminger*. New York: A. S. Barnes, 1971.

Preminger, Marion Mill. *All I Want Is Everything*. New York: Funk & Wagnalls, 1957.

Preminger, Otto. *Preminger: An Autobiography*. New York: Doubleday, 1977.

Ryan, Tom. *Otto Preminger Films* Exodus*: A Report*. New York: Random House, 1960.

Sarris, Andrew. *The American Cinema: Directors and Directions, 1929–1968*. New York: E. P. Dutton, 1968.

Documentaries

Cinéma, de notre temps: Otto Preminger (2012), directed by André S. Labarthe.

Preminger: Anatomy of a Filmmaker (1991), directed by Valerie Robins.

Hollywood on Trial (1976), directed by David Helpern.

Index

About the Editor

Photo credit: Gary Bettinson

Gary Bettinson is senior lecturer in film studies at Lancaster University. He is the author of *The Sensuous Cinema of Wong Kar-wai: Film Poetics and the Aesthetic of Disturbance*, and coauthor (with Richard Rushton) of *What Is Film Theory? An Introduction to Contemporary Debates*.

Printed in the United States
by Baker & Taylor Publisher Services